The historian between the ethnologist and the futurologist

NEW BABYLON

Studies in the behavioral sciences

13

MOUTON · PARIS · THE HAGUE

The historian
between the ethnologist
and the futurologist

*A conference sponsored by the International Association
for Cultural Freedom, by the Giovanni Agnelli Foundation
and by the Giorgio Cini Foundation*

Venice, April 2-8, 1971

Edited by
JERÔME DUMOULIN / DOMINIQUE MOISI

MOUTON · PARIS · THE HAGUE

Library of Congress Catalog Card Number: 73-75801

© 1973 Mouton & Co.

Jacket-design: Jurriaan Schrofer

Printed in the Netherlands

Preface

This book is a record of discussions between a group of historians and social scientists drawn from several countries which took place in Venice at Easter 1971. The obvious person to write the preface was Raymond Aron, who planned the seminar in advance and proved an incomparable chairman of our meetings. However, M. Aron has chosen instead to write a postface which provides so illuminating a conclusion to our discussions that it greatly enhances the value of the book, and so I have agreed, at M. Aron's request, to write the preface in his place.

Some people look upon conferences with scepticism, and as I boarded the plane for Venice I was doubtful how much I should enjoy the meetings I had agreed to attend. These doubts, however, were removed before the end of the first day: I found myself continually astonished, exasperated and stimulated by what was said. Subsequent reflection and the opportunity to read the very skilful record of our discussions which has been prepared by Jerôme Dumoulin and Dominique Moïsi have confirmed the impression which I formed at the time. Whatever may be said about conferences in general, this was one which I found full of interest from beginning to end.

This was certainly not because of any particular contribution which I myself made to the discussion. Although I was driven more than once to flash the red light in front of me and demand to be heard, most of the time I spent in concentrated attention to what was being said by my colleagues – and, perhaps to my surprise, I found what they had to say fascinating.

The reason for this, I suspect – and certainly the only serious qualification I have for writing this preface – is that I happened to have posed the original questions from which the discussion in Venice began. My suggestion sprang from observation of an attitude which is common to many of the present generation of students, their indifference, often hostility, to the study of history as lacking any relevance to their situation.

All radical movements, of course, have been concerned to repudiate at least the immediate past, but many of them have drawn upon history to give force to their indictment of the present state of society. The intellectual foundation of Marxism, to take only the most obvious example, is a particular interpretation of history and without the belief that the materialist conception of history provides a universal key to the understanding of social development much of the attractive power of Marxism would be lost. But it is one of the most widespread and characteristic beliefs of the present generation of students that their experience is so unique, so unlike anything which has been known or felt before, that study of the past – even in a Marxist version – is of no value and irrelevant to them. If this is more than a passing phase, what will be the consequences for a culture which, in Western Europe at least, has been dominated, even in its revolts, by a continuous historical tradition?

One immediate consequence, I suggested, was the avidity with which many students turned to the social sciences as a study which they believed to be orientated towards the future rather than towards the past, and I went on to ask how far the social scientists could meet the expectations formed of their studies if they were to be called upon to play the central role which history had played in our education and culture.

It was our good fortune that the questions I asked – and they were genuine, not rhetorical, questions for I was far from sure even of my own answers to them – interested M. Aron sufficiently for him to accept an invitation to act as chairman of a seminar in which they could be discussed by a group of historians and social scientists drawn from a number of different countries. From this point on M. Aron took control and, in the translation from Oxford to Paris, naturally put the questions in a different way. The theme for the seminar, as it emerged from his hands, now became History between Ethnology and Futurology, a re-wording which added a further dimension to the discussion by recognising that the character of historical study is itself changing under the impact of the social sciences. And indeed, when we finally came to sit down round the table in Venice, it was these changes and the extent to which they invalidated the traditional conception of history which led to some of the most impassioned debates.

At the end of the conference we had no agreed answer to the questions I had originally posed. This was hardly surprising: these are, after all, questions to which everyone must work out his own answers; they cannot be settled by a majority vote. But as a result of our discussions we had penetrated beneath the surface, brought to light the implications of the questions and gained a clearer idea of what is involved in giving an answer to them.

For this, we have above all to thank Raymond Aron who constantly brought the discussion back to the point and who, without ever imposing his own ideas, had (I suspect) a clear view all the time of where it would lead us in the end. This view he has expressed with characteristic lucidity in the concluding chapter, and the record of our discussions would be worth publishing for that alone.

For the opportunity to meet and exchange our views we are indebted to the International Association for Cultural Freedom, under whose auspices the seminar was conducted and particularly to the Association's Director of Seminars, Constantin Jelenski, who undertook the difficult and at times delicate task of organising the conference.

Finally, we are indebted to the Agnelli Foundation, without a generous grant from which the seminar could never have been held, and to the Cini Foundation for providing it with an incomparable setting, designed by Palladio himself and more eloquent than any historia, in which to debate the value of continuing to study the past even in the world of today.

St. Catherine's College   Alan Bullock
Oxford

Editors' note

Certain repetitions in this volume are due to the fact that it reproduces both the papers presented at the seminar and their authors' spoken introductions.

We have tried to preserve a sense of spontaneity rather than tie the debate to a pre-arranged plan, and for this reason a few papers which were of intrinsic interest but did not quite fit into the pattern of the discussion are placed at the end of the book.

J. D. and A. M.

Contents

X *Contents*

1 Rules of the game and landscapes

ERNEST GELLNER

Our current sense of history

Types of horizon

The horizon is generally conspicuous, whereas the surrounding landscape, close to us, is taken for granted. Yet, in the social and historical
world (and perhaps in some measure in the physical world also), the
horizon we perceive depends on our more immediate environment and
its general features. A forest or a savannah, a local hillock or a hollow,
make a great difference to the kind of skyline that is seen. But it is in the
nature of things that what is close and familiar should also be treated with
familiarity and contempt, and that its importance should normally be
ignored. It is its ordinariness, obviousness, which causes us to take it for
granted: but the hold it has over us is immeasurably strengthened
precisely by the fact that we do take it for granted. What is noticed can be
queried, but that which seems utterly obvious eludes questioning.

The horizon, by contrast, errs in the opposite direction. It is often
quite spuriously dramatic. If you walk to the point on the distant skyline,
you may well find, when you reach it, that it is just as ordinary a place as
your starting point. But as long as it remains on the skyline, it occupies
the dramatic point at which the sky meets land or water, the point where
the sun sets or rises. It has a striking suggestiveness, and symbolises our
deeper or more ecstatic aspirations – quite unlike the close and dusty
immediate locality, which tends instead to remind us of our compromises,
shabbiness and mediocrity.

The horizons of a society, or at any rate of many societies, consist of a
cosmogony and an eschatology, of an account of how things began and
how they will end. As the horizon is dramatic, it is often easy to pick it
out: the locals know how to talk about it, and ritual occasions abound

which remind them to do so. Thus it is unlike some of those daily occurrences which may remain unnoticed or which may even be systematically obscured. But, of course, that which is highlighted and that which is obscured may be all of one piece, or at least they may complement each other. It is a commonplace of anthropological method that by skillfully interpreting that which is made conspicuous on the horizon, we may be led to a great deal of that which is hidden under one's very nose.

To ask about the manner in which history enters our vision is, in a way, to ask about the manner in which our horizons are related to the style of our daily life. This being so, one might as well begin with a typology of the kinds of horizon a society can have.

We can develop a typology by using the currently fashionable method of binary oppositions and seeing the types which are generated in this manner. The differences in attitude to history which one should expect to be relevant are these:

1. Naturalistic/discontinuous. A society is naturalistic if it assumes that the events on the horizon are and must be similar in kind to the ordinary events of daily life. Modern societies are naturalistic in this sense. They do not take seriously either an Age of the Gods or an Age of the Heroes, in Vico's terms. But most societies are not naturalistic in this way.

2. Within the class of societies which have non-naturalistic horizons, it is possible to distinguish between simple and ramified background stories. A ramified one will recognise two or more successive stages, basically dissimilar, within the general framework of the horizon story – such as, indeed, Vico's distinction between the Age of Gods and of Heroes. There is then a double skyline on the horizon – something that, after all, also happens in the physical world.

3. Cutting across these distinctions, there is the difference between historical and a-historical societies. A rough criterion would be whether a society accumulates more and more generations with the passage of time, whether the ordinary world within the horizons *grows* in size with time, or whether on the contrary the size of the plain within the horizons remains constant, as happens when systematic omission ensures that the number of generations separating the present from the Founding Father remains constant. There will of course be borderline cases between historical and a-historical societies.

4. The presence or absence of a sense of social structure. By this is

meant whether or not a society recognises a radical difference in type of event, or of sequence, of story, *within* the daily, ordinary, non-horizon part of the world – in other words, whether it has a sense of different epochs, of radically different patterns of social life, where the difference is natural rather than super-natural. A simple society which takes for granted the institutional and conceptual framework within which its members act, has of course no such sense of social structure. Its own structure is invisible to it, and others are barely conceivable. Naively, it absolutises one particular set of conventions. But even quite sophisticated societies or historians are capable of this simplicity. It is arguable that Gibbon's vision was of this kind, and I have heard this claim argued. So clearly, holding such a view does not disqualify a man from the highest ranks of creative intelligence.

The four binary oppositions considered give us 12 possibilities (allowing for the fact that one of the four oppositions applies only to one half of the field, for it only arises if a particular answer is given to one of the other alternatives). It might be interesting to explore the resulting typology in relation to concrete historical and ethnographic material. Our present problem, however, is to isolate features of our own sense of history. For this end, we need only specify our own position within this range of alternatives and then seek to add further refinements to the resulting profile.

Our society is secularised/naturalistic, it sees the world as continuous rather than discontinuous, in as far as it does not take the supernatural cosmogonies and eschatologies, which it has inherited, with any degree of seriousness. It has not openly and generally disowned them, it merely surrounds them with a cloud of ambiguity, according them "symbolic" status or whatnot, and it has been obliged to invent a special term, "fundamentalist", for those who actually claim to take them seriously.

This being so, the question whether the horizon is simple or ramified does not arise. In an important sense, we have no horizon. What is on the horizon is known to be similar in type to the ordinary stuff of daily life.

We are, clearly, an historical society. Generations are not spirited away by genealogical hocus-pocus, or by indifference, but, on the contrary, the slag heap of The Past is ever growing. Some have feared that the shadow it casts may tend to stifle us. Be that as it may, we clearly locate ourselves in a growing, cumulative temporal sequence, which does not obscure change, but records it. This, of course, is the first and most general reason why history is of interest to us. We are not alone in possessing this trait, but it is not an universal one either. Some simpler tribal societies quite independently possess it, and some complex, urban, literate societies do not.

Finally, within the horizon-less and cumulative temporal setting, we do have a sense of successive and radically differentiated social structures. We do not suppose that men throughout history have played the same game, that they were like us, only (at most) wearing different clothes and using different tools and weapons. On the contrary, we know that the games played have changed drastically.

This, then, is the profile of our historical sense. It is a very abstract outline, and a good deal more will need to be said before it becomes really informative. But the additional points which need to be made may be approached through questions arising about this outline. The various questions are cross-related, and they are:

What is a social structure, as opposed to mere historical narrative? Be it noted that reputable thinkers exist who consider accurate narrative to be the only legitimate form of history, and who repudiate the abstract structures sought by sociologists and anthropologists.[1] To answer this question – concerning the nature and status of these "structures" – is in effect to discuss the relation of history to anthropology and sociology.

Specifically, which particular structures, or classifications of structures, do we find relevant in categorising our historical experience – and why?

Given that an important function was performed by the "horizon" in societies which possessed it, and given that we are horizon-less, at least in the old sense, what (if anything) performs that role for us?

If it should turn out that this role is now performed by the social sciences and/or "futurology", just how do they perform it and what kind of sensitivity do they instill?

In the light of all this, how do we need to refine our initial classification of historical perspectiveness by a typology of horizons and horizon-surrogates?

Structure and story

Very roughly, a story is a sequence of events fused not merely by continuity (ideally, there ought to be no gaps), but above all by the fact that they happen to an individual (or a comity) which experiences and conceives them as a unity, as its own fate or destiny or adventure. Perhaps it is of the essence of a story that the sequence should be more than contingent and less than necessary.[2] Such a definition is no doubt question-begging, or rather buck-passing, in that it shifts the burden to the question of just how the individual comes to attribute unity to a sequence of events, and indeed, to how he himself comes to credit himself with unity. One may well suspect that the unity of a self and of a story are correlative, mutually dependent notions.

A very sketchy answer – which is all that we shall offer – to this question is one which invokes the notion of "structure", which is both complementary and contrasted to the idea of a "story". What makes the sequence of moves in (say) a chess game into *one* game, which can (in the case of chess) be turned not merely into a narrative but into a precise and unambiguous one, is, over and above the fact that the moves happen consecutively in one place, the fact that they presuppose a shared set of rules which connect one move with the next. Naive narrative history takes such rules for granted. Sociological history, at the very least, attempts to elicit and specify them. What is the status of these rules?

Some, but some only, are supplied by nature. When the hero of a story undergoes an adventure in which bodily survival is at issue, when he must avoid physical destruction, starvation or exposure, we understand the "logic of the situation" without needing to presuppose any information about his specifically social environment, about the cultural conventions within which he operates. But these natural constraints only account for a small proportion of the connections in a story sequence – for the need to swim to the shore when the boat capsizes, for the need to seek food and shelter on the island. The natural needs also enter as partial constituents into many cultural requirements, without dictating their specific form. Nature decrees you must eat, culture decrees when, how and what.

By far the greater proportion of connections in a story is made intelligible in a manner other than a simple invocation of a natural, physical law. The professional, ritual, familiar, political and other activities of man are constrained by conventions and guided by ends which are not simply or at all derivable from shared biological needs. Those needs certainly set limits to the kind of connections that a society can exhibit, but they most certainly do not determine their specific form. The nexus between an act and its consequences, or between the failure to perform it

and another set of consequences, is dictated not by nature, but is somehow the consequence of a given social structure. A social "structure" is, in
a way, a system of such regular connections and the manner in which
they are enforced. As stated, it somehow ensures that those consequences
flow in a certain pattern (for a social environment is by no means wholly
unpredictable). It somehow ensures it – but *how*?

One facile, occasionally popular, but empirically and otherwise quite
inadequate answer is what might be called the "Brave New World"
solution – the view that concepts are so firmly internalised by members of
given societies that they become, in practice, just as compulsive as natural
necessity. The insulted man of honour "must" fight a duel, the believer
"must" kneel, and so forth. But empirically, it simply is not true that men
are quite so completely enslaved to the concepts and norms of their
societies. Just as significantly, those concepts and norms are generally
ambiguous and less than fully determinate in their requirements, leaving
adequate loopholes for opportunism and variation in strategy. The socialisation process is often less than homogeneous in what it indoctrinates,
and its effectiveness in ensuring the internalisation of what it preaches
varies a good deal.

What, then, is the answer?

We know, roughly, the elements which go into the answer. The manner
in which these elements combine and contribute to the explanation of a
given social situation can only be worked out by a specific investigation
into that particular situation. The elements are the various forms of
restraint and quasi-restraint which delimit human conduct. Physical,
natural constraint, on its own, accounts for a small part: in every society,
much more is physically possible than is socially, "morally" possible. A
social system is a system of un-thinkables and un-doables. A sociological
account of it explains how these limits come to be, but do not, like the
society under consideration, take these for granted. Over and above
physical restraints, it can invoke the range of available concepts, and,
with great caution, the hold these concepts have over the members of the
society. Pure unaided conceptual constraint may sometimes be adequate,
though this needs to be carefully demonstrated in each case. But most
generally, the constraint is situational: the institutions surrounding an
individual limit his options. Some options are barred by a variety of social
sanctions – punishments, ridicule, loss of social credit and standing which
the individual knows he will need for many other ends, and which he

must husband carefully. Such options as *are* open, are generally open only by grace of the social arrangement, so to speak: most actions involve effecting changes which require the co-operation of others, which are beyond the unaided physical powers of the agent. The enlistment of the required co-operation requires, at the very least, that the act to be performed is recognisable and sanctioned within the local institutional framework. Most "actions" can only be performed if they have a recognised local name and status. New "actions" do indeed, from time to time, emerge *prior* to their social recognition and christening: this is the most interesting form of social change. But this process can also be seized and explained by the kind of sociological explanation under consideration.

A model of a social structure must sketch the situation in which the individual pawn in the game finds himself, showing the "rules" which limit his possible moves – and above all, showing how those rules are sanctioned. The pawn cannot do *this* because it would arouse the wrath of his neighbours; he cannot do *that* because the idea of it is simply absent and, even if *he* could conceive of it, he could not enlist the required support because no one would know what he was up to; and he cannot do *the other* because it would ruin him economically, and so forth. In as far as the situation leaves him some choice, this must be taken into consideration in accounting for the constraints placed on his neighbours: what would happen to their position in turn if he, or he and too many others, took this option rather than that?

The "rules" under discussion are of course not the same thing as the normative rules recognised within the society itself, though such normative rules, if well sanctioned, can figure amongst the constraints on conduct. What is at issue are "rules" in the sense of *effective* limitations on conduct. As it is not generally possible to work out an adequate power-and-constraint balance sheet for every individual, in practice it must be sufficient to do this for typical individuals in standard situations, plus some reasons for believing that not too many individuals deviate from this, and that such deviations as do inevitably occur do not disrupt the system but are somehow absorbed by it. It then follows that for similar "ideal types", *i.e.*, social situations defined by similar premises, similar consequences follow. This is a matter of simple logic: from similar premises, other things equal, similar consequences must follow. And as a matter of fact, there is some justification for such a strategy: patterns of constraint do not appear to be endlessly various; there seems to be some justification for the hope that similar premises are crucial for defining more than one society. There do seem to be "structural similarities". Models exist which do illuminate large classes of societies.

Thus generalisation enters indirectly, as a consequence of the applicability of "ideal types". Generalisations of a different kind also enter in as far as they are invoked to explain the connections between items within various models or ideal types. These kind of generalisations, borrowed rather promiscuously from anywhere, are admittedly invoked *ad hoc* and in a rough and ready manner.

Thus generalisations enters somewhat indirectly. On the other hand, the ideal types themselves are an essential, integral part of the method, and indispensable. There is no alternative to using them. The alternative is not some brave, tough-minded history, a pure unadorned narrative of "what really happened", but only a childish narrative which takes the nexus between events for granted.

The account here offered of the nature of sociological method and of "structure", its key concept, is a moderately materialist one. It is materialist in its insistence on starting from the physical constraints given by nature and also in its insistence that conceptual constraints are never self-explanatory, that they can only be accepted as elements in an explanation if it is shown how they in turn are sanctioned, how a situation arises in which men cannot easily evade them. The account is moderate in its materialism through its clear recognition of the fact that the pattern of physical constraints given by the environment, by ecology and available technology, seldom if ever uniquely determines the rest of the system: in other words, there most certainly is no one-one correlation between "base" and "super-structure". It does not exclude the possibility that on some occasions the socialisation process inculcates some concepts so firmly that their internalisation and compulsiveness may be sufficient to explain some particular human conduct: but it is very suspicious of such explanations on the grounds that, in most cases, concepts need to be sanctioned externally as well as internally if they are to be truly compelling. The protestant who follows his faith without external ritual, the revolutionary who defies the external political symbolism of legitimacy and recognises only his own inner political light may exist, but they are rare in their pure inner-directedness. Moreover it is doubtful whether, sociologically speaking, they are often quite so pure: apparently pure inner-directedness often has some covert external reinforcement.

Structuralisme

The structuralism here outlined and commended is meant to be an account of old-fashioned, square, not-with-it structuralism, which is not very close to currently fashionable *Structuralisme*. The latter movement, if I understand it rightly, is a crypto-epistemological doctrine, starting from a point which was once a commonplace in the Idealist polemic against empiricism, namely, that signs are not just echoes of things, trace-marks of experience, but that, on the contrary, they can only function as parts of a system, that to understand them one must see the system of alternatives of which they form a part. The essence of "John" is not its relation to John, but its relation to "Peter", "Paul" and so forth. The system of terms faces the system of things, and *each* is to be understood more through its internal structure and its generation, than through some simple echo-relation between them both.

Modern *Structuralisme* differs from Idealism primarily by not contenting itself with formulating this, in the abstract, as a criticism of empiricism but by endeavouring to be specific, concrete, operational, and showing just how these cognitive systems are constructed and how they work. Chomsky starts from the fact that the boundary between what is and is not an acceptable sentence in a given language can be indicated, and an abstract model can then be constructed which will show how the sentences within the range of acceptable ones can be "generated". Lévi-Strauss, using material which is ethnographic and less clearly self-defining than is the material of linguistics, and procedures which are suggestive rather than rigourous and precise, attempts something which is meant to be analogous in the more difficult, elusive and fluid spheres such as those of mythology.

It seems to me that the kind of old structuralism which I am sketching and commending is both narrower and broader than the currently fashionable *Structuralisme*. It is narrower in that one of its central concerns is not with what a society can conceive or say, but what kind of thing it actually does. It is concerned with conceptual limits in those cases in which they are crucial in limiting conduct; in those numerous other cases where the limits of actual conduct remain well within the limits of the conceivable, it is concerned with those other, non-conceptual constraints that were actually operative. The sociologist and the anthropologist must be concerned with many non-conceptual constraints, and it is not clear that (or how) these could have a logic similar to the generation of possibilities by (say) the combination of polar opposites. Moreover, the sociologist must also be very concerned with that most fascinating form of social change which occurs when conduct breaks through the conceptual barrier of a society, when people do something for which as yet they have no name, no niche within their system of classifications.

At the same time, the concerns of the sociologist are also broader than those of the *Structuraliste*. The range of what is thinkable and the way it arises is something which must itself be explained. The present *Structuraliste* vogue in sociology, with its idea – of jargon – of treating society as a "code", is open to a number of suspicions or cautions. For one thing, the units of social life are far less clearly defined than those of language and much less homogeneous in kind. Linguists are fortunate in possessing a domain whose units are at least relatively self-defining and isolatable. But actions seldom have the comparatively clear outline of a word or a sentence. They are certainly not all transmitted or experienced in more or less the same medium, as language is.

Moreover, a society, if it is a "Language" at all, is a much more loosely defined one than is language in the literal sense. Its sanctions are forever breaking down. A "transformational linguist" can separate, relatively easily, acceptable from unacceptable words in a given language, and proceed to seek the rules which generate the former and exclude the latter. The sociologist has no such initial advantage. There is not much sense in describing any social event as "unacceptable" (sociologically speaking that is, of course, not morally), and there is no clear equivalent in social behaviour to the incompetent user of a language.

Indeed, the whole *Problemstellung* is radically different. Though the sanctions are ever breaking down in social life, giving us but a hazy boundary between that which is acceptable and that which is not (sociologically, of course, not morally), at the same time the concrete nature of those sanctions, despite or because of their frequent failure, is of central interest to the investigation. This is not so in linguistics. The linguist is quite content with an abstract model of the generative procedure and its enforcement, leaving its concrete identification to some distant future advances in neuro-physiology. For the sociologist, the concrete identification of the sanctions is central and cannot be postponed.

The nature of the questions also differs in other ways. The sociologist, though interested in what could happen, is quite particularly concerned with what does happen. In other words, if society were a language, he could be said to be more concerned with *parole* than with *langue*. Moreover, he is quite particularly interested in the actual sequence of "messages" and the way in which earlier items constrain later ones. This is hardly so in linguistics, which cannot have very much to say about the way in which earlier members of long sequences constrain later ones. (Long soliloquies are seldom uniquely determined.) For the linguist, what is of interest is the so to speak vertical nexus between the rules and the individual utterance. (These rules, admittedly, may sometimes exclude certain sequences.) For the sociologist, this kind of interest (which can only very partially be satisfied owing to the looseness of these vertical rules, in sociology) is at least rivalled by the concern with the horizontal nexus between successive events.

Thus, although social actions are presumably generated from some kind of matrix and are selected from a bounded range of alternatives whose possibilities are limited by the elements used by a social system and by the rules for combining them, nevertheless the relationships between social actions, and the relationships between messages, are in many profound ways very different. In the end, a society is a more complex thing than a language. The problems which need to be answered are different in kind. The tempting analogies which seem to inspire *Structuralisme* are suspect. The sociologist must beware of two dangers: Those supposedly hard-headed historians or realists who deny the need of any account more powerful and abstract than mere narrative, and those over-optimistic and eager souls who think they can easily borrow and fruitfully adapt a formal model from simpler and perhaps more fortunate fields such as linguistics or even phonetics.

Self-generating games

Our present concern is with the relation of history to anthropology and sociology. It may be useful to go back to the chess analogy. A game of chess is, most emphatically, a story, a sequence of events meaningfully connected. Moreover, a precise notation exists for telling the story, without ambiguity. A sociological account, however, is analogous to explaining the story to someone, say a child, who is unfamiliar with the rules of chess: the rules must be specified, and it must be explained why and how they constrain certain moves, why some moves are mandatory, others preferable, some forbidden, some allowed but disastrous. To begin with, a sociologist is like a man among a population of chess experts who are so familiar with the game that its rules are nowhere written down. He must elicit the rules from the games in progress and relate them to the development of each game.

But his task is harder still. The rules of chess are very stable, and they are imposed on each game by a convention external to that game, a convention which is a kind of absolute and extraneous datum as far as any one game is concerned. The account of the origin of that convention, and the processes by which it is sustained, is in no way part of the analysis of an individual game. Not so for the sociologist. The tacit rules or constraints limiting human behaviour are not stable, and the mechanisms which enforce them are not extraneous to the story in progress: on the contrary, from the sociologist's viewpoint, they are by far the most interesting aspect of that game. Many societies believe, of course, that the ground-rules *are* extraneously imposed: they shift onto the supernatural the responsibility for their own conventions. But this is an illusion from which the sociologist is professionally debarred. *The constraints, the "rules" within which social life is played out, are themselves a consequence of the game.* (The only thing given extraneously are the rules imposed by nature, but they are minimal and in an important way unspecific: they leave quite open just *how* their imperatives are satisfied. They only require *that* they be satisfied.) A "structural" account of a society is an account of how this comes to be: how the game itself generates and sustains the limits within which it is played. This is the really crucial fact about sociological method. This manner of formulating it shows why the task is so much harder than that of a chess analyst, who has no need to explain just why the players will not knock over the board, why the rook will not move diagonally, and so forth.

It would no doubt be unfair to imply that "pure" historians are like chess journalists who give accounts of the development of given games without realising that the rules themselves must be specified and cannot be taken for granted. In fact historians do frequently explain the nexus between successive events in an historical sequence and indicate what background factors sanctioned, so to speak, the particular connection. But for better or worse, they do it *ad hoc* and unsystematically. I suppose that the most plausible case that could be made out for anti-sociological history would maintain that this can indeed be best done, or done only, in an *ad hoc* manner. Sociology is based on the hope or conviction that it can be done systematically and not *ad hoc*.

Social anthropology is interestingly contrasted to narrative history in that everything is the other way around, as it were: narratives do occur within anthropology, but it is precisely the narrative which is *ad hoc*, illustrative, unsystematic, unbound by any obligation to be complete and rounded off. It is the structural account which is central – the specification of the constraining limits and their sanctions. The ideal sought is a kind of stalemate situation, the demonstration that whatever move is attempted by any participant, the resulting situation must needs remain the same. (This does not mean that the method is committed to some absurd postulate of universal social stability. Noncircular as well as circular situations can be constrained. Circular ones are only the simplest and most manageable ones.) The structure is the thing; the stories are incidental.

It is of course natural that anthropology should have developed these traits. It was initially concerned with milieux that were highly exotic, with games whose rules were far from familiar. At the same time, lack of historical records in the societies in question made long story-sequences hard to come by, and such records as happened to be available were highly suspect. Hence a concentration on eliciting the tacit structures was imposed both by the inherent nature of the material and by the lack of opportunity for other concerns.

But why should a similar attitude be mandatory closer to home, where fascinating and well-documented "stories" are available, and where at the same time the rules of the game are not so exotic and unfamiliar?

For one thing, it seems to me that the familiarity, or at any rate the intelligibility, of the local rules of the game is an illusion. Though a society is not nearly as similar to a language or a code as current fashion would have it, nevertheless I am sure that what Chomsky says in the abstract and negatively about grammar is also true about the rules of social life:

"Clearly, the rules and principles of... grammar are *not accessible to consciousness in general*, though some undoubtedly are... what we discover... is that those principles and rules that are accessible to consciousness are interspersed in some obscure and apparently chaotic way among others that are not, the whole complex... constituting a system of a very tight and intricate design…" (John Locke Lectures, given in Oxford in 1969. Italics mine.)

No doubt we are in thrall to a kind of social Unconscious, to a set of partly obscured conventions or rules governing our own operations, though this unconscious is not at all of a Freudian kind (which was merely a weird and wild caricature of the kind of connections we recognise consciously). Nothing is more false than the supposition that we have easy, direct and privileged access to the conventions governing our own conduct simply because it is our conduct, because we "live" through the concepts which accompany it. We have nothing of the kind.

What follows is that the whole notion of restricting history to an account of "how it really was" is an absurdity. It is common to criticise this idea on the grounds that "what really happened" needs to be selected and interpreted. No doubt. But the really crucial objection is that the connections between events that "really happened" are anything but self-evident, and that such self-evidence as they may seem to have to the participants is illusory.

In some measure, the rapid and dramatic nature of social change has brought this point home. Contemporary history is seldom a long story within a stable and familiar game. It does not encourage the illusion of the self-evident status of the rules of the game. It does not any longer make social structure invisible through excessive familiarity. On the contrary, it makes it painfully problematical. Our social environment is like the controls of a very unfamiliar vehicle. We gingerly press the accelerator and find it to be a brake. We slam the foot on the brake and find it to be an accelerator. In such conditions, the illusion that there are no hidden mechanisms, that the role of the social levers is self-evident and inscribed into the nature of things, and that their instinctive mastery is our birthright – these illusions are no longer so tempting. Profoundly alien and barely intelligible conventions and connections are not exotic and distant, but close to home – and sometimes they envelop us.

All this being so, the sociologising of history, the acquisition of the kind of sensitivity possessed by the anthropologist, is natural and inevitable.

Collapse of horizons

Within its seriously held cognitive stock, our society possesses only naturalistic and tentative cosmogonies, whose role in chartering current social arrangements is negligible; and, in the literal sense, it possesses no eschatologies at all.

But given that cosmogonies and eschatologies, or what we have called the social horizons, did in the past constitute an important part of the vision of societies, one may well ask – what performs their role today?

The answer is obvious. The horizons have, so to speak, collapsed into the present. The crucial events which are the charters of moralities, which mold the decisive features of our life, which limit, articulate and help evaluate our options, are not on the skyline, but, on the contrary, very close to home. The distant horizons, though not necessarily shabby or dull, are not very relevant. Contemporary history is not merely very dramatic, but, more significantly, it is crucial for the formulation, selection, validation of such alternatives as humanity may face. I used to think that we at any rate were a generation which could actually witness the drawing of the Social Contract, by observing the manner in which societies chose to "develop" themselves. So we are, but it is really even deeper than that. We can witness a Creation story. Genesis is something that we read in the present tense.

Let us recapitulate possible types of cosmogonies. The list may not be exhaustive, but it will include those species that make claims on our attention.

a) Traditional Genesis-type stories. Usually located in the fairly distant past. Characterised by the fact that they are structure-blind – the rules of that distant game, the outcome of which was our world, are taken for granted. In this kind of story, the *dramatis personae* are introduced (or is introduced, in the singular) and perform acts which bring about our world. Who or what decreed that they should have the options which they appear to have, and that the options should have the effects which, according to the story, they do have? Answer comes there none, for the question does not seem to have been asked. Take one example: there must, it seems, have been a kind of meta-world within a deity who chose, for ends which must make sense within that world and which would seem to be somewhat vainglorious, to create our world in order to suggest its own prestige by receiving the adulation of its own creation. A curious

story, and one which hardly lives up to the highest moral standards recognised inside our created world. Teachers, or manufacturers of arte-
facts, who openly avow the aim to have themselves praised by their own
products, are somewhat comic figures. But what is relevant for our purpose is that this strange meta-story moves within a framework, the rules
of which it takes for granted.

Charles Lamb has some apt comments on this curious acceptance of
mysterious rules *(Essays of Elia: Witches and Other Night Fears)*:

"That the intercourse was open at all between the two worlds was perhaps the mistake – but that once assumed, I see no reason for disbelieving
one attested story of this nature more than another on the score of absurdity. There is no law to judge of the lawless, or canon by which a dream
may be criticised.

"Our ancestors were bolder or more obtuse. Amidst the universal belief
that (witches) were in league with the author of all evil, holding hell
tributary to their muttering... no simple justice of the peace seems to have
scrupled issuing... a warrant upon them – as if they should subpoena
Satan! Prospero in his boat, with his books and wand about him, suffers
himself to be conveyed away at the mercy of his enemies to an unknown
island. He might have raised a storm or two, we think, on the passage....
We do not know the laws of that country."

Lamb is tactfully commenting on those episodes in which the Other
world impinges on our own, but his point is doubly valid for the Opening
and Closing scenes of our drama, when the Other world initiates or
terminates our play as whole. "We do not know the laws of that country."
Nor do we know those of our own, though when they are stable we may
take them for granted. But just as in stable conditions our own are taken
for granted, so the unsophisticated take for granted both ours and those
of the other country. It takes a Robertson Smith to spell out the tacit
rules which the simple believer knows only through their unquestioned
effects, whose ground rules he does not query. But, once queried, this kind
of cosmogony collapses.

b) The Enlightenment. In its typical form, this is a clear ancestor of
our own vision in that the crucial event is close to home and not somewhere in the skyline. It takes the dualistic religious vision and inverts and
naturalises it: where the Kingdom of God stood opposed to the world of
the Fall from Grace, there now stood Reason and Nature as opposed to
the illusion of the Kingdom of God. But, notoriously, the Enlighten-

ment's understanding of the two crucial options was rather limited. It was the failure to implement its vision after 1789 that forced its votaries to develop a more serious sense of social structure.

c) Evolutionist or Hegelian-type cosmogonies. The two-term vision of the Enlightenment was replaced by something far more ramified and correspondingly less crowded into the historic present. Crucial things may indeed be happening now, but similarly crucial ones had been happening, it appears, for quite a time. *All* history and not just the elimination of infamy was the revelation of a Grand Design. The locus of crucial events remains the historic world, but the cruxes are, so to speak, far more dispersed. Romanticism is of course far less ethnocentric in time than was the Enlightenment. It naturally has a far better sense of social structure and a greater sensitivity to its variety. On the other hand, it tends to overrate historical continuity, the unilineality of development, and the identity of basic underlying plot. As a cosmogony, it is hardly acceptable to us, precisely because it overrates continuity and uses this for facile and unacceptable solutions. "More of the same", where what "the same" is varies as between, say, Hegelians and Spencerians, is no longer a plausible formula when we come to choose our directions.

d) The empiricism-atomistic picture. Officially of course this is not a cosmogony at all, but merely an epistemology. In fact, it does tell a kind of story of how the world came to be built up – *Der Logische Aufbau der Welt* – as one of the authors in this tradition brazenly has it. Moreover – a fact not always noticed – this world-construction story does indeed perform the role of cosmogonies and provides a premiss and charter for a general world-outlook, for a view of human life. It says, in effect, that each man's world is built up anew, from homogeneous sensory constituents, which are the ultimate elements of all things. Its motto might well be – every man is his own cosmogony.

The corollary of this, which in fact we frequently find exemplified amongst modern representatives of this school, is an almost total lack of a sense of history. Though they are sometimes called positivists, they differ markedly in this respect from Comte who bequeathed them the name. Given the importance they attribute to their own vision, one might expect them to be interested in the differences between societies Before and After Positivism. As Christians were sometimes worried whether Socrates ought not to have been amongst the saved, notwithstanding the unfortunate dating of his life, these positivists might wish to face the same problem

in reverse and be puzzled by the occurrences of genuine cognition prior
to their own Illumination. But it is not so. In many cases, their blindness
to history and society is total.

e) The Neo-Enlightenment view – our own. For a variety of reasons,
since 1945 it has become difficult to begin a classification of societies
with any dichotomy other than industrial/preindustrial. This distinction,
so platitudinous now, did of course require clear formulation before it
became obvious, and Raymond Aron will remain associated with its
brilliant articulation. A variety of factors made the categories which were
still in use during the war – such as democracy, capitalism and socialism –
visibly irrelevant. There is no need to rehearse once again the factors which
contributed to this shift of vision.

The consequence was a view which was once again, like that of the
Enlightenment and unlike the intervening Evolutionism, a two-term one,
and one which located the crucial transition somewhere near the present
rather than at the beginning or the end of time. But it is a vision less
starry-eyed than that of the Enlightenment, incorporating romantic
regret as well as progressive hope, and above all, a vision taking over
from the 19th century a far richer sense of the diversity and complexity of
social forms.

I have endeavoured elsewhere to spell out the presuppositions and
consequence of this vision.[3] Perhaps, like other and earlier (and hence
more excusable) writers, I overrated the homogeneity and simplicity of
the transition. Formally, I doubt whether the text could be convicted of
such an error, and the same is probably true of other writers of the time,
and earlier. But what is at issue is not anyone's prophetic record but
rather the recognition of a shift of perception in recent years. Whether or
not one formally excluded it, one did not sufficiently stress the manifold,
complex, multistage nature of the "development" process.

The work of the economist Arrow on voting procedures is well known.
A famous point is that given an electorate with a set of individual pre-
ference-rankings for a set of alternatives, if the alternatives are presented
for voting in pairs, successively (with the loser eliminated in each case),
the final option selected will depend on the *order* in which the choices
have to be made. For reasons which cannot be so neatly formalised, the
development process seems to possess a similar characteristic. A number
of various decisions need to be taken, in the economic, political, social
and other fields. The order in which the various choices are made have

important, perhaps permanent, consequences on the way in which "development" is attained. To take the most obvious example, it makes an enormous difference whether a society embarks on the developmental process with well-established liberal pluralistic institutions, or whether the attempt to acquire them is only made in the course of it. The two traits, economic development and liberal institutions, are not just parts of a syndrome which may be expected to turn up in one order or another: the sequence of appearance or option may be quite crucial for the final pattern.

It is hardly possible here to discuss specific theses in this area, but the kind of awareness described naturally leads to the formulation of questions such as J. Barrington Moore's[4] concerning the effect of the position of the peasantry on the subsequent pattern of development, or David Martin's[5] projected work on the quite diverse social patterns characterisable as "secularisation".

Development is not a single path – unilinealism has by now died many, many deaths – it is a complex network of routes. Even Marx's "Precapitalist Social Formations", if plotted on paper, would look not like a single great road, but more like the Southern Railway's commuter network. But the network is not endlessly permissive. Some early choices perhaps commit one, or damn one, forever. So we are witnessing not merely the Social Contract and Genesis; we are also privileged to observe what normally is transcendental and hidden, that great existential moment when large portions of humanity commit, or hover on the brink of, Original Sin and Eternal Damnation. Admittedly, even when we see them take the leap, we cannot be quite sure that we can reliably distinguish the Saved from the Damned. We may be allowed to hope that in the end God's mercy will prevail and *all* will be saved. But nothing entitles us to reject with confidence quite the opposite hypothesis. This also is an essential part of our contemporary historical sensitivity.

The logic of creation

The price of the collapse of horizons, of the shift of cosmogony and eschatology into the present, is that one acquires only too intimate an experience of the logic of an absolute Creation situation. To be eye-witness of Genesis is not altogether enviable. Creation out of nothing – in other words Creation rather than mere creation – presents some rather special problems. I am not referring to the technical problem of how such a miracle can be wrought. This need not worry us: we know that it is happening, and the "how" can be left aside. The problem which does concern us is how one chooses one's aims, one's course of action, in a Creation situation.

Ordinary, non-Creation situations have a fairly straightforward logic. A stable identity is assumed for the agent, which implies reasonably stable basic aims. Likewise, a reasonably stable, determinate environment is assumed. These two things being given, it follows, for any given level of information, and assuming consistency, that one (possibly more if things are evenly balanced) optimal course of conduct is indicated.

But the point is that a real Creation situation is not at all like this. *Everything* and notably aims and environment are themselves being created. What, then, can dictate, or even suggest, the course of action to be followed by the Creator?

Primitive cosmogonies evade this problem in their naive way by covertly making the creation less than total, by tacitly or otherwise crediting the Creator with a given set of aims (such as a curious concern with his own glory, which apparently can be augmented when endorsed by his own, suitably programmed creation), and a constraining environment which must somehow limit his choice of means in the attainment of that rather peculiar aim. If such constraining circumstances were not present, he could presumably decree the end directly, without the cumbersome and troublesome intermediary use of an often recalcitrant creation. The story of religious creation mirrors the logic of action as we normally know it. It completely fails to give an account of the problem of what genuine Creation would be like. Perhaps this did not matter much when a pure Creation situation was well outside the range of our own possible experience. My point is, however, that what is now known as "development" has forced this unusual experience on us, and we must ponder its logic.

It may of course be objected that our situation is not a "pure" creation situation at all, either because in fact we start not from void but from a complex pre-industrial civilisation, or because we are not bereft of all directives, of all given aims and directives, but on the contrary possess, incapsulated in our nature, some "basic human needs" or something of the kind: the need to cater for these saves us from the moral vacuum, from the normative *premiss-lessness* credited to a "Creation" situation. These objections are invalid. Factually, it is of course true that our historic starting point was not some total void, but a complex social order. So it was. But that inheritance has no authority over us whatever. It is of the essence of the Development process, not that all of the past is abrogated, but that none of it is authoritative. It cannot be invoked; the fragments of it that survive do so either because they were validated by other, non-traditional considerations, or because they came into no conflict, were involved in no issue, and were perpetuated from a kind of indifference. As for those "basic needs" (a favourite philosophical ploy under a variety of names), they are so basic, elementary, minimal and unspecific that almost nothing can be inferred from the need to satisfy them. All important questions concerning the form of life that we are to mold are about *how*, not *whether*, they are to be satisfied – and on this, they can offer no guidance whatever. It could also be claimed that technology is not and will not be so powerful as to free us from all restraints. Certainly this is so. Nevertheless, the range of choice it now tends to offer is so wide that our problem is the choice within that range, and we are not much helped by the consideration that the range itself is not limitless.

The questions posed by a Creation situation have no determinate answer. The very terms of reference preclude it. Yet those terms of reference do, for reasons indicated, correspond pretty well to our general situation.

So? In practice, the problem is evaded. It is true that the old values are suspended. The famous "transvaluation of all values" which preoccupied most 19th century moralists in addition to Nietzsche (such as the Utilitarians or Marx, though they used other terms) was really only a suspension of the old values: all those moralists are convincing when they suspend the old and unconvincing, ambiguous and vacillating in their choice of new ones.

But in practice, all the new options turn up, as we stressed in the discussion of the complexity of the development process, not all together, not on one agenda, not in one fell swoop, but in dribs and drabs, one by one. Moreover, so far at least, and by all appearances also for quite some time to come, the options arrive well before we are in full and untrammeled possession of the new technological powers. They come when there are still strong pressures on very scarce resources, in circumstances which, by accident rather than from long-term and considered design, dictate this or that interim solution. So, by the time we do have full technological elbow-room, the options will have been prejudged by the more or less accidental pressures which operated when the relevant crossroads was first reached. Interim solutions became parts of viable, habituation-hallowed cultures.

This, then, is another curious and ironic role history has within our general vision: it helps to prejudge questions for which, if we had to face them rationally, we could simply have no determinate answers. All the premisses would be too slippery. One great interest of contemporary history is just this: how does the sequence of alternatives, and the pressing circumstances in which they make their appearance in diverse societies, help prejudge the questions of value, which otherwise would be beyond the scope of rational decision? Traditional societies credited their ultimate choices, over which they had no control and which they did not much understand, to the nature of things or the whim of gods. We have (we like to think) some understanding of how the choices arise, and our history intrigues us by narrowing our range of choice, thus saving us from the embarrassment of excessive free will.

NOTES

1. For instance, Mrs. Shirley Letwin writes (*Spectator*, 9 January 1971, pp. 52, 54):
    "...historians are not concerned with what might have happened, they try to explain what actually did happen. They do not explain an event in terms of its connection with universal laws; they trace its connection with other events. ...as long as he remains a historian, he... (does not use) events to illustrate laws."
    Mrs. Letwin, who clearly here speaks as the representative of a whole school, proceeds, rightly from her viewpoint, to repudiate Max Weber, ideal types, and the whole Kantian notion that rational explanation must mean subsumption under general law. The contrasted ideal appears to be accurate narrative, rational in some other, non-Kantian sense.
2. *Cf.* Bryce Gallie, *Philosophy and Historical Understanding*. London, 1964.
3. *Thought and Change*. London, 1964.
4. *Social Origins of Dictatorship & Democracy*. Boston, 1966.
5. Notes for a general theory secularisation. *Archives Européennes de Sociologie*, Tome X, 1969, No. 2.

Discussion

RAYMOND ARON: The idea for this seminar originated with Professor Bullock, and the starting-point was the question of what might be called, for want of a better expression, a change or decline in historical consciousness.

This might mean a number of different things. It could refer to an alteration in what the Germans call the "*geschichtliches Bewusstsein*" – *i.e.*, to a different sense of our own place in history, a change in the general mental image of history. But it could also mean a decline in curiosity about the past, or, in the absolute sense, the beginnings of an indifference to what has been and an obsession with what is and will be. It could also signify an increased interest in that part of the past which is not called historical – in other words, in the past of archaic societies. Finally, it could refer to a falling-off of interest in the activities of academic and professional historians as compared with those of experts in the social sciences.

ERNEST GELLNER: I shall be dealing with the relationship of historical and anthropological methods. The feeling I have when faced with a pure narrative historian is a sense of just incompleteness in my failure to understand. This seems to me the relevant point about the relationship of the two disciplines. This sort of negatively ideal type of the pure narrative historian strikes me as a man who is too much at home in the world, an attitude which I find disturbing in anyone; the kind of sense of being-at-homeness which assumes that the game that is being played is totally familiar. According to me, people occasionally have this misguided feeling because they immerse themselves in the material, and they have the illusion that the game which is being played is somehow obvious.

I don't know whether the interest in the common societies which are the

paradigmatic hunting grounds of the anthropologist has brought home
the fact that the contexts in which social games are played out are by no
means self-evident. The anthropological tribe has itself its traditions about
the epistemology of anthropology, about how people are specialized and
trained to be anthropologists; the "folklore" consists in a kind of baptist
theory of knowledge, by total immersion. The anthropologist is meant to
be thrown into a society which is utterly alien to him: the trauma of suddenly having his connections dislocated and the need to reestablish them
is what really trains them. This is the belief anthropologists have about
their own method and the kind of ritual therapeutic and cognitive value
of fieldwork. What strikes me about the world we actually live in, not
some tribal and alien world, is that it is anything but intelligible. I suppose
my resentment against the people who feel terribly at home in the world
springs, like most resentments, from envy and jealousy. Whenever I
switch on the news to get a bit of narrative instalment on contemporary
history, I can more or less understand what the newscaster is saying, but
the reasons why the range of alternatives should be what they are assumed
to be seem to me not at all obvious. The essence of the social sciences,
taken in a broader sense and perhaps excluding economics, is that they
endeavour to specify the structure within which the game is being played.

I won't attempt to define structure formally. But the very least a structural account does (and I mean structural in the old-fashioned sense, not
in the sense of the *"structuralistes"*, who I think are inspired by a very
misguided analogy with language) is first of all to present the alternatives
which are available, and secondly to explain what sanctions, what constraints define and delimit those alternatives. Pure narrative history fails
to do this.

Economic phenomena, for instance, are a very important part of the
structures which envelop us, and the complaint I constantly have against
the economists is how very little they help us to understand the alternatives which face us, for reasons which are the very opposite of the reasons
which may inhibit historians. They are not preoccupied with narrative,
but with a kind of abstract account which seems to me the wrong kind of
abstraction. By the time you have a long-sustained abstract argument you
are so far away from your premises and so many errors have entered at
each step that the likelihood of your being relevant is very small. Economic phenomena always struck me as being disguised by two sets of
assumptions and two languages. On one hand, we find the private tribal

language of the financiers and the actual practising City men and that of the economists. On the other hand, economists make a double mistake: first of all they take the first language seriously rather than adopting the kind of sceptical strategy which anthropologists adopt towards the language of the tribe they study, and secondly (having taken the City much too seriously), rather than explaining what constraints and what camouflages operate, they give a theoretical account which is very questionably illuminating.

I can be a little more constructive in my offerings: I would like to refer to a passage which struck me in some lectures of Professor Trevor-Roper in which he is explaining why he finds European history more interesting than the fashionable extra-European Third World kind of history. I can't remember the actual words, but Professor Trevor-Roper found it difficult to take an interest in the gyrations of tribes one succeeding another in a kind of chaotic manner, which is what Afro-Asian history certainly often looks like. But any kind of first immersion in the available histories of extra-European territories tends to look exactly like this. One of the few theses of research I've undertaken did concern a territory the history of which can certainly be presented as a kind of meaningless tale of a succession of tribal movements.

Well, I didn't get at all bored with it; what made it interesting was that it had a structure under the apparently chaotic mood. It isn't a structure in the sense of the *"structuraliste"*; it is a structure in a semi-materialist sense in which there is no onesone correlation between the economic base and the conceptual and institutional alternatives which a society possesses. The exploration of that kind of structure is of interest not merely because it enables us to understand a society which otherwise would be a dull kind of tale-tell by an idiot but also because we lose our conceptual virginity or naïveté with respect to our own society.

RAYMOND ARON: Both in the study of the archaic and in that of the historical past there is an attempt to discover "the other". And even if the other is more other in archaic societies than in our own past, might one not say this quest is something the anthropologist and the historian have in common?

How far does the notion of structure, introduced by Mr. Gellner in a very general sense to criticize a kind of chronicle no longer found in any modern history book, differ from the notion of historical content or of comprehension of a given period? Dissatisfaction with mere narration is not a novelty due to the influence of ethnology. Burckhardt, for example, was convinced that historical comprehension consisted in the discovery of the rules of the game, or the constraints, of a certain period. In other words, to show how the ethnologists' structure differs from that of the historians', one must go beyond the idea of constraints, rules of the game, and value systems characteristic of a society. Speaking of the ethnologists' curiosity, Lévi-Strauss says we only really discover the "other" who enables us to understand ourselves when we go and look for him in some other place. For him, Rousseau is the ethnologist par excellence, the man who helps us understand ourselves because he does not only look for the other who is near, the other who is inserted into the historical process, the other who is a moment in the cumulative, intelligible process you have described, but for what might be called the absolute other.

FRANÇOIS FURET: The image of the other has changed a good deal in the last two hundred years. If one takes the eighteenth century, Rousseau for example, uncivilized man is "the other"; but at the same time he is subtly linked to civilized man in that he represents the latter's infancy. It was the economic development of the nineteenth century which made the non-European world the embodiment of absolute other-ness. History then became the study of change, ascribing to all human activity the spectacular rhythms of economic activity, whether according to Marx or to the Manchester School. It was probably then too that the non-European universe became the reverse of the historical one – an unwanted assortment of immobile societies that did not change. Today we are witnessing a kind of planetization of the globe: there are no more faraway worlds; in a way, all are familiar. On the other hand our own world, as Mr. Gellner says, becomes completely mysterious to us, as it drifts towards some unknown future devoid of any eschatological, cosmogonical, or even evolutionist vision; we are witnessing a kind of enormous crisis in linear progress. Strangeness has come back into our own world. The dialectic between "the other" and "the same", between the historical and the non-historical world, is in the process of disappearing from our consciousness, in so far as, mankind having become one, no one knows its future any more, though all know it will be the same for everyone.

For all these reasons it seems to me that the ethnologist's and the historian's views of the world of today are quite close to one another. It is no longer possible to give a good definition of history, even a rough one: history has benefited a great deal from the social sciences, economics, demography and ethnology; it has developed almost parasitically on the body of the social sciences, so that it is difficult to say whether it includes them or they it. There is always this ambiguity.

According to Mr. Gellner, what characterizes the epistemological "bridge" between ethnology and history is the notion of structure, not in Lévi-Strauss's sense of a code or language, but as a complex of constraints within which a society makes its choices. To me this seems insufficient: history's borrowings from the social sciences are much more definite than that. For example, the Paris and Cambridge historians who have reconstructed the demography of France and England between the sixteenth and nineteenth centuries have purely and simply imported demographic concepts and put together the demography of the *ancien régime* just as a modern demographer reconstructs the history of populations. There is no difference between the work of Louis Henry or Peter Laslett and that of an expert in present-day demography. The same is true with economics. History is importing concepts all the time.

ERNEST GELLNER: Is there any difference between preoccupation with structure and interest in context? I should have thought not. They are both vague notions; anything is part of context. But structure contains the notion of constraints and the concern with how those constraints are generated. It is quite possible to go a long way in history without having this strong sense of structure. Assuming the correct account is given it is quite possible to do interesting work on the assumption that people are very much the same in all places and times, that the basic game that is being played is the same one. This is very mistaken. But it is interesting that you can go quite a long way believing this.

PETER WILES: The semantic confusions are going to dog the whole of this conference. The first is whether we mean by the word historian a gentleman who draws his salary from that part of the academic register which is marked clearly "Department of History" (which I think some of us have already tended to mean), or whether we simply mean somebody who is trying to find out about a reasonably remote period, by whatever methods come in handy to him in his particular enquiry. I have in mind, for instance, Professor Trevor-Roper, whom I would accuse of having been a rather distinguished, middle-period sociologist when he wrote those interesting things on witches.

My other semantic warning is the usual one about *science* versus *Wissenschaft;* in the English language "science" means something that you can prove by some form of causal reasoning and generalisation from a statistically comparable universe, and therefore has tended to mean natural sciences, and when we say social sciences in English we mean that kind of science. *Wissenschaft* is not such a word at all, but it means study, *social studies* as it is sometimes called by the kind of Englishman who does not believe that the *Sozialwissenschaften* are sciences.

RAYMOND ARON: As regards the confusion between *science* and *Wissenschaft*, the French word *"science"* comes, of course, in between. If we take it in the sense of science, we should say there is only one real "science" in the social field, and that is *"la science économique,"* leaving aside of course the economist of the *Faculté de Droit*, who would not be regarded as scientific by the rest of the international community.

It seems to me there is a fairly clear-cut distinction in the notion of structure and context. Very few historians today are interested purely in describing what simply happened as an event. What you want is to find its meaning or find a pattern of explanation. The Russian Revolution happened but you can explain it as part of Russian development, or as part of working-class development, or as part of the rise of a new class. The difference here between a historian and a sociologist is then fairly simple. If I take for example my colleague Mr. Bracher, he is trying to explain a whole historical context which is the Nazi period. He is trying to explain a set of events within a bounded time. I am interested in his work as a sociologist because my interest is in the nature of patterns of domination, the relation between domination and authority, the relation between domination and consensus, not in order to define laws (because I don't think there are such things as laws), but at least to see if there are certain types of relationships which could then carry over into other circumstances.

KARL D. BRACHER: The question "What is history and what is social science?" depends really on how we look at each of them. Are we interested in their differences or in their interdependence? You can say history is part of the social sciences; in this case, I would use the German term *Wissenschaft;* but you can also say social sciences are part of history, and the interest you may have personally depends entirely on the subject you are dealing with in your scientific research. You may, for instance, be interested in the question of historical alternatives in certain situations. Take the Russian Revolution or take the Weimar Republic: you will ask the question "What could have happened if...," a question which the pure historian might have turned down. But I don't think he will turn it down today any longer. You need a systematic framework within which you can ask that question, for instance parliamentary democracy, or a certain type of social structure, and so forth. When I use the term structure, I would not agree entirely with the definition given by Mr. Gellner because I don't think social structure can be defined merely or mainly in terms of constraints. I think that social structure is to a certain degree the way in which human beings are enabled to act as historical beings, to develop human activity at all.

WALDEMAR BESSON: The question has come up whether context and structure are different. It is not too important to clarify the difference because it is obvious if you take context in the broad sense, it doesn't only mean a series of constraints but also a system of alternatives for action. It is not constraint alone, it is an opportunity for human beings to act and to create the future. On the other hand, I would feel that in social science and in history there is a definite tendency to underestimate what I should call the narrative element in historical writing in so far as, after all, social and political life is a growing thing, a process, a series of developing actions and events in which it is obvious that the purpose and resolve of those who act do not meet; but this is a triviality and this has always been, today and 2,500 years ago. Then, of course, what Mr. Gellner has pointed out becomes clear: that events apparently still have a feedback on the series of rules and regulations, constraints or system of alternatives. I would then call history an accumulated experience of ways to act without being determined once and for all as to what we are going to do in the future. Social science today neglects this aspect of determining the future by the accumulated experience of the past, without being forced to follow it blindly.

Today we have the necessary means to solve certain problems of the Greek city-state. Plato and Aristotle certainly didn't have them: they were as far away from solving the problems of their time as we are from solving the problems of our own. Therefore, the position of the historian, the man who thinks about what the past means for today and the future, has not changed at all.

ALAN BULLOCK: One of the easiest ways for myself to think about the relationship between history and the social sciences is to observe the change that has taken place since I was a student in one or two fields with which I am familiar. Like Professor Trevor-Roper, I began my interest in history with classical history; in those days (in the 1930s) the tradition was still that Greece was a unique culture; the people we admired were the folk who soaked and steeped themselves deeper and deeper in the knowledge of that society. I am quite sure they were aware of structure and of the fact that this society was different from them, but the way in which they dealt with the problem was to go deeper and deeper within that area. And if anybody had said to my teachers that Greece was just one example of a number of similar societies, they would have been scorned and this scorn ultimately would have sprung from the intellectual snobbery of the European tradition about this. It is true that anyone who studies the ancient history of Greece today would recognise that Greek society was one of a range of societies and that while, no doubt, it had very special characteristics of its own, there was merit all the time in seeing whether by looking at other societies you could not learn something about the civilisation of Greece. This is a real change. It does not mean that the man who still steeps himself in Greek culture does not excite our admiration as a scholar. But we would think a man who only does this and refuses to acknowledge the existence of comparable societies is in fact narrow-minded. Mr. Gellner has not quite made up his mind whether he is pleased to see that history borrows from the social sciences or resentful of the fact that it does so while still retaining chairs of history.

ERNEST GELLNER: I have no resentment at all against historians; my son at a very early age quite clearly wants to be a historian, which seems to indicate that the family atmosphere is not hostile to historians.

RAYMOND ARON: It could be interpreted both ways.

ERNEST GELLNER: Yes, it could be Oedipal.

STEPHEN GRAUBARD: I think what distinguishes the historian from the ethnologist is that the second is generally speaking about something which only he and a few others know anything about. He is constantly making discoveries: if he begins to work on a tribe, it is very frequently a tribe that only he and three others have ever examined. As historians, we are working with things everyone believes he knows something about. When we move into modern history, we find it is those of our colleagues who know the least but who write what seems to be the most widely distributed history who, in fact, answer to the needs of the greatest number of people.

WOLFGANG J. MOMMSEN: History as it is done now by professional people is more and more separate from everyday history, and this refers to political history just as much as to other kinds of history. In Germany, at least, every young historian wants to be a social scientist or to use as much as possible of sociology and related sciences in his work.

RAYMOND ARON: The notion of "not feeling at home" seems to me to have taken on two quite different meanings in the course of the discussion. To be ill at ease is a feeling very widespread in human history in general, and today in particular. But what Mr. Gellner is getting at is the illusion, which we all nourish, that we know our own society and how to act in it. This has nothing to do with the feeling of being at home or the reverse.

The virtue of anthropology consists in reminding us that we have to discover the rules of our own society just as we discover those of archaic societies. A sense that we are unconscious of the rules of our own behaviour is not the same as a sense of the unintelligibility of our society.

ERNEST GELLNER: I accept the two senses of "not being at home," except that I wouldn't go as far as to say they are completely opposed. The sense of unintelligibility and cognitive "not at homeness" seems to me a species, one particular form of a general *Angst*. I accept what Mr. Bullock said about his mentors having had a sense of structure, but they merely combined it with a kind of admiration for the Hellenes as ancestors and a lack of interest in others. This ethnocentrism does seem to me to cast some doubt about how clear-minded they were about structure. Once you have this notion, the only way of getting evidence about how a structure works is to see how the elements are varied. To take a contemporary classicist, Moses Finley, I'm interested in some of his work precisely because when he writes about the Greeks he tends to look over his shoulder at the Berbers who share with the Greeks their experience of being a Mediterranean culture and a certain number of interesting features and similarities. Of course, anybody who does history from the viewpoint of awarding moral marks, anybody who does a sort of Clark history of civilizations will be interested in those two peoples from precisely opposite obvious viewpoints. The Berbers have been there for a very long time, and their main interest is that they've changed very little and that they've achieved relatively little, whereas the Greeks achieved a lot and then in their old form disappeared.

I'm not doing a plug for my own work because it was not on oases but up on the mountains. But the mountain and the desert, the nomads and the mountaineers, exemplify the principles of segmentary organisations which is a fairly well explored theme in anthropology. Something quite interesting happens in the oasis: the oasis continues to have clan organisation, but the fact that they are in an oasis, in other words living very close to each other and have to cope with certain problems by joint action, forces them to become a semi-civic organisation. You get a very interesting cross between segmentary opposition of opposed kin groups and some kind of city organisation. I think some of the material assembled on oases will throw some light on the way a city state may emerge from a more nomadic clan organisation when it is packed into one valley and has other interests than protecting its pasture and dividing up internally.

The distinction between the kind of social structure which I am preaching and the fashionable structuralism is really worth stressing. There is an enormous difference between society and language, and the real weakness of the structuralist fashion is the terrible overrating of the similarity. What makes language such a unique phenomenon is that the problem of social control seems to be so easy. Linguistically speaking, mankind is terribly well behaved. It is true that people form their own language and speak ungrammatically from time to time, but on the whole the extent to which they obey the rules is really quite remarkable, given the complexity of those rules and the enormous richness of the material. The paradoxical thing is that the number of things you can do in society is much smaller than the number of things you can say. Yet whilst our range is far smaller socially than it is linguistically, we obey the social rules far less. In society control is a major problem, whereas in linguistics it is curiously unimportant because, for some mysterious reason, people observe the rules: for this reason most of Lévi-Strauss's programme seems to me rather suspect.

FRANÇOIS FURET: There is not only the fact that we feel we know the rules of historical societies. There is also the fact that we have elaborated that kind of history in order to be able to "place" ourselves in the concatenation of time, so we feel in a filial relation to it. But no one feels in a filial relation to Malinovsky's Trobiands or to Lévi-Strauss's South Americans (except Lévi-Strauss himself!). To a certain extent the existential choice of the anthropologist is a marginal one. On the other hand, a Frenchman in relation to the French Revolution, or an American in relation to the Boston Tea Party, or a Russian in relation to 1917, all these feel in, so to speak. familiar situations, before events which lack strangeness insofar as they have been interiorised. It is for this reason that revolutionary phenomena are only weakly conceptualised: everyone thinks he understands them because we have interiorised what might be called their contemporary interpretation. If you look at the French Revolution you find that in fact the interpretation of it was given in 1789 by Sieyès before it actually broke out; and 170 years of commentaries and historical studies have really added little since, at the conceptual level, to the general interpretation. History makes us sons while anthropology makes us strangers: the two types of knowledge resemble and approach each other through the strangeness each kind of researcher feels in relation to his subject.

WALDEMAR BESSON: Social scientism in history, trying to get away from the narrative side, has now reached a point where very important analytic tools are lacking in our understanding of what is going on. I have had an opportunity to look into the Russian Revolution in a larger context. For me, it became quite clear that if you do not follow very closely the chain of events of 1917, 1918 and 1919 you don't understand why and how this new state and society really could emerge. The fashion of the science side has reached such important aspects of historiography that I feel we are now deficient in something we may have overdone in the past. Some people write the history of National Socialism as if a person called Hitler never actually existed. And this tendency can only occur when you underestimate the narrative side. One sees throughout the countries of the West that social science apparently doesn't increase the amount of rationality in our society; on the contrary. There is a new romanticism growing because of this concentration of the present issue, forgetting that after all people have thought about this before. So again my plea is for a rather classical history, out of sheer interest in the rational approach to human events.

ERNEST GELLNER: In one sense the only evidence you have for structure is sequences of events. But in stable structures, what you mainly look at is repetitive patterns. When you speak about the Russian Revolution, you say you can't understand what happened in the twenties unless you look carefully at '17, '18 and '19; I had this experience with looking at Third World countries. After the achievement of independence, these countries, when they allow researchers in, tend to be flooded by Ph. D. students. They come in to do research on national integration, nation-building and other favourite topics; many of them are sociologists, and they sin, in this respect, more than anthropologists. They come equipped with certain techniques which are meant to be structure-sensitive. I don't simply mean that they are quantitative, that they have questionnaires, but the questionnaires are designed to elicit the class structure, the composition of interest groups and so on and the whole methodology is geared to the assumption of a stable structure. They arrive two or three days after independence, and the one thing they are totally insensitive to, because of the toolbox they have brought with them, is precisely the equivalent to your 1917-18: the impact of the trauma when power got redistributed.

In the area in which I did research, people remember what happened when the powers changed, who got killed and why and how at the transfer of power, and also the abortive attempts before. If you want to understand their political behaviour, you have to know the one crucial event which has not been repeated in many cases.

PETER WILES: Mr. Gellner, I am still bothered by the fact that you feel not at home. Do you believe that there really is an underlying structure in our society today as in societies studied in departments of anthropology? Or don't you just admit on second thoughts that what's gone wrong and why you don't feel at home is not because the announcer on the BBC isn't an anthropologist, it is because there isn't any structure. It's all gone. If I am right and if there isn't any structure, then isn't surely anthropology the least useful of all the social sciences for the study of the modern western world at this time? And don't we just, on the contrary, need the pure historian?

ERNEST GELLNER: As a listener to the news, as a citizen, I try to understand the economic predicament, for instance, of the country we inhabit, which is obviously important, and quite frankly I find it unintelligible. I am very fond of the aphorism attributed to Lord Home that the country faces two sets of problems: the political ones are insoluble and the economic ones are unintelligible.

KOSTAS PAPAIOANNOU: I should like to say a few words about that quest for other-ness which tends too much to be regarded as the privilege of ethnology. In the first place it is congenital with history and is a specific characteristic of the historical consciousness of the modern as opposed to the ancient world. To explain further what I mean, Herodotus was the type at once of the ethnologist and of the historian. But take the great texts in Plutarch's *De Iside*, where it says that "basically the gods of the Egyptians are our own gods": the fundamental tendency of ancient historiography is to abolish other-ness as such and to discover identity. On the other hand, what has characterised modern historical conscious-ness from its birth, *i.e.*, since the Renaissance, is the invention of the past as an aid to self-criticism. When the Greeks were brought back to life again, when Machiavelli spoke of the city of antiquity and deplored the degradation into which Christianity had plunged modern Italy, it was not in order to lay claim to ancestors: the Greeks were not ancestors at all; on the contrary, they represented the absolute "other," more formidable and threatening than all the "ancients" put together. The reference back was made above all in order to criticise a whole tradition and to relegate a thousand years of Christianity into the darkness of what are called the Middle Ages (as if the expression had any meaning). Similarly, all the other resurrections which have succeeded one another in the modern history of the West have all been part of a continually renewed challenge of the very foundations of the present. Take the resurrection which follow-ed that of the Ancients – that of the Noble Savage. This figure always makes me think of those strange verses by Ronsard, asking Villegaignon not to civilise the savages because he will make them *"comme nous qui par trop de raison trop malheureux sommes"* (like us, who through too much reason too wretched are). Here, long before Marcuse, is the theme of reason as repression. The same is true of China, which was literally invented to challenge the Western tradition, in the same way as the Schlegels transformed India into a land of wisdom by way of reaction against the rationalism of the seventeenth century. One could extend the list down as far as the discovery of African art by the Cubists. What characterises the modern historical consciousness and distinguishes it from all others is the desire to turn the whole of the past into the common heritage of all mankind. From the point of view of this kind of historical consciousness there can be no difference between ethnology and history. Both form part of the same historical universe, the only one we consider habitable.

The function of the historical consciousness is fundamentally critical: Marx reproached traditional economists with regarding bourgeois society as the only natural one, and thereby eternal, whereas it was by definition transitory and ephemeral. Hegel's, I think, will always remain the best definition of the historical consciousness. According to him it consists in feeling *"bei sich im Anderssein"* – at home in other-ness. History is simply the discovery of other-ness as such, an education of the mind aimed at making it feel at home in the being of "the other". Ethnology in the strict sense of the word can only be regarded as one means among many of bringing out both other-ness and the feeling of identity which should arise out of the experience of other-ness.

ALAIN BESANÇON: Mightn't one make the sequence not history and ethnology, but two types of history and then ethnology? The first type of history might be described as defining the ideal put forward by parents. Xenophon, Plutarch and Bossuet address themselves to a child or a prince to show him the exemplary way his ancestors lived. All that is not exemplary is outside the sphere of history. The second type of history tries to discover the genealogy of the self. Ethnology would then be a third attitude, trying to discover neither the ideal of the self nor the self as inherited, but a possible self. Savage man is not only primitive man but also the wolf-boy of the Aveyron forests or the Indian jungle, a man without mother or father. Perhaps this might help to clear up the notion of feeling at home or otherwise. The first type of history, exemplary and exalting, has a style that is extremely self-satisfied. But the history of the self, confronting man with the quest for his origins, will be disturbing, perhaps painful. As for ethnology, as its attitude is negative it will necessarily be revolutionary and nihilistic – an uncomfortable situation in which indeed one doesn't feel at all at home.

ALAN BULLOCK: I should like to comment on a point which arises from one's experience in teaching, especially teaching people who are not graduate students. It is a very prevalent view amongst the young that somehow or other social science enables one to take a shortcut to history. There's this dreary historian, who wants us to study what happened in 1933 in Germany or in 1917 in Russia – but why, since the social sciences make possible a shortcut through the ideal-type? It will enable us to dispense with the laborious, tedious work of the detail. That splendid word detail, which is so despised by many young people who come to be taught at universities, will be superseded by glittering generalisations. Every social scientist here will fall upon me and say "This is not what we are trying to do." Nonetheless, I think it is very important for them to make clear to us that they do not believe this is the case: when as a young historian I first encountered the social sciences I shared some of this feeling. I felt I could escape from the limitation of particular time and place by looking for the general elements in any given situation. But in the end the historian has to bring the insights which he gains from this excursion back to the particular area he is studying. It is this return to historical study after you have been examining all the evidence from other disciplines which is particularly painful and at the same time particularly salutary.

ERNEST GELLNER: One can understand students' desire for shortcuts in history: take for example the thesis of hydraulic society, a very schematic and very simple ideal-type which gives the students precisely one of these shortcuts to the whole of Asian history. If there is one geographic area where you would expect this thesis to apply it would be Mesopotamia, for instance. Here you have a society dependent on irrigation; what's more, unlike the Nile, the way the floods come is unpredictable. In order to survive the people of the Lower Mesopotamian valley are particularly at the mercy of efficient irrigation schemes which you would expect would call for centralised effort well beyond the powers of local groups. It happens that there have been some semi-historical and anthropological studies on the manner Southern Iraqi society co-exists with the irrigation problem; and the main result was that the thesis was entirely wrong and that the Southern Iraqi irrigation worked much more efficiently when it was not coordinated centrally, but when it was left to the interplay of uncentralised local tribal groups. When the Turks and the British got more efficient at suppressing the tribes and running the thing, it worked less well. But all these micro-studies which were done on Southern Iraqi irrigation wouldn't have had the interest and would have been rather dull if there hadn't been the stimulus of the hydraulic thesis to begin with.

Back to the definition of the term "structure", I think the notion is absolutely crucial. I could go so far as to say that it is co-extensive with scientific explanation as such. It is much more than the Monroe Doctrine. It is very difficult to define, I love it and I can't define it – I *could* give you definitions which would merely lead back in a kind of circle. What I would say is that one does very much notice when it is absent. One of the things which seems to me very striking about the whole protest movement of the sixties, particularly in America but elsewhere too, was its lack of a notion of structure. Whatever alternative you propose, there will be some distribution of power and of resources; you can't simply reject the present with a few slogans and assume that society can get on without structure. When people don't have a sense of it, you notice it.

The biography, the fate of individual human beings is always interesting. If you consider the recent success in England of the television series on Henry VIII and Elizabeth, the appeal was the kind of biographical treatment of dramatic events, but, in fact, the series was successful because it highlighted the difference in the rules of the game. Roughly speaking, most people's reaction watching it was something like the story about the Victorian lady's comment on Anthony and Cleopatra: "How unlike the home life of our own dear Queen"; the rules have changed. So that even in what you would call "crude" narrative history, which is the supplying of adventure stories for general consumption, there is room for tacit intelligence about structure.

FRANÇOIS FURET: I don't think it is possible to draw an absolutely strict line between structural and narrative history. Even the most empiricist of narrative histories implies a minimum of causality. Of course this sometimes takes the elementary form of *post hoc, ergo propter hoc:* whenever anyone organises material in the form of a narrative he presupposes a minimum genetic relation at least between couples of events. Narrative history does not leave the organisation of its material to chance: it implies a minimum of structural links between the events selected. If one turns to the more "scientific" history, it is clear that even that can never be a knowledge that can be formularized or a deductive science functioning, like theoretical political economy, through an abstract model from which truth may be deduced.

RAYMOND ARON: I wouldn't claim to summarise the discussion, but I should just like to take up two points which seem to me important. Professor Gellner's proposition that an explanation is essentially such through structure is surprising taken in relation to the epistemological literature on history, and very far from the Hempel-Drey discussion. I won't go into the question of how helpful it is to say at one and the same time that real explanation is through structure, and that structure is indefinable or cannot be satisfactorily defined. At all events it is not usual, in the logical and analytical literature on historical knowledge, to make use of the concept of structure to distinguish a valid explanation from an invalid one.

Professor Bullock's description of a return to history after passing through the social sciences links up in a way with the fundamental distinction established by Max Weber between sociology and history. Everything Weber wrote might be considered as belonging to historical knowledge. A book recently published in France calls him the great historian of the modern age.[1]

My third and last remark is that something would have been lacking if our discussion hadn't brought in left-wing students and university unrest. We should all be grateful to Professor Gellner for having put forward the recent troubles at the London School of Economics as the expression and symbol of unintelligibility.

FRANÇOIS FURET: I'd like to refer to a part of my paper which we didn't talk about in the general discussion this morning and which deals basically with the shift in historical curiosity. It seems to me that in the last twenty-five or thirty years there has been, all over the world, and in any case in Europe and the United States, a sort of great shift in the objects and methods of history, and I think this internal re-structuring of the historical field has some influence on the rapprochement between history and ethnology. So much so indeed that if a historian were asked today whether there is a fundamental difference between history and ethnology I think he would have some difficulty in replying because, it seems to me, there has been at one and the same time a historicisation of ethnology, arising out of the independence of formerly colonial nations and the advent of new political forms, and on the other hand an ethno-logisation of history. Some of the reasons for this are external ones, but I should like just to stress those reasons that are internal to history itself. In France the problem is usually set out in the form of the opposition between what we call *"histoire événementielle"* and *"non-événemen-tielle"* (or what Professor Gellner might call structural history). What is this history based on events? Perhaps we might try to define it. I would say it is a history which attempts to reconstruct what has happened in terms of special facts selected on the time axis and promoted to the dignity of "events." These events are not chosen systematically but in terms of a linear historical structure which generally, at least in the nine-teenth century, was teleological, *i.e.*, it was directed towards an end, to-wards more progress, more democracy, more reason, and so on. And however patiently the historian reconstructs, according to very strict critical rules, the historic fact which constitutes the event, the event conceived of as such derives its meaning from the external world and only does so because it is integrated into a sense of history, whether Hegelian, Manchester or Marxist, which is received so to speak from without. In my view one of the great transformations in the treatment of historical fact in the last twenty years has been the setting out of historical events in series and as recurring units over given periods. In a history where the data are set out in series the event is no longer a stage in some progress or march towards an end. An event is defined by its comparability with other facts which come before and after. In other words, history has simply imported the procedure of the economic curve, transposing it to the various levels of history, since clearly there can be curves of recurring events in economics and demography, and in certain areas of culture and politics. But this completely alters the definition of a fact or datum: the fact is no longer a datum in itself, but in relation to a body of similar and comparable units. From this point of view the corpus of historical fact is exactly similar to that of anthropology, economics, economic history, ethnology or demography. The only difference is that historical series may be diachronistic whereas series concerning, for example, kinship structures in a Pacific tribe are synchronistic. But ethnological series are not necessarily synchronistic, nor are historical series necessarily diachronistic: you do get bodies of historical fact which are the first, and bodies of ethnological data which are the second. As I said, the deciding factor comes from without. This is so much the case that at the level at which the historian works it seems to me that the difference has been completely effaced between the sort of historian who deals with series and, say, the anthropologist or what the British and Americans call the social scientist. I am not saying that this type of history – what we might call serial history – can be applied to all kinds of historical data. Obviously the historian who is writing a biography or, say, one who wants to make a price curve for corn in Rome in the second century B.C., will not find any series. What I do say is that the generalisation of this method over various sectors of history makes these sectors almost completely parallel with the social sciences as a whole. And this being so, what differentiates history is that part of it which it is impossible to organise, much less to set out as data comparable to that of the other social sciences.

This methodological transformation of history has been accompanied almost inevitably by the definition of new historical subjects. Once the historian starts interesting himself in series he is constructing a subject much more abstract than the concrete, individual man of traditional history. As one sees, for example, in Goubert, he is no longer concerned with Louis XIV but with the peasants who lived under his reign. He can reduce this peasant to an abstract demographic unit; in other words, one peasant is equivalent to another. Or he can reduce him to an abstract economic unit: the peasant is then seen as an economic agent, or in other words as a man stripped of his individuality. Whether he comes from Limousin or Wales, he is just a unit, *homo economicus* or *homo demographicus*. And to this extent there has been a shift from the great man to the anonymous man, who is at the same time abstract man. To this extent also, and by a rather amusing misunderstanding, the history which aimed at being the most scientific has met up with that which aimed at being the most democratic, through its preference for "the little man," through the kind of popularism which has invaded contemporary history during the last twenty or thirty years, and through the neglect of Caesar, Louis xiv, Pitt and Napoleon in favour of the traditional peasant, the revolutionary mob, the life-span and marriage-age of populations and their average number of children – in other words, for the statistical distribution, according to strictly probabilistic calculation, of historical population. Here again, the probabilistic analysis is of the type traditional in the social sciences, and imported from them by history. Once more, what I have been describing does not constitute a norm, and I do not claim that this type of history explains the court of Louis xiv or the Battle of Waterloo. But I do say that this kind of history has established itself as a consistent whole linked to the social sciences, beside which there continues to exist the history of the event defined as the improbable, *i.e.*, something which cannot be calculated according to probabilities.

Another aspect of this displacement of historical curiosity is that the history interiorised in the nineteenth century as a sense of progress, the history that was experienced as an extrapolation of the rhythms of production of material goods and of economic advance, has to a large extent given way to the history of inertias, and paradoxically enough to the history of non-developments. One of the most brilliant works of history in the last ten or twenty years is Leroy-Ladurie's *Histoire des paysans de Languedoc*, in which the author outlines a kind of homeostatic history. That is, he shows that between the crisis at the end of the Middle Ages (1350-1450) and the beginning of new activity in the 1750's, there is a long underlying cyclic history which follows a Malthusian rhythm governed by the relation population-subsistence. During this time there is no take-off; the factors here analysed demographically and economically are so organised as to block all growth; they produce thirty- or fifty-year sub-cycles which constitute the economic structures barring development under the French agrarian *ancien régime*.

This form of history, which might be termed abstract and anonymous, has also spread to political history. If one takes a part of the English School writing on the French Revolution – I'm thinking of those of Marxist tendencies: Rudé, Hobsbawm and, in a way, Cobb as well – the Revolution is seen from below, through the succession of units which make up the masses and which then have to be reconstructed according to the ultimately anthropological concept of collective behaviour. Both the anthropologist and the historian have difficulty in working with this concept, since one can never be sure where the transition from the individual to the collective takes place, or how far one may extrapolate from the individual to collective behaviour. I would go so far as to say that this type of historical analysis has spread beyond the demographic, economic and political aspects to reach certain forms of cultural history. There is a tendency now for history to go beyond what might be called the noble history of ideas, or in other words the history of noble ideas – those ideas we have designated as classical and of which we feel ourselves to be the offspring – and to discern for example in the eighteenth century in France not only Voltaire and Rousseau but also, at the village level, the delayed arrival of the counter-Reformation. This was spread out in time, arriving among the élite at the beginning of the seventeenth century, reaching the roughly urban level in the second half of that century, and, through a whole body of pious literature, spreading to the country people in what is supposed to be the anti-religious, anti-clerical eighteenth century. The same could be said about folklore and peasant mentality – the vast, basically unknown world of what might be termed an uncivilised peasantry. I see very little difference between the so-called primitive inhabitants of an underdeveloped society today, and the peasantry of the eleventh or sixteenth century, which though potentially our parent remains a world completely foreign to us. The deciphering of what little evidence we have on the culture of a peasantry at such periods is a great problem. It is aggravated by the fact that we can usually come at the peasants only through police records, or in other words through repression: a riot that escapes repression also escapes history. But we do have some positive things: we can trace history back on the basis of the folklore that survives in popular story, which, though threatened by industrialisation and rapidly disappearing, leads us back to similar evidence in previous centuries. I would willingly agree that this type of history has basically a conservative function because once you start to compare not such events as marked changes but factors that remain the same over a period of time, you are in danger, both by hypothesis and by definition, of discovering inertias. Such history is, therefore, I think, a good antidote to the Manchester-Marxist history of the nineteenth century, though being cumulative it cannot show what is extraordinary in the history of the West in the nineteenth century. In other words, I would say the ethnologisation of history is one of the great steps forward in contemporary history in that it has enabled historians to rid their minds of traditional images of change and to rediscover all the underlying inertias, blockages, crises and tensions. But it needs to be linked to a history or problematic of change, in order to rediscover at a higher level the richness and complexity which might be lost by too simple a history of inertia.

RAYMOND ARON: Do you think the event is necessarily linked to the linear structure of history? In reality there is neither a logical nor an intellectual nor an ideological link between them, except according to a rather peculiar conception of history revealed by the slip which makes you, Professor Furet, a historian of the French Revolution, take the French Revolution as the event par excellence. While a cyclic conception like Toynbee's has critical points such as the Peloponnesian War signifying the collapse of the civilisation of antiquity, the notion of an event is not at all linked to a unilinear view of things.

FRANÇOIS FURET: I agree, but an event is always selected in terms of an over-all significance.

RAYMOND ARON: There again I don't agree. Unless one misuses words, the "*événementielle*" conception is that which attaches greatest importance to events. But this conception often denies that there is any meaning in history. Take Seignobos, the most typical modern French representative of "*événementielle*" or, as it would seem to the Annales school, caricatural history. For Seignobos, political history consists of events signifying nothing and leading to nothing, except perhaps to the revelation that they do signify nothing and that men's acts are all foolishness.

FRANÇOIS FURET: I'm sure that if you looked closely at Seignobos's political history you would see that his treatment is that of a republican historian...

RAYMOND ARON: Yes, I grant you that...

FRANÇOIS FURET: ...and that he selects his events in terms of his own idea of the history of the republic in France. I don't think any "*événementielle*" history can choose its events with no regard whatsoever for meaning.

RAYMOND ARON: Of course, consciously or unconsciously every historian makes choices. But it doesn't seem to me inevitable that a narrative history of events, in particular diplomatic history or the history of international relations, must be in any way an oriented history. There can be a succession of states, wars, treaties, signifying nothing. Empires rise and fall. It's the very type of chaotic, incoherent history.

FRANÇOIS FURET: It's only apparently chaotic. If you take a historian who deals with the wars of the seventeenth century, his choices rest, though he doesn't say so, on the history of the Hapsburgs and the Bourbons. His selection of events means that for him human, or at least European history at that period consists in the conflict between the Hapsburgs and the Bourbons.

ALAN BULLOCK: There has been an enormous extension of the field of history which most historians would welcome. But one is still left with the question "what do we make of political history?" Some people would take the view that by turning to the history of the common people, of the people who do not participate, we are turning to a more virtuous history. Political history is basically about the exercise, the conquest, the distribution of power; I am afraid some exponents of the new fields of history are considering the issue of power no longer important. I believe that history as it has been written in the past, at least the rather far past, has neglected all the things you have spoken of. But if this is to be taken as showing that the decisions made by governments, the decisions arrived at in wars and diplomacies are in some way no longer important and no longer affect the life of the common man, this is a mistake. You have brought into being a new kind of history which enormously enriches the discipline, but I can't believe that it invalidates its old form.

Another point is, why is it essential that you tie together the idea of a history of events with the whole idea of unilinear development of progress? I wouldn't substitute for that a cyclical one like Mr. Aron, but simply no movement at all: people make decisions, power is exercised, it doesn't move but there are plenty of changes. We have a difference between change and movement here and what we are saying is that there is a history of change which is not necessarily tied up with the belief that it is a movement towards anything.

FRANÇOIS FURET: I've no prejudice against political history. I think it is the most difficult to write and the most complex, and that since the great school of Namier and his successors nothing fundamental has been added on the methodological plane. History is capable today of describing systems, but not the system of systems. So we need to be modest. I mistrust any over-all synthesis because I think such a thing is beyond the reach of history in its present state.

WOLFGANG J. MOMMESEN: Mr. Furet, you argue that in the traditional history each "*fait*" in the "*histoire événementielle*" receives its importance in an ideological context. I would raise the question whether your "*série*" does not have almost the same character; you select series not only because they are available but because they have a certain importance in a larger context.

FRANÇOIS FURET: I think nevertheless there is a fundamental difference. Suppose we take demographic history as an example of serial history. Between 1945 and 1950 people in France and England started to reconstruct population figures for the past. What is the ideology behind that? There isn't one. All that happened was that history imported a model from contemporary demography – a very different matter from a historian selecting his facts in accordance with a definite problematic. One of the things discovered in the process is that under the *ancien régime* in both France and England, in the period from the seventeenth to the eighteenth century, women married at the age of twenty-six, instead of at fourteen as in Shakespeare and Molière. This unexpected discovery was a heuristic one – derived not from the description of an event selected from the concatenation of time, but from the building up of a body of data as in contemporary demography. Of course, the problem of causality remains unsolved: it is an open question whether it was for cultural or ecological or other reasons that women married at twenty-six. But a field of history had been revealed which is absolutely non-ideological and scientifically certain.

RAYMOND ARON: How do you define serial history? Do you use it to mean simply the history of a particular aspect of reality, or the history of an aspect of reality which presents certain particular charactristics?

FRANÇOIS FURET: I define serial history as a history with a particular way of selecting facts, based on the existence, or more exactly on the construction, of similar, homogeneous and recurring data.

RAYMOND ARON: A profession of faith! "*Evénementielle*" history is an obscure idea because it was used polemically by the *Annales* school to dismiss those who practised it. François Furet has exposed it to a further degree of scorn by implying that this history or arbitrarily chosen events in fact concealed an ideology – though, talking of ideology, there is also an ideology implicit in the history of the *Annales* school.

WALDEMAR BESSON: What criteria does the traditional historian choose to make the selection of his facts? This has always been, of course, the great problem, and there have always been two schools of thought at every stage of historical thinking. One is to select facts according to the priorities you have in your own time and ask questions relevant to your own situation. That would amount today to an increasing interest in the fate of the common man, to which earlier historiography did not accord such importance. The second school is the one in which some attempt is made to select the facts according to the priorities of those who are under scrutiny: in other words, to understand and systematize the values and perspectives of those who are the object of the historian. It seems to me that history nowadays is completely focussed on the first school. Obviously, you can't get rid of the perspectives you have in your own time. You are not only biased, you are also probably forced to make judgements about the past. But you have to take into account the fact that the past obviously had other priorities. We have to put past events into a sequence of events, and therefore we are probably bound to judge them according to their relevance to our own time; but any past event has its own open and undetermined future. There is always a choice of alternatives, unless you construct the trend and assume a philosophical basis.

FRANÇOIS FURET: A new element has entered into the drawing up of the problematic of history. History is no longer just a dialectic between the past and the present, but involves the importing of concepts worked out by other disciplines.

WALDEMAR BESSON: But would you not agree that the influx of social science into the study of history has a certain tendency to shift the balance between the historian in his own time and his object in another time, to the disadvantage of the object in the past? By introducing all these methods which are adequate for our own time to solve the problems of our industrial situation, are we not losing the sense of a time that was very different from our own?

FRANÇOIS FURET: There's undoubtedly a danger of that, especially if a researcher neglects to come "back to history" after making use of these other concepts. But there is also a corresponding advantage. Take Weber's notion of the charismatic leader. This sociological concept is very useful to us for the understanding of the kings of France and the functioning of sacred kingship. There is greater danger of anachronism, but there is also an opportunity for a new understanding of old phenomena. Basically it all depends on the skill of the historian.

PETER WILES: I believe the English for "*histoire événementielle*" is "and then, and then" history. Mr. Furet gave an interesting demographic example which, without further explanation or comment, seems to me to be very precisely a new type of "*histoire événementielle*," using new techniques, interesting itself in different facets of human existence, but still "and then, and then," unless it gives some explanation of what caused this rise in the age of marriage.

FRANÇOIS FURET: Girls married at twenty-six. In England they had a lot of illegitimate children first. In France they didn't. The national images are reversed, and it's England that's licentious and France that's Victorian. One could consider various hypotheses: the influence of religion, sexual frustration linked to a whole series of socially deviant forms, brakes on demographic growth, and so on.

STEPHEN GRAUBARD: This new history you are describing reminds me very much of positivist history in the 19th century. It begins by saying that large questions, like political history, are too complex to be treated scientifically. Therefore you will do what the positivist historian believed you could do: a monograph. Theoretically, others would do monographs too and eventually out of all those monographs would come a larger history. But as we all know, it never happened that way, in part because you always had to move from what you call fact (and incidentally what the positivists also called fact) to some kind of causal interpretation. According to you, the facts tell their own story. The historian doesn't choose. Yet I think it is precisely the element of choice that becomes the important one: the moment the historian ceases to concern himself with the facts, and begins to relate them, he enters upon what I would call the more dangerous territory where he is exposed to refutation. It seems to me that "*histoire sérielle*" is very close to what a good number of people were doing who were positivists in the tradition of the late 19th century. This is what really interests me: this concern with being scientific.

KOSTAS PAPAIOANNOU: What are the ideologies underlying the various historiographies? Perhaps the only really "*événementielle*" history is the chronicle kind, as in, for example, "Theophanes Continuatus," who tells the story of Byzantium by means of anecdote. But to turn to a far greater man, Herodotus: he writes the history of the war so that the great deeds of the Greeks and Barbarians shall not fall into oblivion. That is his ideology, and he is fully aware of it. To students of ancient Greece it reveals two important things. The first is a conception of truth according to which being is actually threatened by oblivion. The whole of the epic thought of Greece is a fierce struggle against oblivion, which is seen as identical with death. The second thing is that this conception presupposes a certain ethic: the aristocratic ethic, according to which man only exists in order to display *virtue* or worth. This is found again in the morality of that king of France who at Crécy, I think, ordered his knights to carry out a move which would destroy their own infantry: "Or, tuez-moi carry out a move which would destroy their own infantry: "*Or, tuez-moi toute cette ribaudaille parce qu'elle nous empêche la voie sans raison.*" This is a different kind of reason from Hegel's, but it is perfectly possible to understand a history organised on the basis of such a conception.

Today, ideology is centred on "the common man," "the little man." Look at Goubert and Leroy-Ladurie. Between 1350 and 1750 there is a great non-historical mass, a sort of Spenglerian "fellah" vegetating at the base of society; and yet things happened between those two dates. I wonder if the democratic conception of history, which is certainly a fertile one, gives an answer to the most decisive question: what does the historicity of societies consist in? Societies exist in a world which has nothing to do with history and may even know nothing about it; but history is certainly there somewhere. Must we not then come back to the old historiography, that of *Haupt und Staat Aktionen*, or to cultural history as Burckhardt saw it, or Hegel, if one subtracts his linearism and more or less narcissistic progressivism?

FRANÇOIS FURET: If one defines historicity by what changes, the history of the great cyclic oscillations of the masses does not come into it, or only marginally. For this reason these oscillations are comparatively easy to structure: the factors of alteration and improbability are much less important, and it is quite easy to import models from social sciences. But it shouldn't be forgotten that the definition of history as change has cost the twentieth century a certain number of misfortunes: terrible archaic resurgences like Hitler's Germany and Stalin's Russia. The history of inertias is not only a good discipline; it is also a good therapeutic against a view of historicity inherited from the philosophy of the Enlightenment.

TATSURO YAMAMOTO: My main preoccupation is with the kind of criteria used for the selection of the facts. Many Eastern historians have very little interest in some historical studies carried out in Western countries. For example, if we take the Indian textbook of world history for general education in high school, the criteria for selecting the facts are completely different from the Japanese ones. The Indian text lays great emphasis on ancient history; most problems come back to religion.

We are now writing world history: what criteria could be used more or less universally?

RAYMOND ARON: In theory there are two possible answers to that question. The answer of those who believe in the social sciences would be that it is possible to determine, in a way that is universally valid, fundamental categories applicable to all societies. Thus on the basis of a system of concepts taken from the social sciences one could make an analysis of the various aspects, sectors, authorities, sub-sectors and sub-systems which go to make up any society.

The other answer takes its stand at a certain point in the historical process, and in terms of a notion of humanity as one, or to become one, regards some things as worth preserving as the common treasure of mankind. Thus Charles Morazé, in his book *La Logique de l'histoire*, tries to re-think history in terms of the phenomenon of *"planétarisation."* I don't think he succeeds, but the attempt is conceivable, in the abstract.

Of the two kinds of answer, the second is humanist, voluntarist, or political. Only the first could be scientific; but in the present state of things it is hard to imagine it actually being realised.

Parsons has tried to work out supra- or trans-historical concepts formalised enough to make it possible to reconstruct all historical societies. But up till now I don't think he has succeeded: no one uses Parsons' concepts except Parsons himself.

KARL D. BRACHER: After listening to this discussion, I wonder what kind of progress we have really made during the past eighty years in clarifying what the historian is really doing. As far as I can see, the so-called pure historian never existed, and certainly not in the 19th century. If you look at the historians – and not only the German ones – what they really did was write total history as far as this could be done. At that time social science did not exist, but men like Treitschke or even Mommsen used every material they could. The most fascinating aspect of the task of the historian today – and I think it can be done much better than in earlier times because of the mass of material and of the tools we have – is, instead of looking at history as a pure history of a more or less necessary development, to think of history as a history of alternatives. We have to find out why, within different possibilities, the decision was made as the development came about the way it did. Here we need all kinds of semi-historical or even non-historical help, and I would say the basic problem is not how to distinguish history from other disciplines but how to put them into proper use.

RAYMOND ARON: The only progress that has been made since the nineteenth century has been the discovery that one can't write total histories; or rather why, if one does write them, one does so inevitably from a definite point of view. The basic problem is not how to write a history which at one and the same time includes birth and death rates, how often Louis XIV took a new mistress, all the battles that were fought, and so on, but how to group these various factors in a way that is neither accidental nor incoherent. But we have learned that it is difficult to use one factor to determine others. Marc Bloch's great book on the society of the Middle Ages is a reconstruction of a whole society which leaves a good deal out, Burckhardt's *Civilisation of the Renaissance* could be written today, if there was a historian with enough talent, but we shouldn't call it a total history, in the sense of the only possible reconstruction of that period. It is just one view, one vision, among others.

The reference to the problem of the multiplicity of alternatives re-minded me of an article – naturally a very witty one – by Peter Wiles. It was called "The Importance of Being Djugashvili".[2] Was agrarian collectivisation, as practised in 1930, really necessary? According to Mr. Wiles, Stalin's aims could have been achieved without it. Historians often ask themselves this question concerning alternatives, and their answer is not very different from that of historians in the past. There is always an element of doubt. In economics there are comparatively firm data which make it possible to form hypotheses with rather more confidence. But if you ask the question: "Should Hitler have attacked Russia in 1941, or would he have done better – from his point of view, not ours – to attack Britain and the Mediterranean?" – no one can give a categorical answer one way or the other. All those who write the history of the Second World War put the problem in those terms.

A global reconstruction of history made with the aid of the social sciences will not thereby possess evident or unique truth. It will still be one view among others, whatever partial truths it may contain.

HUGH TREVOR-ROPER: I have sometimes felt this discussion was artificial and indeed rather parochial. The distinction between "*histoire événementielle*" and "social history" is itself artificial and parochial insofar as it is suggested that this new kind of history is a development of the last twenty-five years. It makes me wonder whether the social historians really read the older historians. In what category (linear history, *histoire événementielle*, social history, *histoire des Annales*) would we put Pirenne, for instance, whose *Histoire de la Belgique* is certainly a history of events and yet has precisely that social and economic dimension which distinguishes what we are told is a new kind of history? Or Niebuhr, who constructed a social system, rightly or wrongly, out of non-historical evidence? But as a matter of fact we can go back beyond them. The great historians of the 18th century were social historians. Of course, they had a less refined technique. They hadn't quite so many polysyllabic words with which to define the branches of science they used; they referred generally to philosophy and to branches of philosophy which they didn't so exactly specify. Voltaire perhaps can be dismissed as an amateur. But there were contemporaries who were, in our sense, more professional. The historians of the 18th century used a massive accumulation of the erudition of the past century, just as our modern historians tend to use the massive accumulation of erudition of our past century. Gibbon is a historian who certainly had a very highly developed sense of the different social structures of the past. It's a certain intellectual pleasure to compare Gibbon's text with the footnotes and the references: they show the materials, often non-historical, from which he very skillfully constructed an entirely different form of society in the past, not only the Roman Empire, but also Medieval Europe and the Mongol Empire. Think of Hume's famous essay on the populousness of ancient nations published in the middle of the 18th century. Here is an essay on demography which totally reversed the accepted views of the populousness of ancient nations which had been held ever since the Renaissance, and did it entirely by the kind of methods, *mutatis mutandis*, which are recommended to us today. Even in Hume's history, which is in some respects an amateur work, nevertheless there are excursions into social and political history which are marvelously constructed out of non-historical evidence. Great historians of the past have always written "*histoire événementielle*" in depth, carrying along with them the extra dimension of social history. I suppose there is some connection between this and the time in which historians write. We live today in a period of very quick social transformation and this has forced us to think in these terms and sometimes to suppose that we are thinking newly in these terms, just as the historians of the past have been coerced by their own external pressures. Machiavelli was forced to introduce a new method of looking at history by the disasters of Italy in his time. Clarendon was forced to look at English history in the mid-17th century in a new way because of the totally unpredicted disasters which had overwhelmed him. Even our very discussion may be forced upon us by new external circumstances and not by the development of historical expertise.

NOTES

1. *Comment on écrit l'histoire, essai d'épistémologie*, Paul Veyne, Le Seuil, 1971.
2. *Problems of Communism*, Vol. XII, No. 2, 1963.

2 Futurology or projection of the present

DANIEL BELL

Prediction versus prophecy

When the Commission for the Year 2000 began, we felt that the persons most aggrieved by being lfet out of the enterprise might be the historians, so we tried to mollify them by adopting an epigraph to indicate the division of labor between the historian and the futurologist: we said, the past is never finished for the future is yet to come.

I suppose that the first contemporary futurologist was an American journalist named Lincoln Steffens who in the early 1920's went to the Soviet Union and said with great astonishment: "I have seen the future, and it works." He had neither seen the future, and clearly it hasn't worked; and to the extent anyone is aware of the foolish extravagance of Steffens's statement he understands the limitations of what is called futurology.

Although the topic for discussion this morning is the system of values, I will, initially, sidestep the subject because of the number of misconceptions about what is called futurology – I don't like the word, I don't use it. What I would like to do is to spend some time dealing with the methodological problems of prediction and forecasting.

Let me say first, perhaps to the surprise only of those who have a naïve view of the enterprise, that the purpose of "futurology" is not to predict the future – I don't think one can; and there is no such thing as *the* future – but at best to make explicit the present-day, on-going structure of society: to know what societal changes are under way and to try to explain why they go in the direction they do. Futurology, thus, is really an exercise in sociology. It is an exercise in self-discipline, in forcing one to say why it is that one picked out a particular element rather than another to identify societal change. I make the fundamental point: the purpose of futurology is not to *predict* the future but to make *explicit* the structure of a society.

As to the relation between futurology and history: if history deals only with events, and what happens, then sociology and futurology have nothing to say. In specifying what happens one tries to reconstruct the antecedent elements that have preceded the event. If the problem is to reconstruct an event, there is no methodological intervention which a sociologist can make. Nor is there a methodology for predicting particular events, and especially their timing. Events are a concatenation of so many particular elements that these are inherently unpredictable. But if the historian is not concerned with events, but seeks an explanation, then one has to identify a pattern, and a pattern implies some continuing structure into a future; otherwise it is not really a very useful pattern. I can't say *the* pattern, I would say *a* pattern. I make a distinction, a very simple one and yet obviously a very important one, for in explanations there is never *one* pattern alone: events are like mosaics which fit into various patterns; and these depend upon the standpoint of the analyst, and the reasons why he considers them important. The standpoint becomes an overriding consideration.

The standpoint I adopt is the standpoint of a sociologist, namely that society is a structure of relationships in which men occupy differential, often hierarchical positions vis-à-vis each other: positions in a class structure, in economic sectors, in power relations, etc. Mr. Bullock said that history is really a set of changes in decisions and policies, but for sociologists these are relevant changes if these changes in decisions and policies affect the *ordering of these differential* relationships. So the start for us has to be some image of a society in which people occupy different positions, usually hierarchically ordered, and if we are going to talk about change, one has to specify the differential effect of these changes on such positions.

Social changes – to make an analytical distinction – are of two kinds. One we call crescive; that is, they are slow, gradual, and usually the aggregate of multiples of individual decisions; demographic decisions are of this kind (they are made by individuals, yet have aggregate, multiple effects), and also market decisions. Second, there are enacted decisions, where there is a deliberate intervention for change, whether it be a legislative reform or revolution. The question for analysis always is how one orders the relationship between these two kinds of change which are simultaneously taking place in the structure of a society.

That, it seems to me, is the fundamental standpoint of a sociologist:

that one doesn't simply deal with changes in power alone, but in changes in power which have a consequence for the differential structure of a society.

If one turns to a problem of how futurology was conducted in the 19th century, there are a number of interesting contrasts with the exercise today. We can begin with Condorcet. If you look at the last chapter of the *Sketch of the Progress of the Human Mind,* this man sitting in a garret under the threat of death, a condition which as Dr. Johnson says concentrates the mind wonderfully, made some very remarkable predictions. He predicted things as detailed as social insurance, equal rights for women, the end of colonialism, the spread of democracy. Or if one turns to the work of Tocqueville, *Democracy in America* is really an identification of a set of on-going societal relationships. He says that democracy is a social system in which what the few have today the many will want tomorrow. He predicts the onset of what we call today mass society, which is the destruction of the *pouvoir secondaire* and the problem of relationship of the individual to centralized power. If one turns to Jacob Burckhardt, in his letters he predicts the militarization of society based upon the spread of an industrial discipline.

If one analyzes the work of Condorcet, of Tocqueville, of Burckhardt, and asks what is it which allows them to make their predictions, it is the assumption of a master idea, that is, one overriding idea which acts as a secular trend in history even though there are momentary interruptions. The key, then, is the identification of an irreversible idea.

If one looks at the early sociological predictions – using *early* here as the turn of the 20th century – the emphasis is not on the power of *ideas per se,* but on *processes.* If one takes the model of Durkheim, particularly in the *Division of Labor,* it is a model essentially which has no "ideas", in terms of ideology or philosophical content or a metaphysical thought. It is an identification of processes or the change of types of social solidarity which involve a number of different dimensions: interaction or competition between people, structural differentiation, that is, a set of complementary relationships, and finally a change of scale. The theme here is the idea of growth and the identification of determinate social processes through which growth would proceed.

If we take the writings of Max Weber, there, too, the emphasis is on a basic social process by which society is transformed – that of rationalization. For Weber rationalization – in law, economy, polity, culture, etc., was the master process of the twentieth century.

Now two predictions together identify a fundamental framework of 20th century life, namely the tension between *equality* – which is the underlying idea behind what Burckhardt and Tocqueville and Condorcet were talking about – and bureaucratization, which is what Weber and to some extent even Durkheim were describing in their work. If there is a single axis along which one can identify the major themes of the 20th century, it is the contradictory tensions which are generated by these two fundamental principles.

I don't think there are any persons who have a sense of history as sweeping as that of the earlier philosophical historians, or analysts or individuals who have a sense of process as comprehensive as those of Durkheim or Weber. What we have is a greater sensitivity to methodology and technique, and our task is to identify the different techniques which are appropriate for the different kinds of forecasting that are possible.

There is first technological forecasting. To allay any misapprehensions, one cannot predict a specific invention; an invention is like an event, it's always a matter of surprise. But what one *can* do is to predict what might be called classes of inventions or *rates* of change within the defined classes of inventions. One can take speed trend curves from jets to missiles; one can take memory capacities of computers and project the capacities of the next class of inventions. This is possible for two methodological reasons. Technology is a closed system, and it has finite parameters because one is subject to the limitations of physical laws. One can only go as fast as 16,000 miles an hour on earth; after that you are in orbit. You are limited in computer speed by the character of the transmitting unit – originally vacuum tubes, then transistors and now integrated circuits. To that extent, there are these classes of finite parameters which allow one to specify the limits of change at any particular time.[1]

A second type of forecasting is demographic forecasting. Here one operates by extrapolation, and it works on two levels. It is fairly easy for example to figure twenty years from now the limits of the future labor force of any society when the children are already born. By using actuarial data on the mortality rates of the children, we can simply plot what the labor force will be like twenty years from now. It is important for an economist to have a sense of the demographic profile twenty years ahead based upon the number of births. But the question, at any particular time, of how many will be born – the actual fertility rate – is indeterminate. Here we have a fluctuating element because one does not fully know the decisions of the multiple aggregates of individuals as to how many children they will have. What most demographers do is to make an array of projections, a fan of projections, of high to medium to low and con- stantly re-check, by sampling, these extrapolations. We have here a mod- ified closed system.

If we take economic forecasting, these are of two kinds. One is the familiar extrapolation of time series with the assumption that there is no break in the system through the intervention of some exogenous variable. Second is the possibility of setting up a simplified model of the economy which can be expressed in econometric terms – even though this may involve thirty-six sectors and 125 equations which have to be solved simultaneously. Econometric forecasting is possible because one can set up a system of interacting variables. We have here a modification, again, of the technological sort, namely a closed system, but one in which the finite parameters are chosen by the analyst and are not physical laws.

If I turn to political prediction, we find a fundamental limit of so-called futurology because politics, more than any other human enterprise, depends upon single events, personalities, contingencies and the like, and it is almost impossible *methodologically* to predict political events. Wise individuals can make judgments, but we are talking here about method- ological foundations for prediction rather than simply the talents of individual persons who have detailed knowledge and sound judgment.

There is, however, a way in which one does political predictions which can serve as a model. I take as an example the first prediction study I ever did, which was about sixteen years ago, a study of the probable outcome of the Russian Five-Year Plan. The question was, would the Russians be able to meet the targets of the Plan. It turned out that one could chart two basic factors: the growth of population and the fact that the Russians had reached the limit of extensive agriculture. At some point ahead there would be a crunch; population would run up against food supply. It was a classic Malthusian problem. It seems that the Russians had three altern- atives: they could open up new lands in order to extend agriculture; they could buy wheat from abroad, which is what many countries have done; or they could cut back on heavy industry and convert capital resources into light industry, fertilisers for intensive agriculture.

At that point I went to the people who were doing national estimates of Soviet intentions and I said, this is the data I have, these are the projec- tions I make; what do you think is going to happen? They replied that the course was very clear: the agronomists say that new lands are too risky; the Russians will never buy wheat from abroad because that would damage their prestige; the *rational* course would be to cut back heavy industry and go into fertiliser, and that is what they will do.

Well, being a little naïve, I wrote the article and took that advice. I predicted that the Russians would have to cut back on industrial production. Lo and behold, the crunch came. The first thing that Khrushchev did was to go into virgin lands. And, after a while, that failed. The second thing he did was to buy wheat from Canada and even from the United States. Finally, many years later, they turned to light industry and to fertiliser.

Despite the "failure," there was a very important lesson, methodologically, in the exercise: in doing prediction you can identify a *problem;* you can identify the *constraints;* you can identify the *alternatives,* the *options;* but you don't know *which option* will be chosen because that's a function of what might be called inside intelligence. One doesn't know the inside play of forces within the decision-making groups. Khrushchev may have felt, for example, that if he had taken one path he would have been opposed by the army, or by a party group; his decision may not have been a response to the so-called economic rationality but to a form of political rationality. But let me point up the fundamental gain: that one can identify a problem, identify the constraints, and identify the options; and this, it seems to me, is a very useful and powerful advance.

There is a form of forecasting which is very different from all of these, different from technology, demography, economics and politics, and this is what I call sociological forecasting. It is not an effort to project specific social trends but to conceptualize a social framework. It makes one assumption that is very different from the other modes of forecasting, namely that there are axial institutions around which other institutions in the society are draped. To some extent this argument goes against the tendencies of the last twenty years or more in the social sciences which deride the idea of so-called single factor causation and talk about multiple interaction of different variables. I would go back and say that there is in any society what may be called axial principles which are the "bone structure" of a society.

The axial principle is a conceptual scheme: it is neither true nor false. It is only useful or useless. One can look at history in terms of feudalism, capitalism and socialism. This is not a theory of history, but a conceptual scheme along the axis of property. And it is useful or not useful insofar as one can test the proposition that the axis of property is the most important axis around which other institutions cluster. An historical scheme, such as pre-industrial, industrial and post-industrial society, is based, in one dimension, around the axis of technology. It assumes that not property relationships but technology itself becomes the axis around which the other institutions of the society are draped.

The choice of a scheme depends upon the standpoint of the observer. When Raymond Aron, for example, created the concept of industrial society, what underlay this was the fact that he had gone to Japan and said that, from the standpoint of Asia, the differences between the Soviet Union and the United States are less relevant than the fact that they are both industrial societies, they are both societies organized around principles of production using machinery, factory organization and the like. The key point here is the standpoint of selection. From another standpoint, the Soviet Union and the United States are vastly different.

By setting forth a social framework as a conceptual scheme one identifies an axial institution, one defines on-going structures, and one deduces problems which have to be solved by the society – even though one may not be able to predict how they may be solved.

The idea of a post-industrial society, however disputed the concept may be, involves, for example, the idea of an axial principle. The axial principle is the centrality of theoretical knowledge. It argues that there is a new kind of relationship today between science and technology, that today theory precedes empiricism so that the advances in technology today, as distinct from the way in which nineteenth century industry developed, depend primarily on the codification of theoretical knowledge; that nineteenth century industry developed largely from talented tinkerers and inventors who were ignorant of the laws of science; that today the science-based industries, whether they are chemistry, polymers, holograms, lasers, optics, electronics, computers, etc., are basically science-based industries depending on a centrality of theoretical knowledge. From this one can deduce an entire set of problems confronting a society: the problem of the human capital, which becomes more important than money capital, as a condition of growth; the determination of science policy, the organization of science, the centrality of the universities as research institutions or the organisation of research institutions as distinct from the university, all these become important social issues of the future.

Now let me point out an important qualification regarding this kind of sociological prediction. To talk of a post-industrial society is not to say that it is a picture of the whole society. A post-industrial society can be organized in different ways, just as industrial society has been organized in different ways. The Soviet Union, Japan, Nazi Germany, post-Nazi Germany, the United States are all industrial societies, yet politically they are organized in different ways. Social forecasting makes sense or the social frameworks make sense only within the social structure.

I define social structure here (more narrowly than many of my colleagues) as the economy, the technology and the occupational and stratification system of the society. In addition, there is the polity and the culture. One can do sociological prediction when one can identify constraints and alternatives within known normative rules and stipulated resources. If that is the case, we have reached the limits of futurology.

Analytically, there are three dimensions to a society, but each is ruled by a different principle. The first is the social structure, which I defined as the economy, technology and the stratification system; this operates under the constraint of functional rationality – of efficiency, optimization and the principle of replacement at least cost. The second is the polity, the political system, which is the management of power, the management of conflict between social groups. This is fundamentally non-rational because it deals with bargaining between groups or, at the extreme, revolutions to change the group in power or the mode of power. Finally there is the culture, which is the realm of expressive symbolism and meaning, or on a more mundane level, the constituents of life-styles. Here I would say that culture operates on a principle of limited possibility. In the human imagination, there is a limited repertoire in the number of moral possibilities and the number of styles of life simply because culture always confronts certain basic existential questions – death, tragedy, aggression, sexuality, etc., and there are probably no real surprises in culture.

In these realms, we have different principles of change, and here is where the real problem of analysis enters. Social structure is cumulative and quantitative because there are given rules for replacement. The rules for replacement are essentially economic – low costs, high efficiency, ready utilization of resources. Therefore the realm of social structure has a directional element by the fact that it is quantitative and cumulative.

Politics, I would say, is centrifugal. It operates around the fundamental problem of conflict and consensus, domination and cooperation and the alternative modes of either securing consensus or ensuring domination. And that is why one can find works such as Mosca's and others which deal with such perennial themes as central.

In culture, even though there is a principle of limited possibility, I do not think there is a "*ricorsi.*" I do not believe in cycles of history. But I would say that culture is *mimetic:* culture, in a sense, always copies from *some* past and, therefore, operates on the principle of mimesis. The economy and technology are not copies from nature; they are not copies from the past. They are cumulative. Culture is some form of mimesis.

Mimesis is not pure imitation – one can choose different elements from the past and combine them in novel ways. In modern times this begins, say, with Schopenhauer, who translates the Indian Vedas and tries to create a new image of life by fusing Indian philosophy with the traditional romanticism of German philosophy. It is mimetic in this particular way.

Now, one finds variations. A technocrat, for example, is somebody who takes over an economic principle from the social structure into politics, and it doesn't work for that reason because it comes from a different realm. A rebel is someone who takes over a social style, or expressive element, into politics and that too doesn't work because it doesn't last.

This type of analysis runs counter to what has been the major tradition of sociological thought in the last half century or so. Basically, most social theorists have thought of a society as integrated through some single principle. Marx thought that all of society could be organized in economic relationships and that exchange relationships dominated all of the aspects of society including culture. Someone like Sorokin thought that all social relationships were mediated through culture and that there is a common sensate mentality which permeates all of culture. Talcott Parsons assumes, for example, that all of society is integrated through the value system. He would say, for example, that in the United States there is a common value system, which he calls "instrumental activism," which unifies the culture.

I would say two things are different today. First there is the relative autonomy of the political sphere, and this is a theme about which Raymond Aron has written upon eloquently. And second, there is a growing disjunction between the culture and social structures because of the principle upon which each operates: the social structure is functional, meritocratic, efficiency-oriented, whereas the culture is antinomian, anti-institutional, anti-intellectual, anti-cognitive.

One can talk of a common economic system, or even of common political systems, but any *particular* society is an idiosyncratic combination of these diverse elements of social structure, culture and politics organized around history and tradition in an ideographic way. This is why particularity prediction about any *single* society from a common type is difficult.

There is, too, a different limitation on complete prediction because social change involves four dimensions: *constants* (such as topography or climate), cyclical changes, secular changes and contingencies. And methodologically it is difficult to fit these together. Finally, there is a third barrier to "total" prediction because of the different principles of change in the different realms of society: the different principle operating in social structure that generates its own rate of change vis-à-vis the other sectors; the polity which has to return centrally to the same problems of conflict and consensus or domination and cooperation; and the culture which is inherently mimetic.

I want to say a final word about the culture – for today this is the most "open" realm, and the one subject to the widest fluctuations. In the history of human society, there seems to be a dialectic between the principle of restraint and that of libertinism. Today, we are in the widest swing of the pendulum of release. By the very fact that culture can become increasingly mimetic and open to choice, one is able to choose and put together new styles in order to emphasize this form of release. In that phrase of Yeats' there is "a widening gyre," and in the everwidening circles more and more taboos go under.

To come back to the question of futurology itself, I would say that to the extent that there is a value to the kind of enterprise, it is limited primarily to social structure and to a lesser extent to culture. We can identify situations or issues that a society is called upon to solve, but because they can be solved in different ways, the actual courses are not inherently predictable. Second, we can deal with culture by identifying likely cultural modes which might be chosen on the basis of mimesis. But the combination will remain novel. In short, we can work with alternative futures, but we do not know which alternative will be taken. This is my principle of futurology. All the rest is exegesis.

Discussion

RAYMOND ARON: In French, speculation of the future has already been given the rather inelegant name of *futurologie*. There is no doubt that it is something that belongs to the *Zeitgeist*. I won't claim that it was born in France, but some twenty years ago certain Frenchmen, one of whom was Bertrand de Jouvenel, cautiously began to embark on speculations which they called "*futuribles*", and this attempt was taken up and developed in a big way by the American university machine and by the American foundations. Speculation on the future has become one of the favourite subjects of pluridisciplinary research in the United States; the Japanese have echoed the Americans with even greater enthusiasm; Germany has not been spared; as usual, one country has put up a certain amount of resistance – Britain regards the subject with suitable scepticism.

PETERS WILES: Daniel Bell began by saying that he didn't really claim to predict the future, and then he started to praise Condorcet for having done so correctly. You ought to come out flatly and admit that you do wish to predict the future; that is what the word "futurology" means; it's what we are paid to do, and it's a useful activity if it can be made a reliable one. You mention the large numbers of short-term predictions in econometrics and demography; but great institutes of futurology have not been founded simply to encourage econometrics and the study of the population. Of course, there is a connection: the longer forward in time the econometrician or the demographer goes, the more useful he is likely to be to the proper futurologist; but still it is an essentially different activity. As economists, for instance, we have been completely incapable of predicting the present cost inflation in Britain. There was absolutely nothing in the Phillips curve, or in any Keynesian analysis, or in anything ever said, that would lead one to believe that within one year from now all wage-claims would be running at the rate of about ten per cent or more and that most of these claims would be being actually met by employers. We have now in Britain a completely different short-term situation on which no econometrician threw any light at all.

Demographers have predicted the most astonishing things decade by decade. I am even old enough to remember that the world was going to be depopulated. The whole of Western Europe was going to be converted into a sort of desert by the failure of people to give birth. This was indeed the demography upon which I personally got my degree.

To take another example, what is going to be the relation between the enterprise and the central planner in any East European country, let's say, five years from now? Here I admit we come to the crucial problem: the autonomy of politics rears its ugly but indisputable head. It has been said by specialists in Poland that if the Israelis had not won the Six-Day war, the Polish economy would have been decentralised. I will not take up your time now to demonstrate this connection, but it is an indisputable one. Or, to give you another country, completely unpredicted by myself, Bulgaria has chosen to re-centralise. The Hungarians have gone towards the other way. I would have completely failed to make correct predictions if I had been unwise enough to try.

Going forward to futurology properly speaking, who chooses your axial principles? Marx chose the principle of property. It hasn't worked all that well. It hasn't worked very badly either. You have to justify the choice that you have made. To use Marxian terms, the forces of production instead of the relations of production as the main thing. It is possible that some totally different axial principle should have been chosen, which will become quite obvious to us all in one decade from now, and we will all kick ourselves for not having observed that the real thing had something to do with telepathy or tarot cards or God knows what. I think there is in fact in many of these long-term forecasts a certain lack of imagination. Didn't Condorcet make any errors? Is it that the only futurologist whose errors we concentrate upon is Karl Marx, just because he happens to have a movement named after him in the modern world? Every time I look at ancient thinkers who have been much praised, I find an awful lot of rubbish in addition to their brilliant insights and I merely ask, as I genuinely don't know, would Condorcet really stand up to severe criticism of the type that Marx has been subjected to? And indeed, further, must we execute Bell in order to improve the quality of his predictions?

DANIEL BELL: Peter Wiles has raised the question of these short-run predictions which have been so faulty. He talks as a man who was once a young lover and who has become an old "roué" in these matters. I remember, about fifteen years ago, an interesting debate which took place in *Encounter*, in which "Statistical Wiles" was making a prediction much higher than anybody else regarding the rate of Russian economic development. In fact, Peter, I also recall a seminar at Columbia in 1963 at which you were telling us that the Cuban economy would be developing much faster than anybody else would ever think about because it was now a planned, socialised and centralised economy. So I can understand some of your scepticism...

The demographers in the past made simple straight-line extrapolations. No census office today ever does such a thing. If you take a look, for example, at the American census projections, they will give you five runs (a) to (e) and will very carefully stipulate the assumptions on which (a) to (e) are made and constantly re-check them. You are limiting, in a sense, your margin of error; this doesn't mean that there won't be uncertainty.

Peter Wiles asked the question, who picks axial principles? Obviously, any particular person is the one who picks, but there are two things involved here. For the last thirty years, we have been subject to the notion of multiple interacting causes. Every student who grows up in contemporary sociology learns equilibrium analysis in which no cause is more important than another because they are all interacting. And to some extent I think they have been limited and impoverished in their ability to identify certain crucial elements. Going back to the notion of "axial principle," it is an effort to identify what I had simply called *the bone structure* of a society, even though the flesh and blood may be placed differently. Who chooses it? We all do it and are subject to the correction of our peers and of evidence. And this is not different from what any intellectual and scholarly procedure consists of.

We concentrate on Marx's errors and not on Condorcet's for the very simple reason that people try to impose Marx's errors on the rest of us. Indeed, Condorcet has made errors, all of us have made errors and we all will continue to make errors. The problem is to reduce them. We are not greater than Condorcet or greater than Tocqueville or greater than Burckhardt; what we try to do is to make explicit the assumptions upon which they worked.

RAYMOND ARON: It's easy to say economics acts according to the principle of rationality, politics according to that of centrifugality, and culture according to that of mimesis. But there are dialectical relationships between these three spheres.

Economic rationality cannot be separated, in its actual functioning, from political irrationality. Peter Wiles is at the heart of the methodological debate when he says the fundamental problem of futurology is not sectorial extrapolation but the relations between systems and subsystems.

You say that in the last twenty-five years sociologists have only interested themselves in the mutual relationships between factors. This is true of the Parsons school, but not of European sociologists of the Marxist tradition. The idea of an axial principle takes up, with a certain amount of epistemological neutrality, the idea that the different sectors are not equivalent. The Parsonians' inability to select one factor as more important than the other resulted from their particular approach and was of no scientific significance.

Lastly, I hesitate to regard culture as a *mimesis* of limited possibilities, because, at least as far as art and creation are concerned, culture seems to me precisely the realm of the limitless.

DANIEL BELL: When I talk about culture as mimesis I don't mean creative culture *per se* (although it provides elements) but life-styles, cultural groups... In modern times, there is intrinsically and increasingly an adversary relationship between the culture and the social structure. This theme was enunciated originally by Lionel Trilling. The culture has now an economic basis to sustain itself in the large amount of support from television, movies, record industry, etc., and to a considerable extent, some aspects of the youth revolt are a reflection of this adversary tension between the culture and the social structure. I think this contrary relationship is going to increase, so as to make life more and more difficult within Western society.

ERNEST GELLNER: There are two arguments about culture. One is what might be called "the questionnaire theory" of culture – that cultures can be classified by handing each one a questionnaire: How do you stand with regard to death, tragedy, sex and so on? This gives you a limited number of possibilities. If this analysis were correct, it would merely mean that the culture of the year 2000, for example, will be one particular hand dealt from this pack of cards; one could speculate about which cards are likely to be played in late industrial or post-industrial society.

The other theme, which I suspect to be the correct one, ties up with the uniqueness of our time, the uniqueness of what is being brought into being now. The student protest movement may be a kind of hint of the future. In the past, people thought that the nature of things, or a divine revelation, provided a set of premises which limited their cultural possibilities. The modernist movement seems to be a systematic evasion of those premises, and if it's not illusory, this undercuts the whole questionnaire approach to culture because there's something quite new: the socio-economic basis of this kind of violently free-floating culture is that the constraints have been removed. To put it in very concrete and crude terms, the economic base of the protest movement in the United States is the simple fact that you can work for a very short period of time and then live for a long time after. Projecting culture in that kind of context becomes rather like predicting developments in architecture if there are some new building materials and techniques available which enable you to use almost any material in any old way; the fantasy of the architect has free play and all kinds of other constraints are removed as well. I suspect this is the correct tack in futurology on culture.

DANIEL BELL: One can always find there is a range of continuum in Western society; many of the elements which are present today existed in the past. Read, for example, the history of certain gnostic groups... If there is something new, it is essentially the change of scale. What once used to be private is now public; what people would once keep as small enclaves, in an isolated area, and practise quietly and secretly, now is flaunted openly. In the youth culture, there is very little which can't be found in the life of Rimbaud, whether it be the taking of drugs, going on homosexual vagabondage with Verlaine, running off into darkest Africa. But today you have 150,000 Rimbauds in this respect – without the poetry.

ALAIN BESANÇON: Baudelaire is certainly one of the first modern poets. But we shouldn't forget that in *Pauvre Belgique*, the last thing he wrote, he expressed the panic hatred he felt for a world entirely devoted to trade and completely cut off from the spirit. He called progress "the great heresy of decrepitude" – which makes him close to Dostoevsky and Nietzsche: they were all prophets of the same catastrophe. You are right to say culture is *mimesis:* I think it is quite simply mimesis of itself. But one never knows whether what is said in a new way is a rupture or a repetition. Coco Chanel said something very profound when she was

asked if she was an artist. She answered, "No. The business of fashion is
to create beautiful things which soon look ugly. An artist creates things
which look ugly but gradually reveal their beauty." I don't really see how
futurology can make it possible to foresee that what is ugly now will soon
be beautiful. In other words, I don't think it can help artists to be in
fashion.

Let us take incest, which has always been a fundamental problem in all
our societies. Suppose we imagine everyone soon sleeping with everyone
else: it will only be the democratisation of a transgression that used to be
reserved for the king or the chief of the tribe. Here again it will only be
a mimesis. After all, incest is a mimesis par excellence – a mimesis of what
the father does. Unfortunately, it's a mimesis that is forbidden.

DANIEL BELL: Today, everybody demands for himself the same
privileges and rights that were previously accorded to the genius. But the
very nature of the democratisation of genius ultimately results in the
breakdown of standards and distinctions.

WOLFGANG J. MOMMSEN: I was slightly worried when you quoted
Tocqueville, Burkhardt, Condorcet as ancestors of modern futurologists.
How does futurology evade the danger of imposing half consciously the
present-day values on its predictions? Indeed, there are the famous letters
of Burkhardt describing the coming *Militärstaat*, but this turned up in a
context which was highly against any form of democracy.

The boundaries between political and social systems are constantly
likely to change. The borderline between the political order and the
social order in the Communist system is different from that in the West.
If you look back into the past, for instance into the social system of the
Middle Ages, it is perhaps difficult to say there is a real distinction between these two sectors of social life.

DANIEL BELL: I would agree that the particular impulse out of which
Burckhardt wrote is a fear of the masses, a fear of democracy, but at the
same time he was able to point to a fundamental problem, which is the
inherent tension between liberty and democracy, a problem which still
exists today. There are many people (including to some extent myself)
who say: "I'm a libertarian first and a democrat second." I'm not a believer in democracy *per se* because I accept some of the Burckhardt
problems and therefore I would say there is a prior question of liberty
before democracy. It is not that futurology predicts what will happen: it
predicts the kinds of problems which will arise.

TATSURO YAMAMOTO: In Japan and other East Asian countries, contrary to what happens in the West, there is a growing interest in the past and a so-called "history boom." In my country, the younger generation is very interested in the past. This interest is closely connected with the future: future-oriented history is now one of the main aspects of historical works in Eastern countries, and this for three reasons. First, we have to preserve our tradition. Second, Marxism raises much interest in the younger generation. Third, in discussing the term modern (or modernism or modernisation), we are thinking of something the whole world has in common.

DANIEL BELL: Regarding the West, modernity and modernism have two fundamental characteristics. One is an attentiveness to the new, not to the past; to change, not to tradition. The other is the idea so central to Marx, that a technical world will replace the natural world; the idea that men have new powers which will create new wants, no longer derived from nature but from a sense of mastery over it. To that extent, the end of history in the classical sense was the end of the natural world and its replacement by a technical one. But soon you have a reaction, which emphasizes the natural against the technical; this begins with the first impact of Nietzsche on the Western world.

I know very little about Japan, but what you said didn't sound so different from the reactions to change in the West. A more interesting comparison might be between Japan and China, where there is a great sense of the future as well, but at the same time an extraordinary effort to repudiate the past.

KOSTAS PAPAIOANNOU: Futurology, in the sense of rational interrogation of the future, is only possible, within a given system, defined first and foremost as a system of values. A rational exploration of the future really presupposes a linear time: it excludes by definition the moment when time completely changes direction. Let us take a classic example: Tocqueville's predictions about democratisation. He includes everything, even the sadness that will afflict man in the mass society of the future. This extraordinary prediction presupposes a certain type of *demos* as the subject of the historical process. The future really appears when the *demos* changes its nature. It is then found, with amazement, anguish, and perhaps with eschatological expectation, that "the people" has become something quite different. The phrase "massification of leisure," for example, seems quite rational: we know very well that working hours are growing less. But in fact the argument comes from within a specific system: that of the nineteenth century, where people worked fourteen hours a day and free time was just the time in which they did not work. But from a certain point on, free time extends so far that one can no longer speak of free time. It becomes empty time, which can only be redefined insofar as one has a different system of values to refer to. And it's here that we see the limits of futurology, in the strict sense of the term. When we hear the expression "Paradise now," the future appears fundamentally "other," and we can do nothing but be silent.

ROBERT NISBET: If I did believe that the present we live in emerged from the past, then I would be obliged to believe that the future will emerge from the present, and that by dint of sufficiently sophisticated and astute analysis of the present one might very well arrive at some notion of the future. This would be the greatest single defence of futurology. But if one does not believe in a linear series of past, present and future, then futurology can only throw light on the present.

DANIEL BELL: I would agree there is no such thing as "the future"; it has to be the future of something...

RAYMOND ARON: From what you have said one might think futurology is consciously and entirely a reflection of the present, or even "the sad consciousness of the present." Condorcet and Tocqueville lived at the beginning of what you call the modern movement. Each pointed out certain characteristics: Tocqueville, the progressive equalisation of the conditions of the individual; Condorcet, the progress of enlightenment. They developed the consequences of these fundamental characteristics to infinity, without really considering the relations between the different aspects of society. Sometimes they ended up with alternatives. Tocqueville's alternative was: "Democracy is inevitable. It will be either liberal or despotic." With Weber there begins a dialectic between the contradictory tendencies of modern society.

What interests me is that the futurology you might have done fifteen years ago would have been appreciably different from the futurology you are doing today. If I may refer to Peter Wiles' previsions on the development of the Soviet economy, he said one day, "My forecasting was right for seven years – it's a good long time." Your present futurology seems to me to be dominated by the current experience of American society, that of an economic system which has produced comparative marvels in the course of the last twenty or twenty-five years, and which, to the surprise of everyone (including the futurologists), is going through a severe crisis in the realm of culture. This contradiction between economic success and cultural crisis leads you to a theory concerning the sectors of society which is very much better than that of Parsons. But one didn't need the crisis in American society to prove the worth of certain of Max Weber's ideas, among others, the idea that politics cannot be forecast simply in terms of a certain organisation of the economy, and that only certain correlations can be established between these systems.

You are struck by the contradictions between culture and the socio-economic system in modern civilisation. A whole section of the intelligentsia (for a long time the reactionary intellectuals of the Right) were critical of the mass society, rejected economic rationalisation, and saw in democratisation the end of all higher values. But there were also thinkers of the Right, optimistic rationalists, who saw in the creation of a modern economy and the development of productive forces the conditions which made possible a democratic society worthy of the name. Nowadays the most violent critics of the rationalist society come from the extreme-Left, using arguments typical of the former reactionaries.

As Max Weber said: "You must be a puritan to create capitalism. Once capitalism exists there is no need any more for a system of specific values." Does the economic system whose rational success you describe to us imply the maintenance of some of the values which helped create it? Where does the contradiction between cultural models and the economic society actually occur?

DANIEL BELL: The cultural contradictions of capitalism derive from the fact that you have a production system organised entirely on the most highly functional rationalistic principles of technology, and an economy which is producing a hedonistic way of life. This is an extraordinary contradiction: in the past, early bourgeois society produced goods to satisfy the basic necessities of people. Today, a capitalist society, which is organised economically and technologically in the most extreme rationalistic way as Weber described it, is producing a hedonism and therefore creating a fundamental split between the sectors of production and consumption. You want people to be rational, career-oriented, seeking delayed gratification, Protestant in the area of production; you want them to be spontaneous, free, pleasure-seeking in the area of consumption.

GEORGES DUBY: Cultural life always presents two very different faces. One is traditional and "security-seeking," made up of a number of norms facilitating the survival of the establishment: these are cultural models handed down by educational systems, which are resistant to change and guardians of continuity. But opposite this cultural inertia there is always a desire for modernity or contestation, and it is here that creation comes in, always eminently ludic and gratuitous vis-à-vis tradition. The carriers of these elements of contestation are aristocracies in the widest sense of the term, and youth; the first in a way which is permanent but ambiguous, the second in a way which is transitory but particularly vigorous.

DANIEL BELL: Within the last hundred years the major source of change in Western society has been in the economy and in the technology. This still continues. But the major constraint against the innovation of technology is increasing cost and, by and large, one finds in many societies this effort to escape increasing cost, more usually by the creation of elements like multi-national corporations and the like. To a considerable extent the primacy of change may now have passed into culture. It is easy, in a sense, to innovate in culture, because you begin in the imagination and there are few costs of change. Yet in the past it has been difficult to do so because you had a traditional culture and traditional institutions. One of the extraordinary things about modern times is that nobody any longer resists the new in culture. In fact, that's the reason why in effect there is no longer an avant-garde – because anything which is new is immediately accepted rather than resisted. In the past, one of the functions of universities was to test the new by relating it to tradition and testing it by saying "Is it valid or not?" Today what is new is no longer challenged. It becomes a source of conflict when people try to turn these cultural changes into political forms.

RAYMOND ARON: When I read works of futurology (science-fiction apart), what always strikes me is the lack of imagination: there are only our present experiences, transposed, projected and produced. Nothing to cause the least surprise to anyone with the slightest knowledge of the present or of history. Futurology aims at being a rational and not an imaginative exercise: no doubt it can only be rigorous if this is so. Perhaps history requires more imagination...

PETER WILES: Mr. Bell, I wonder why have you excluded science-fiction from futurology.

DANIEL BELL: There is a whole range of futurological works. One can find in the magazine *Future*, for instance, this sort of imaginative prospective. But it has a kind of cranky quality. Let me call your attention, for example, to a series which was published in England in the twenties, called *Today and Tomorrow*, and written by eminent people. Bertrand Russell, J. B. S. Haldane, J. F. C. Fuller wrote and signed with names like Icarus, Prometheus, Daedalus... These little books used a soaring imagination and proved to be wrong. Now, if one looks at the Commission for the Year 2000, in which I've been engaged for five or six years, it arose from a simple impulse: the fact that when the Kennedy administration came to power in 1960, it suddenly confronted a housing problem, a health problem, a black problem and so forth... and people said: "Give us a programme, tell us what to do." The model for me, curiously enough, was not these volumes of the twenties, but a book put out in 1931 in the United States called *Recent Social Trends*, the research director of which was the sociologist William F. Ogburn. If you look at that volume, it is fascinating how the contributors were able to predict quite well certain trends, for example, in health (the fact that there would be a doctor shortage), in the growth of suburbs. In the Commission for the Year 2000 there was an effort to reintroduce some forward planning for society. We have economic indicators in terms of elements of investment, consumption, etc.; we have no social indicators in terms of: "Are we healthier or not? Do we have less crime or not?" A book by Professor Klaus Moser called *Social Trends* tried for the first time to put together data of this kind and to begin to create a system of social accounts just as we have a system of economic accounts.

There may be a poverty of historical imagination because we're less concerned with the large *Weltbilde* and more with making a society responsive to the social issues of the time.

RAYMOND ARON: What are the trends which you admit at the starting point to be (a) irreversible and (b) inevitable? In the French system of planning, they speak about hard trends (*tendances lourdes*), which implies that a certain kind of sectorial evolutions are inevitable, and from then on they try to find out the options.

DANIEL BELL: There are a number of such "*tendances lourdes*." I think, for instance, of the desire for participation. It can be used as a catch-phrase by the French government, but it's quite real. People feel to a considerable extent that they are somehow lost in larger organisational structures, and they want to find ways of becoming more involved in the decisions which affect their lives. I think this is an irreversible tendency. A second kind of trend which is part of the extension of industrialisation into a post-industrial phase is the movement towards a service society: a change from a goods-producing society to a service society. A pre-industrial society is a game against nature; it involves diminishing returns. An industrial society is a game against fabricated nature because you are transforming nature into a technical form. Whereas a post-industrial society is a game between persons. In that situation, the relationship between people is a very different kind of social structure from the relationship between man and technical artifacts or the man-machine relationship in this particular way. How will you reorganise work and the use of leisure time? I'll mention the scarcity of human capital. More and more, in a technical society, the key resources are talents. The whole educational system is antiquated because it is not responsive either to the technical requirements or even to the cultural requirements.

HUGH TREVOR-ROPER: Mr. Bell says that one trend which was irreversible was the desire for participation. I would like to know on what evidence this statement is based, because it was presented as a dogma, not as a reasoned statement. Historians know that in the past there have been many ephemeral movements like those heretical movements which have been referred to; mere fashions, thought to be permanent acquisitions today, disappeared altogether tomorrow. Why, theoretically, may not this desire for participation be merely what Mr. Bell calls a lot of noise?

DANIEL BELL: I think that a process of this sort takes place on many different levels. It first takes place on the level of what might be called ideology or normative belief. Once it becomes accepted on this level and is accepted as a principle in society, then people have a standard of judgment and are able to see whether it has been carried out or not. To take a simple analogy, in the United States there is a legitimating instrumentality which you don't have in many other countries: the Supreme Court. Elements which are established in legal processes come up to the Court for decision; and the Court is not only a legal court but also a philosophical one. The turning point, for example, in the Civil Rights movement in the United States came essentially in 1954 when there was a case called Brown versus the Board of Topeca which in effect struck down a previous decision about separation of the races and in effect brought in integration as a new principle. Thereafter most of the resources of the society, even though in an inadequate and halting way, were turned towards that

particular effort. The desire for participation was accepted (and institut-
ionalised) first of all in a very key area, in the trade union movement on
the factory floor. The whole history of trade unionism is essentially an
attempt to deal with the nature of arbitrary authority and to limit arbitrary authority in this particular way. Trade unionism is a form of participation in which you share power on the factory floor. What happens in
our society is an extension of this into many other sectors as well, and this
is why I would regard it on a philosophical, normative as well as institutional level as an irreversible process.

HUGH TREVOR-ROPER: I'm afraid I remain unconvinced. I don't believe that even a decision of the United States Supreme Court renders a
historical process irreversible. Going back to other periods of history, I
remember, for instance, the Leveller movement in seventeenth century
England. It was thought to be irreversible at the time by its advocates. In
fact, the forms accepted by the Leveller movement as a small vocal
organised minority were never accepted in the other organs of society,
and for that reason a whiff of grapeshot in the end disposed of the movement. It seems to me that the same sort of reasoning can be used about
"participation". Supposing all the universities in the world accept
participation, unless society endorses it, unless apprentices in trade or
new employees in industry or first-year civil servants are going to have
full participation in their world, then this is a mere university phenomenon, confined to a single organ of society, and it may wither away like
the agitation of the German *Burschenschaften* in the early nineteenth
century.

DANIEL BELL: May I just say that Cromwell never accepted the Level-
lers but de Gaulle accepted participation and if you may not want the
United States Supreme Court you may have to take de Gaulle as a
legitimating authority in this particular way.

I gave you the example of the English trade union movement. It shows
a desire for participation, in the sense of sharing the power, not in the
sense of running or taking over factories.

RAYMOND ARON: It is very interesting to me that to my question
"What are for you the irreversible trends?" you took as an example
"participation." If I had put the same question to a French futurologist
he would have answered, almost without any doubt, demographic or
economic trends. It may be a question of nationality.

ALAN BULLOCK: When I was a tutor in history, any student who ever used the word "inevitable" I wouldn't allow to pass. Has anybody carried out an inquiry, since the First World War, into the fate of those trends which were widely stated and believed to be irreversible and inevitable? What strikes me very much is the short run we are taking to base the extrapolation.

RAYMOND ARON: What Mr. Bell has explained in his study about the future is mainly a way of better planning. It is largely a pragmatic outlook. One of the dangers of the method is to accept as inevitable certain elements which are perhaps not so. Five years ago it seemed irreversible and inevitable that there should be a competition for the rate of growth of the G.N.P.; today, it is no longer obvious that the ultimate objective of national policy should be to have the maximum rate of growth. When you say "inevitable and irreversible" you are leaving aside the possible destruction of the system; but even inside this framework there is the danger of accepting as determined by fatality what is after all a decision of the people.

DANIEL BELL: I should have cavilled more strongly at the words "inevitable" and "irreversible" and come to the formulation I prefer, which is the nature of something being "renewable." It may well be that there is for this moment a momentary halt in the will for growth; I would assume however that as most people do want a better standard of living this is a renewable kind of impulse.

ALAN BULLOCK: When we come to the human and social attitudes adopted by people in face of change there is a limited number of roles and attitudes. For this reason, Mr. Bell's notion of "renewability" is a very helpful one.

GEORGE NADEL: It is sometimes said that the principal American tradition in the system of values is change itself: paradoxically, you could see change itself as a form of stability!

STEPHEN GRAUBARD: The task of the historian is to propose explanations after the event. Let us take some of the major events that have happened in our own century. The end of the First World War was also believed to be the end of a certain kind of Europe. Europe in the 1920's and the 1930's felt a sense of decline, of the termination of an epoch. After the Second World War one tended to collapse the two wars together, into a sort of Thucydidian European civil war.

In many respects, and this seems most interesting, those very things that were thought to be so innovative in the nineteenth century have become even more pronounced in the twentieth century. Thus, for example, the nineteenth century prided itself on the fact that it was the period of the creation of the nation state. But, in fact, it is the twentieth century that has really been nationalist, in the purer, and even more rampant, sense.

Similarly, the nineteenth century had an anticipation of the growing power of the masses in every respect. But again, none in the nineteenth century fully anticipated the kind of educational developments that the twentieth century experimented. The university enrolments since the 1950's have gone far beyond what most Europeans and what most Americans in fact imagined to be possible. One has only to examine the books of history of the early nineteenth century and those of the late twentieth century to see the extraordinary changes that have come about in the way in which we explain things and perceive phenomena. Take an American example: the most fashionable discussion about the "generation gap." Looking at American history, you realise that partly because of the frontier and partly because of other phenomena, parents did not have the same capacity to control their children that you find in certain parts of Europe; therefore, they used to send them to universities in order to control them. Certain questions which seemed to belong to the past are not of the past at all. In the nineteenth century, Tocqueville was not quoted as frequently as he is today, and it is precisely because we understand more fully the relevance of certain things he said that we have returned to him.

KARL D. BRACHER: Revolts against technological changes and against the complexity of modern life can combine very well with conservatism or reactionary tendencies.

What strikes me in looking at world history is that the rate of change has not been much modified. Look at the political development of the last 200 years, which accompanied the industrial and technological revolution, and compare it with the political development in Ancient Greece, or in Ancient Rome, or even in the Middle Ages: the clearcut correlation between the technical process and the political one becomes then very dubious.

DANIEL BELL: There are probably very few changes in the nature of political conflict; the major change here is a change in scale.

If you read Thucydides, you can find the speeches of Cleon very enlightening for the case of Lyndon Johnson, and the Sicilian campaign very suggestive with regard to the Vietnam war; yet the scale is fundamentally different. For it now involves an enormous number of people who can suddenly, in a very rapid way, destroy each other.

ALAN BULLOCK: The problem about futurology may be the ambivalent attitude of those who are not futurologists. We foist upon futurologists ambitions they have never claimed and and then turn round and denounce them when our ambitions don't come to pass. We are constantly pushing their claims up because secretly we can't make our mind up whether we are going to get the greater satisfaction if they can do it or if they fail.

NOTE

1. There is a different kind of technological forecasting which deals with probabilities. For example, if we wish to identify the impact of technology on international relations in the next twenty years, we could say that there are four technological *areas* that will be decisive: ocean engineering, energy production, satellite communication and weather control. These are areas which are "natural" extensions of present-day work based on the likelihood of new capacities. So, as we deplete earth crust resources, increasingly we turn to underwater sources for oil, minerals and metals. The extraordinary demands for electrical energy "call forth" the use of fission and fusion processes. The spread of international communications – television and telephone – make satellites a key area of expansion and experiments in cloud seeding and damming of seas could change ocean currents and weather. In the interplay of technology and international politics we have a relevant area of "futurology."

3 The historian and scientific economics

PETER WILES

The necessity and impossibility of political economy

"Of all social sciences", my instruction for this conference tells me, "economics is supposed to be (justifiably, it seems) the most advanced". But this is because it is hardly a social science, and those sectors in which it has made the greatest advances are precisely the least human. Economics stands at the point of man's interaction with nature, not other men, and it borrows its predictability from the inanimate side of its subject matter. Increasing returns to scale, diminishing returns when one input is fixed, the inexorability of material balances in an input/output table, the rate of technical progress, the fact of scarcity – in a word the "logic of commodities": no wonder Marx thought of man's struggle with nature as the predictable part of man's history. No wonder, either, that he hoped it determined the superstructure. But that is the trouble: it does not determine, it only constrains. And this is what makes a successful political economy so improbable.

Moreover when economics turns to consider man it takes a most inhuman view of him – he is a Benthamite, a maximizer of a simple and constant psychological function. The problems he faces, too – those of exchange and choice between alternatives – are the same every morning, and his unique faculty of memory alters nothing fundamental in his behaviour. It only makes him a better adjuster of the same kind. There is, then, no history, but only a chronology of demographic and technological change, and capital accumulation. Ideas may develop, but motivation is always the same. Political power may change hands, but unless it expresses itself in adequately enforced legislation men's behaviour is always everywhere the same.

The astounding thing is that this assumption works. Not perfectly, of course. It does not well describe the behaviour of most primitive tribes;

nor of complicated organizations in complicated exchange situations like
trade unions and large capitalist corporations; and least of all governments, which are fundamentally not in this kind of situation at all. But
for the rest, including individuals in a Communist society, Benthamism
is an evidently workable assumption about economic behaviour, fruitful
of correct predictions. It *may* be that, say, sociology or psychology will
discover a similar basic simplicity, but I see no sign of it. Men, in other
facets of their lives, are more complicated to begin with; and their memory
of how they or their predecessors behaved continually changes their own
principles of behaviour. So the statistical "universe" is never the same, or
if you prefer it, the principle of the uniformity of nature cannot be
assumed. Governments and marriage customs evolve, economic man
does not.

So, first, economics has the advantage of a basic, workable, simplicity.
Then, too, its methodology is much more advanced. Today, indeed, it is
no longer the jackal at the feast of mathematics and statistics but the lion
himself, hunting new prey and providing the feast. In linear programming
and in control theory mathematics has made advances for the sake of
economics, and the accusation is no longer valid that we are making do
with techniques developed by and for physicists. We also demand large
and specialized computers! And all this makes us very proud, and inspires
a host of imitators in politics and sociology who seem to be mainly
wasting their time. For we tend to forget, and our imitators seem never to
have heard, the all-important phrase: Garbage In, Garbage Out. *I.e.*,
your results cannot be more reliable than your data, and no mathemati-
cian or computer can tell you what those are.

Data are petty bourgeois; methodology is aristocratic. In the Century
of the Common Man everyone is an aristocrat, so in each social science
methodology has bolted, like uncropped asparagus, to heights where
there are no data at all. If *this* is what "advanced" means, Heaven keep us
backward. I certainly would not wish to say, having looked a little at
conflict research, that economics presents the widest gap between methods
and data, since after all it has more of both. But I do believe it has contributed to the gap in its sister sciences, by setting up a "revolution of
rising methodological expectations" that nothing can fulfil.

The obsession with methodology and with simple assumptions is
accompanied by an excessive faith in mere logic, or nowadays mere
mathematics (which is only a particularly powerful kind of logic). That is,

economists try to deduce complicated and yet practical conclusions, usable in real life, from much ratiocination and few data. Our energy goes into the ratiocination, and we do not examine the data. Nay worse, *we confine our questions to those that can be answered in this manner*. None of these questions touches political economy. For that study requires very many data, collected by imaginative yet scrupulous people, and can support only short flights of reasoning, since some of the necessary data are always missing.

Long chains of reasoning are a hopeless waste of time in political economy; the input, often reused, leads to explosively large errors in the output. Needless to say, no amount of logic can actually generate, or substitute for, factual input; yet this hoary fallacy seems not to be quite dead. Garbage In Garbage Out applies to logic as well – logic is, after all, a sort of computer.

Finally, and also similar, there is the flight into the normative. Economists love to tell us what we ought to do. Some of them are even careful to circumscribe the occasions when we ought to, and to give quite valuable advice. I am far indeed from criticizing this activity, but shall only point out that it is not scientific in any sense helpful to a historian. History is positive, it is about what we do, or did. Normative economics is, by definition, not about what we do; it is also a great deal easier than positive economics, and that is why it is so widely practised. It is of course another excellent field for the construction of large logical edifices on scanty data.

Moreover economics is a very large subject. It contains large fields of study nearly untouched by modern methodology and yielding but the sparsest scientific crop. Notably among these are economic motivation, the distribution of income and capital, the conduct of large corporations, the comparison of economic systems. Moving still further out, we find nothing that even pretends to be a theory of governmental economic behaviour. The whole of the subjects known as public finance, monetary policy and detailed planning is normative. We might want to call a tightly knit logical structure of normative propositions scientific, but it isn't positive so it hardly concerns us. *Moreover it is just these areas that impinge most nearly upon, nay that constitute, political economy.*

Indeed what in economics is truly scientific? What does justify our reputation as the most advanced social science? Let us take a specific example: econometrics, the establishment of quantitative models that describe the behaviour of whole national economies. Parameters are derived empirically[1] that relate the component magnitudes – quantity of money, rate of interest, output of durable and non-durable consumer goods, fixed and circulating investment, budget surplus, balance of foreign payments, etc. – to each other. One feeds in an initial situation or a brief pre-history, assumes certain future values for variables beyond one's control and sets the model in motion. The actual future course of the economy is predicted – sometimes quite well.

It is true that econometrics often makes horrible mistakes. The initial data can be wrong, and so can the assumptions about the future of the exogenous variables. The parametric relations of the variables may change very quickly and without warning, which is much as if a physicist had to deal with substances that boiled at different temperature year by year. Above all the econometrician may *intend* his prophecy to be falsified. Thus his model predicts unemployment, so he shows it to the government, which takes corrective measures. But take it all in all, econometrics is a remarkable scientific achievement, far more successful than its cousin in the natural world, meteorology.

Now what has all this to do with the political economist, let alone the historian? They will note the *effects* of the application by governments of greater econometrical knowledge:[2] fuller and more stable employment, and more rapid growth, in every advanced capitalist country than at any previous recorded period. Now these direct effects can be inferred pretty rigorously from the model; indeed they are a part of it. But not so the effects of these effects: say that Communism has been halted in Europe, or that Social Democracy has veered rightwards, or that laissez-faire has been abandoned to extremists. There is of course nothing in econometrics that tells us how man will react politically to a radical change in the performance of capitalism.

It is easier to educe the constitutional changes that the technical necessities of practicing econometrics impose on a government. Thus, the central bank must – and everywhere has – come more under the control of the Ministry of Finance. For "it says in Keynes" that fiscal and monetary policy are alternatives and must be co-ordinated. But the bank cannot dominate the government, so the government must dominate the bank. Clearly, a historian of the period must know all this, but somehow we have still not got very far. It is rather like saying that the telephone has diminished the role of ambassadors, or that nuclear weapons increase civilian domination over the military. These three propositions really belong to "political technology": they tell us how governmental structures can or must be altered because someone has invented something.

But take another proposition, not strictly about econometrics: Keynesian macro-economic manipulation has nothing whatsoever to do with Communist central physical command planning; it does not even lead to it by an insensible progression, with a second generation of detailed controls being piled upon the first generation of lax controls, because the latter fail to achieve their objective. This is the opposite of what Hayek asserts in his *Road to Serfdom*. Never mind which of us is right: obviously the proposition and its negation are "political economy" in the true sense. How could one confirm or deny it?

The historian will look at all the countries that have adopted Keynesian policies and ask which of them made the Hayekian progression. The answer appears to be, none. For twenty five years or so sixteen advanced capitalist countries have practised the Keynesian economics, say 400 country-years. Not one has trodden the Road to Serfdom. Central physical command planning has been introduced only by governments that liked it anyway, and which had *not* first tried out Keynesian methods and found them wanting. Governments or countries finding these methods wanting have rather retreated to laissez-faire. The Nazis, upon whom Hayek incorrectly based his proposition, even retreated towards laissez-faire in the middle of a war (under Albert Speer); and in any case they never came very close to a command economy.

That, then, is what I call the historical method, though some purists would object that counting and comparing things isn't the rigorous "and then and then" stuff on which they got their Ph. D.'s. I would reply, the previous paragraph is most certainly "and then and then" stuff, in that it is entirely unanalytical and avoids all explanation. If it throws up a plausible generalization nevertheless, we should not be surprised; the method had merely been underrated by its advocates, it is entirely capable of generating good predictions, but not explanations. Pure unthinking statistical analysis, such as the establishment of a connexion between lung cancer and cigarettes, or of the superiority of movements in the quantity of money as a predictor of the national income – all measurement without theory – *is* the "historical method".

But there is no such thing as a historical explanation. That is by definition the province of some science, in this case one of the social sciences.

Measurement without theory, to repeat, can predict but not explain. What passes ordinarily for historical explanation is political explanation. Much of what historians write is not narrative but analysis. This analysis is *never* particular but *always* appeals to some implicit generalization. In other words when we say "history is past politics" we mean that the average historian is a low-grade political scientist. I mean no insult by the qualification, for political science is so rudimentary and unreliable that it is not worth while to be a high-grade exponent of it.

Now political economy is partly politics and partly economics. But the aspects of economics which it touches are very precisely the least developed, as we have seen. As to politics, it has no pretensions to scientific status: no generalization is yet possible on how power is acquired or on how it is used. Therefore there can be no scientific political economy. The nearest we can come to it is the purely positive, virtually untheoretical, amassing of relevant historical data, as in the answer given above to Hayek's question: Does a little planning lead to a lot of planning? This, I submit, is a truly politico-economic question. It is about the likely political reactions of governments and peoples to certain economic events, about the way in which power will be used over the economy when the economy has reacted to an initial use of power. It is also a very important question, to which the world would welcome a scientific answer. Hayek and I have both given positivistic answers, based on the facts. His answer is wrong, mine is right; but neither of us goes very deeply below the surface to enquire what makes some governments try to control the market, and why they react in the way they do when at first their methods seem to fail.

One man, possibly the only man, to go deeply below this surface was Karl Marx. His name is often coupled with the British school of political economy – Smith, Ricardo, Malthus and J. S. Mill – but I am quite unable to do them so much honour. Not one of them studies, let alone makes clear, the connexion between the political and the economic order. Ricardo comes nearest to it, in his theory of income distribution among the three factors of production. These were land, capital and labour and he wrote in this manner at a time and a place when feudal land relationships were not exhausted and political power lay with land owners; while capitalists were a self-conscious class seeking a share of that power, and labourers were indeed an incipient proletariat but could do no more than stage ineffective revolts. And no doubt it was precisely these contours of the political lanscape that stirred David Ricardo, M. P., to produce that theory of income distribution. But the theory is as valid or as invalid in any market economy, no matter what the political configuration. And then it becomes mere economics. It was political economy for a brief half-century.

The insights of Marx were a great deal more illuminating. He was a worse economist and represents in many ways a regression from Ricardo; but an infinitely better politician. Such a question as Hayek's would have been meat and drink to him, and he would have answered it with a truly scientific, though probably incorrect, theory: something about the concentration of capital leading to state capitalism and then to revolution and socialism. This kind of thing genuinely purports to explain *why* governments do this or that to the economy, as well as to to predict *what* they will do. For we must, to repeat, always remain insecure in our predictions of what so long as we do not know why: it is our scientific duty to isolate that carcinogen in nicotine.

My objection to Marx is that though he asked the right questions, and fluked a few good answers, he had the lowest possible standards of proof, logic and definition. Indeed he didn't know the meaning of these words. He was, after all, more German than Jewish: he believed in the power of mere phrases and the omnipotence of thought. The whole of his dialectic is nothing more than this. Moreover *"umso schlimmer für die Tatsachen"* – I blush to translate it into an empirical language – was not, but might well have been, his phrase. He spoke frequently of revolutions but never defined or dated a bourgeois revolution; he confused capitalism with industrialism, and spoke often of mercantilism but never fitted it in; he gaily substracted China, India and even Russia from his theory of history but never reexamined the theory; he spoke of two classes in modern society, but his best book (*The 18th Brumaire*) deals openly with three, etc., etc.

Marx had innumerable successors who were soberer, less arrogant and more scientific: the *Kathedersozialisten* of late 19th century Germany and their contemporaries, the economic historians of Britain. Economic history for a time aspired to be the queen of the social sciences, and to provide both a general view of human history and even guidelines for public policy. Schmoller and Tawney bestrode the world: what has become of this aspiration, and why are our colleagues in that field today such humble drudges? Partly, no doubt, it was the loss of the *Methoden-*

streit. For their great predecessors fought the timeless and bloodless analysis of modern economics, discussed above, not with Hegelian dialectic but with nothing at all. The mere heaping up of data was somehow to reveal something. Partly too, they claimed too much: policy matters like the economic effects of protection or how to cure unemployment really are better tackled analytically, and the good scientist intuitively knows where his own methods will not yield much. But political economists they were, and they should have stuck to their guns.

For political economy is possible and will be useful provided that we do not ask too much of it. It needs no new methodology, only the Marxian habit of asking the right questions, a touch of Marxian genius in the practitioner, and a wholly un-Marxian humility before the data. For the revelant data are numerous and their collection is laborious. But above all we must be humble about our results. For before we have derived this or that proposition from a year's work the "statistical universe" will change before our eyes, and we shall have to begin again. The laws of political economy are like those of politics: temporary and probable generalizations on which to found good bets but not certain predictions, and only valid for an epoch, the boundaries of which the student must establish for himself.

These constant changes of the "statistical universe" merit some concluding, and emphatic, words. The nightmare of the physicist is the political economist's everyday problem. The former dreams of superheavy or super-hot stars on which the natural elements lose their ordinary properties and gravity its usual strength; but these things are only speculation. Marx, however, was constrained to recognize that *Kapital* concerned Europe alone; the Benthamite must admit that Trobrianders are not *homines economici* but may be becoming such as contact with the white man increases. He must even admit that the hippie also breaks most of his rules – deliberately, and after too much "contact with the white man".

There are no rules about the changing of the rules. Sometimes such changes can be foreseen, but mostly they can not. We can predict, perhaps, the development of the Trobriander into *homo economicus*; for other primitive people, albeit quite unlike him, have undergone this same transformation. But none of us foresaw the hippie. The Marxian claim that dialectical materialism tells us how the rules will change, that it is precisely the science of the necessary succession of one statistical universe upon another, is false. The futurologists' attempts to do the job have been no more successful. It would be nice to have such a science, but we haven't, and I doubt if we ever will.

NOTE

1. Sometimes, as in the case of the Chicago School, the crassest empiricism suffices. No theory underlies the proposition that the quantity of money today is the predictor of the national income tomorrow. It is simply alleged to be the best predictor in fact, by econometrical tests. But true science must explain *why*, just as the proposition that smoking causes cancer cries out for the isolation of the carcinogen.
2. Effects, by the way, of the first and least sophisticated advances in the science: those made by Keynes himself. It would be impossible to show that subsequent complications and improvements had contributed anything to any nation's economic performance.

Discussion

PETER WILES: I shall forget about three quarters of my paper and draw your attention to the notion of historical explanation. Obviously, the historian is arbitrary in the object of his selection; he follows market demand for his books, he follows foundation supply for his means of production, and the vogues of interest among his peers. Mr. Furet hinted that the only kind of historical explanation he knew about was that of the social sciences. According to him this kind of explanation only applied to bits of economic and social history; and there isn't any political, politico-historical type of explanation. I think it's obvious that economic and social history are merely past economics and past sociology. So we have, as I see it, three levels of explanation. There is the man-nature interaction first of all, which is fairly easy; my paper draws attention to it with its remarks on Karl Marx and the importance of the forces of production as opposed to the relations of production. Secondly, there is what I rather tentatively call the man-man interaction in commonplace, repetitive, statistical relationships, which is the rest of economics and most of sociology. And here explanation is a good deal less easy. Thirdly, we have historical explanation in the political field. An inattentive listener might have supposed that Mr. Furet, since he didn't know how to generate explanations in this field, was therefore against writing history in it, for the reason that we must not contemplate studying things we cannot explain. However, as any reader of this brief *curriculum vitae* will observe, he isn't really against that kind of thing. So we seem all of us to agree: firstly, that social science can explain past events if the data are appropriate, that a lot of history is past social science, and that the mere time at which the events took place is quite irrelevant; secondly, that political history really is different, or as the futurologist has it, that politics is an autonomous sphere; thirdly, and here begins our trouble, political history is *"événementielle"* – it is "and then, and then" history. Can we do something about it? Fourthly, Alan Bullock has already drawn our attention to the fact that this low-level lexicographical aspect of the historian's work is of extreme importance and complication. It isn't really obvious who executed whom in 1649: you've got to find out, and there might be very unpleasant surprises if you go back to the original sources. In this sort of low-level sense, *"histoire événementielle"* lies underneath the man-nature interactions and the statistical man-man interactions as well. After you have got your sources, the social scientist can take off with considerable ease, whereas the political historian cannot, and it is useless for him to pretend that he can do something more than simply write *"histoire événementielle."* And so my fifth point on this score is that, after all, if most of history is past economics or past sociology, the rest of it is past politics; and what we are really considering when we come to the difficulties of historical explanation are nothing else than the difficulties of political explanation. It is the fact, as I put it rather cruelly, that political science is just a *"Wissenschaft,"* not a science at all. This is not an insulting remark: that is how things are.

Then, what is political explanation? I have a certain admiration for the mere accumulation of data, for the mere accounting of statistics of political events. The particular case I chose was a political non-event, namely the failure of any country to tread Hayek's *Road to Serfdom;* I suggested that you take a year as a suitable period of time and a country as a suitable object of study and then you have four hundred non-events in this particular field. This is, at a very low level, something that generates political predictability; political economy is practically politics. We have here a first stage towards a historico-political explanation generated by a rather formidable statistic. It is of the nature of such statistics and you can extrapolate from them without understanding them, and the parallel that I chose was that smoking causes cancer, which was for a very long time perfectly obviously correct, although nobody had identified the carcinogen. You could therefore go straight ahead to forbid smoking, or cigarette advertising, without waiting for the explanation itself. There is therefore value simply in the heaping up of historico-political data of this type.

But that, of course, is not historical explanation. This seems to me to be by definition the province of social science; a measurement without

theory can predict but it cannot explain. What passes ordinarily for historical explanation is political explanation, and its nature is often of a very
crude and simple type. It's often simply a decent, honest inference from
our ordinary knowledge of human nature. Thus, why did Caesar cross
the Rubicon? Well, because he thought that if he didn't his enemies in
Rome would kill him. And they agreed with this, and everybody else fully
understood that this was his position, and so it fell within the general
structure of the time that this was a permissible ploy. Caesar wanted to
remain alive. These are generalisations, explanations, as I see it, of the
behaviour of Caesar by reference to what other people would have done,
or had indeed done, at that time, by reference to a structure of anthropological type in Ernest Gellner's exposition. This is a scientific historical
explanation of Caesar's behaviour. What I think makes us so aghast at
such a claim is that we expect something more glorious, more technical,
something you could stuff into a computer. Well, it isn't like that. But
I believe this to be good enough and to be of the same type of explanation. Explanation means reference of the particular events to other
similar events which have already been studied. Let me finally draw your
attention to a grave defect in this type of analysis. After all, political explanation of this type is indeed a kind of generalisation, but it is valid only
for an epoch, and the politician, or the political economist, faces daily the
nightmare of the astronomer and the astrophysicist, namely the superheavy star, or the super-hot star of which the natural elements have lost
their ordinary properties. These things are mere speculation for the astrophysicist, whereas for the political economist and the political historian
they are everyday occurrences. The boundaries of the epoch for which
your generalisations apply must be discovered by the student himself.
In other words, I have signally failed to show just how we establish that
this is the end of a period when people crossed the Rubicon for that kind
of reason; there's a period beginning, let us say, with Marius, and ending,
let us say, with Augustus. And I am quite mystified as to how one knows
that it couldn't have applied fifty years before Marius or fifty years after
Augustus.

ALBERTO TENENTI: Historians in general have not thought very much
about their *métier*. They don't present a very united front against the
economists, even though they have agreed to take the economic dimension into account. They breathe the air of economics without always
knowing it.

History is going through a great mutation under the influence of scientific knowledge. All the other human sciences simply accept the suggestions of science; it is a phenomenon of civilisation, not merely of gnoseology. A whole area of historical explanation now approaches the area of what is called scientific explanation. The subject of history becomes the collective rather than the individual, the recurrent rather than the unique, permanence rather than creativity. There is no single answer to the question "What is history?" History is at one and the same time a kind of knowledge (or attempt at knowledge) and a cultural form which though perhaps not universal or eternal is certainly long-lasting. The problem is whether the requirements of history as knowledge can go along with those of history as a cultural form. Within the idea of history one can distinguish a narrative history several thousand years old; a philosophical history or philosophy of history, scarcely younger and not always aware of itself; a history of history, or historiography – *i.e.*, a critical analysis of the forms of narrative history and of those of the philosophy of history; and lastly (if one may risk the word), a history which is a social science.

Up till now, historical explanation applied itself to man as a being in himself. Historical analysis made use of psychological explanation: man was considered not reductible to things. But with the advent of scientific analysis historical man ceases to be an essence and becomes an element of reality. He stops being an actor of history, or agent, and acquires a dimension that is economic, ecological, demographic, or magic... Where is all this new knowledge taking history?

If we look at economics alone, we see that it is present in historical research in various different ways: as a requirement that cannot be dissociated from human affairs in general; as a motive force in the social dynamic; as an external explanation of phenomena regarded as non-economic; and lastly as a factor inseparable from most social behaviour. History seems to want to extend the notion of measure to all historical reality. Quantitative history itself aims at being global history.

The economic approach only continues the spontaneously imperialist and hierarchical ambition of the history of the nineteenth century; it involves a classification of peoples and countries in which the criteria of inequality are based no longer on beliefs or power, but on development.

On the other hand, the scientific history inspired by economics tends to dissociate itself, in certain respects at least, from the role traditional history used to play in the conservation of the general cultural heritage. Or rather quantitative history, while renouncing that role, goes on playing it secretly; although it is a technical or scientific knowledge of man as one object among many, it still rests on a system of values even though it claims to reject any ethic. While it doesn't rule out the study of non-economic, including cultural, phenomena, and is perfectly within its rights not to, it does tend to neglect all that is singular, creative or reactive in history in favour of certain anonymous energies which produce quantifiable results. But to live history as an experience can still be an aim of historical knowledge. It is doubtful whether men would want to pursue the study of history just in order to be "informed". History is more than an aggregate of knowledge: it is also a heritage, and a form of human consciousness.

FRANÇOIS FURET: What strikes me about the development of history in recent years is the way the concept of the problem has come to replace the concept of period. The historian of today thinks not so much in terms of seventeenth century, Middle Ages or Renaissance as of economic problems, demographic problems, and so on. Let us take, for example, the model of the input-output table. It can't be used just as it stands in empirical economic history because we lack the data to fill up all the spaces. But the historian can make use of substitute materials. On the basis of, say, a series of tithes (*i.e.*, ecclesiastical levies on agricultural production), you can arrive, if not at absolute figures, at least at an over-all production trend. The introduction of economic concepts has led the historian to investigate and make use of new materials.

But the result of importing concepts from the social sciences into the field history is that we now have a fragmented history, and we have great difficulty in putting the pieces together to reconstruct a global history, a history *à la Voltaire*...

ARNALDO MOMIGLIANO: Who tells us that explanation is the chief or the only business of the historian? As the chairman of the Commission of the Year 2000 B.C. I must report some work in progress, basically jumping into the unknown. It is a point which has not been made that there is a polarity between discovery and explanation. This is a fact. The most important element in the evolution of historical research in the last hundred years has been the discovery entirely out of the unknown of new civilisations. We have discovered the Hittites, the Mycenean civilisation, the Dead Sea scrolls, sometimes absolutely by chance, by mistake even,

simply by buying things and discovering that they were something different from the price we paid for it. This, of course, implies some problems
about the methodology of interpretation, about the relation between
interpretation of remains, and explanation in general, and to me this is not
entirely unrelated to the problem of what the ultimate explanation is.
Unless you introduce into your methodology of explanation the methodology of discovery, you are far from making progress.

MORSE PECKHAM: Mr. Wiles's notion of the low order of the explan-
atory power in history is very well taken. I think the basic appeal of
history is the appeal of fiction. In my own case, I used to read novels but I
now prefer to read history, possibly because no novelist can relate pro-
ceedings so fantastic as those of the historian. But the appeal of history in
this sense (both its charm and the charm of fiction) is basically the charm
of gossip. The rhetoric "and then, and then" is the rhetoric of gossip.
Gossip is one of the most refreshing things in the world because it relieves
us from having to provide explanations for events.

I would like to make a further point. Like anyone trained in literature,
I have been interested not only in the content but also in the form of the
discussion. There is the logos of the present, the logos of the past and the
logos of the future. The realistic novelists of the nineteenth century, beginning with the Goncourts, and Thackeray and Turgenev, realised that
the techniques used in the historical novel could be applied to the present.
The realistic novel is in this sense an historical novel about the present. If
you look at the various rhetorics of our history and of sociology and of
futurology, the rhetorics of the "pastology," "presentology" and "futurology," there is no striking difference in the discourse (in the kind of
content presented or in the way the content is used for explanations).
The difference is simply a difference of tense; the rhetoric of the historian
is primarily a rhetoric of the past tense. One of the most interesting
things, however, is that he is constantly eliding into the present tense
when he wishes to provide explanations. The rhetoric of the sociologist is
rhetoric of the present tense. He discusses the same material as the
historian does and picks his examples from the same documents and
sources. But the discusses them in the present tense, and the futurologist
of course in the future tense. This is not an unimportant difference. By
rhetoric I mean a linguistic overdetermination, perceived against the
background of ordinary language. Perhaps there is no such thing as
"*la langue*," but only "*la parole*," which consists of various rhetorics.

Therefore it is not surprising that history, being basically gossip, does not easily generate explanations and should constantly import them from the various social sciences.

RAYMOND ARON: Mr. Wiles, it seems to me there is a deliberate ambiguity in the second part of your paper. Sometimes you treat as a lower form of intellectual activity that part of history which because of the very nature of its subject does not reach "scientificity" of explanation. But at other times you deliberately suggest that this is the only kind of history that is really interesting. In other words, for you there is no necessary correlation between the degree of scientificity and the degree of interest. But you bring in another factor. Instead of saying directly "there is no correlation between how interesting a certain aspect of history is and our ability to treat it scientifically," you say we must treat scientifically that which in fact cannot be treated scientifically. You reconcile the two propositions by adopting a rough form of the Hempel model (which you probably don't believe in any more than I do, but which you pretend to believe in). The only way you can get us out of the impasse and into scientificity is by the truisms of Scribner, which give us the basis of a historical explanation.

PIETRO ROSSI: Mr. Wiles referred not only to absence of scientificity but also to different degrees of it. It seems to me his paper presupposes that there is only one form of scientificity or explanation. But when he says there is no explanation in political history he appeals to an idea of explanation which itself needs to be explained, or at least defined. I think the thesis that there is only one form of explanation, with different degrees within it, is a neo-positivist myth running completely counter to all the attempts toward methodology produced by history and the social sciences in the age of Max Weber, who tried to define different types and forms of explanation, and hence of scientificity.

I also wonder whether Mr. Wiles chose quite the exact word when he said there is no *genetic* explanation. Julius Caesar's conduct and political acts cannot be explained without reference to Marius, but such a reference is not purely comparative.

WOLFGANG J. MOMMSEN: Is quantitative history in such a superior position, as far as the word *"scientificité"* is concerned? Take, for example, the question of the impact of an economic crisis on the overall society. One can quantify to a certain degree its effects on the stock exchange, on manpower, etc... but it is really a matter of discussion to what extent this really influences the general course of things. This brings me to the level of the global explanation. Look at Rostow in *The Stages of Economic Growth*: is he in a better position than the ordinary political historian? If you leave the level of fairly basic data you will be much in the same position as political historians. I can easily say, being one of them, that a specific decision was made at a specific moment: it is just as precise as a series of data seriously and carefully collected. So, can we really say there are two types of history, one of them more scientific than the other?

PETER WILES: You are quite right in suggesting that to a large extent the economic historian is little better off than the political historian. But, you see, there is the "doctrine of the quality of the author." You were quoting Rostow, were you not? This is a very important consideration here. Those same weapons having become quite sharp in a more skilled hand might perhaps have persuaded you that the task of the economic historian is a little easier than that of the political historian.

4 Illusions of temporal continuity

ROBERT NISBET

History, sociology and revolutions

Whatever else the word "revolution" may connote to our age, substantial change is clearly the essence. Whether we have reference to the French Revolution, the Industrial Revolution, or the Scientific Revolution – to select three varying and widespread uses of the word "revolution" – the implication is the same in all three: that large-scale, far-reaching, and somewhat convulsive change is involved. I would suggest at the outset of these remarks, then, that the study of revolutions is but a special case of the larger study of change in society and that whatever difficulties may inhere in our approach to the understanding of revolutions probably are rooted in our general approach to the understanding of change.

Professor Aron asks toward the end of his memorandum to the Seminar: "Why do historians continue to tell the 'story' of the French Revolution or the Russian Revolution?" He also asks: "Why did (do) sociologists have so little to teach us about the Revolution or revolutions?" These two questions will be, in a considerable sense, the organizing themes of my paper. I shall begin with the second of them and will, as a sociologist, give it the greater part of my attention here. The first question must not be neglected, however, for answer to it is almost equally important to the larger problem I am concerned with in this paper. That problem is: Why has our understanding of the processes of revolutions, and those of large-scale change generally, improved so little during the past two centuries when, beginning almost immediately after the Revolution in France at the end of the 18th century, concern with revolution and change has been so conscious, so direct and widespread, and, on a constantly expanding scale, so systematic?

Lest my stated question seem rhetorical only, I should stress my conviction here that, taking the French Revolution alone, which is the most important and also the most studied of all revolutions, we have not added significantly to the theoretical understanding of this great event that may be found in Tocqueville's great book on the subject or in the more general Marxian theory of revolution. I do not deny that interesting and often useful insights have been added, though for the most part as corollaries rather than as new propositions, or that substantial bodies of new fact have been brought into existence or older bodies of fact given fresh treatment through statistical techniques. I argue only that whatever increase in actual theoretical understanding of this revolution has taken place during the past century or century and a half has been small and out of proportion to the vast amount of attention given the study of this revolution particularly and of revolutions generally.

If I am right in this argument, the reason would appear to lie not in lack of data, nor in number of investigators working on the matter, nor in insufficiency of funds to support research – the reasons we most often give when our knowledge is insubstantial or confused – but, rather, in lack of proper concepts, of proper methods of approach, or, perhaps most fundamentally, lack of proper statements of the very problem of revolution. I shall proceed, in any event, on this supposition, and begin with the question, why are sociological explanations of revolution, whether Marxian or structural-functionalist (assuming there is a really significant difference between these), so clearly inadequate?

The metaphor of growth

The answer, or large part of the answer, lies, I suggest, in the metaphor of growth that is for the most part the sociologist's way of approaching the problem of change in human society. It is, of course, a very old metaphor and approach in Western thought, going back, certainly, to the earliest Greek rationalists such as Heraclitus who, for want of better model, took the one nearest at hand: the model formed by the processes of growth in the organic world the Greeks were so fascinated by. Aristotle's entire system of philosophy was based in very great part on the derivations he drew from observation of the processes of growth in the individual organism. We need look only at the famous treatment of the nature or *physis* of the State that is given us in the first part of his *Politics*. For Aristotle the nature of the State was indistinguishable from the inherent, self-generative, genetically continuous, processes of internal development he declared to lie in, not merely the State, but in all social, as well as biological entities. The very idea of *physis*, that most vital of Greek concepts in the understanding of the world around us, is drawn from the analogy of all things to the organism-in-growth. We are obliged to call this metaphoric understanding, for we do not see, not in any literal, empirical sense, processes of growth in human institutions and social structures. We see only the effects of changes, real or imagined, large or small, discontinuous or continuous. *Growth* is, for social entities, not fact, as it so plainly is in the plant or organism, but, rather, a theory or hypothesis advanced to account for the effects of the perceived changes.

Of all perspectives or master-ideas in Western thought, none has been more influential than the idea of growth, or development, as we prefer. Everyone knows that the theory of social development, as we find it in the literature of the 19th and 20th centuries, is far from being a simple application of Darwinian evolutionism to social phenomena. For, only too plainly, theories of social and cultural development long precede the publication in 1859 of Darwin's *The Origin of the Species*. The more important point, though, is that even after the Darwinian idea of natural selection, of statistical variation around a norm through reproductive survival, came into being, even indeed after the radical ideas of Mendel became widely known at the end of the 19th century, neither Darwinism nor Mendelism had much effect upon the sociological (and also ethnological) efforts to explain change in time. For these efforts, throughout the 19th century and even very widely today, are for the most part rooted in, not 19th and 20th century perspectives of natural selection, mutation, random events, and others that scientific biology is rich in, but, instead, in the age-old metaphor of growth, in the analogy of social change to processes of immanent growth in the single organism.

There is neither space nor need here to elaborate on the history of the metaphor and the analogy as these are to be found throughout the course of Western thought.[1] What I want to do, what must be done, here is indicate a few of the derivations or corollaries that have flowed into sociological thought from the single source of the metaphor of growth, from the assumption that what happens in time in social institutions and structures is comparable to what happens in time to the organism. I am bound to say at the outset that apart from these derivations and corollaries very little exists in systematic or theoretical form in modern sociology so far as the problem of change – or the problem of revolution – is concerned.

Change may be defined as a succession of differences in time in a persisting identity. All elements are crucial to the definitions: "succession of differences", "in time", and "persisting identity". Without them in combination we may have simple differences, the flow of time, or the persisting identity. But we do not have change. From the point of view of the sociologist or, for that matter, historian or ethnologist, the fundamental problem of change is to account for it, to explain it when we find it. Once we have made allowance for the usual confusions of change with processes that may involve motion, action, movement, interaction, and so on but not necessarily *change*, we seek to find cause for it, and also the mechanisms through which a given change may pass into wider areas of the structure itself and of the society and culture surrounding the structure. Here is where the philosophy or theory of growth comes into use and has come into use for many centuries down to the present. This philosophy or theory, having made the initial – and massive – assumption that social structures are like, or very much like, organisms in character, proceeds to the following conclusions about social change, which I shall state here very briefly and synoptically:

1. *Change is natural or normal in any institution or structure.* It would be hard to think of any proposition more universally accepted in Western thought, ever since the pre-Socratic rationalists in ancient Greece, than this one. Heraclitus declared that the *physis* of anything, physical, organic, social, was its life-cycle, its pattern of growth. Analysis must therefore concern itself with those forces internal to the entity under consideration which generate the growth or change. At no point since in Western history, not even during the long spell of Augustinian Christianity, has there been more than occasional serious doubt expressed with respect to this proposition, this axiomatic insistence upon the naturalness of change or, restating it, upon the thesis that every entity, social structure or institution, as well as biological organism, has mechanisms of change more or less built into its component elements.

2. *Change is immanent.* In a way, I am restating here what has just been said, but I think it important to underscore heavily that flowing from the metaphor of growth has come not only the view that change is natural

and normal but that it proceeds from forces contained within it; that is, from elements of structure such as roles, statuses, and norms deemed to be in constant condition of stress or tension sufficient over long periods to result in change – provided nothing interferes or thwarts the tendency toward change. Leibniz wrote: "When I speak of the force and action of created beings, I mean that each created being is pregnant with its future state, and that it naturally follows a certain course if nothing hinders it." Every educated Greek or Roman would have taken that for granted, and it is hard to think of a single major Greek scientist or philosopher who did not state it in form pretty close to Leibniz's. One would look in vain for a major philosopher of change in the 19th century in whose theory this Leibnizian assertion is not fundamental. Marx, Comte, Maine, Spencer, all took it for granted that the forces of change are to be found *in* the entity, be it as large as civilization as a whole (where alone the contention is indisputable on logical grounds, unless one is committed to theistic intervention going on incessantly) or some single institution, social organization, nation, or political system. The sovereign goal of the so-called science of change was that of discovering the specific forces and mechanisms responsible for the change that was deemed in advance to be both natural and immanent. Nor is the situation different today in social science. Whether it is sociologists and their structural-functional or social systems analyses, economists and their business cycles, or political scientists engaged in studies of political development abroad, the naturalness and the immanence of change to a given institution or nation or system are accepted virtually without question.

3. *Change is continuous.* The idea of continuity is one of the most important and also one of the oldest derivations from the metaphor of growth. The essence of the idea of continuity, with respect to change at least, lies in the assumption that change is, normally, slow, gradual, and cumulative. The last is the key word. It carries the implication that social change, like organic growth, is not merely constant in time, not merely additive, but that each later change is the consequence of a cumulation of earlier ones in the life of any institution or social system. The "chain of being" that Aristotle descried in nature was matched perfectly by his "chain of change" in the *Politics*, his declaration that the *physis* of anything social lies in the continuous and cumulative change it reveals in time.

In the 18th century Leibniz, borrowing from the metaphor of growth, declared: *Natura non facit saltum.* He also declared that "the present is big with the future" just as the past was once big with what lies around us now. It would be hard to find any phrase more widely quoted in the 19th century than Leibniz's on continuity. We find it in Comte, Spencer, Marx, Darwin, and a host of other writers on change. We find it today in many works. To vindicate the principle of continuity is, in a sense, the sovereign objective of sociological students of change. So is the objective of historians, though in a different sense, as I shall indicate shortly. Large changes, including revolutions, are held to be the iron cumulation of smaller, genetically related changes taking place in the entity – "feudalism", "capitalism", "the social system" – under examination. Whether in Marxism, developmentalism, evolutionism, or functionalism in the social sciences, the concept of continuity is basic.

4. *Change is necessary.* There is no need to elaborate on this, for, plainly, if change is declared to be natural, immanent, and continuous in a given thing, it is, at very least, "necessary." Necessity means something more, obviously, in developmental theories of change than mere omnipresence, or asserted omnipresence. It means also *logical necessity.* From the time that Socratic philosophers introduced teleology into the study of nature and society, the fateful idea of logical necessity has exerted profound influence upon Western thought about the problem of change. It is the notion of logical necessity that lies behind the often-observed penchant of developmentalists to find "stages" or "phases" which are declared either necessary or highly probable – always assuming of course, in Leibniz's phrase, that nothing "hinders" or "interferes with" the putative naturalness, continuity, and necessity of the change. No one argues from the doctrine of the necessity of change that each and every phenomenon goes through its natural course of necessary change; not any more than the physiologist would so argue of his organism. After all we do live in a world of accidents and interferences. Nonetheless a scientific or sociological theory of change, in contrast to one in which change might be thought random and the result of external and fortuitous forces, is quite evidently – looking at nearly all texts and treatises in contemporary sociology – one in which the processes of change are regarded as necessary – in the sense that growth is necessary in the organism.

5. *Change proceeds from uniform causes.* This is only another way of saying change must not be allowed to be thought dependent upon the merely casual, the fortuitous, the accidental, above all, the randomly external. For, if change is envisaged this way, how, then, can there be a true *science* of change – in contrast to mere cataloguings, descriptions, and annalistic recordings? When the doctrine of uniformitarianism became powerful in the late 18th century, with first Hutton, then Lyell, and finally Darwin in the 19th century giving it expression, the adversary these men opposed was not simply the belief in divine creation and intervention. There were some in that age who, whatever may have been their attitude toward Scripture, simply declared the geological and biological record unintelligible save by reference to periodic, unique, event-like, catastrophes and convulsions. But the catastrophists and vulcanologists were pretty well put to rout by the theory of uniform causation. Especially was this the case after Darwin put his name to uniformitarianism, though in a degree that led to Lyell's distress and to an extraordinary, self-sealing kind of logic in Darwin's *Origin of the Species.* In the social sciences, certainly from the time that the "natural history" was in vogue in the 18th century, there was never the slightest doubt that uniform causes, causes held to have operated through all human time, to operate now in the present, and on into the future, were the only proper subject of scientific – in distinction from merely "historical" – inquiry. Whether Adam Smith's instinct to "truck and barter", Kant's "unsocial sociability", Marx's – and many others' – factor of perpetual conflict, or the contemporary functionalist's "dysfunctions" of norm, role, and status, the doctrine of uniform cause has been an influential one. And the search for this Holy Grail has, of course, been an unremitting one, especially by all with utopian or revolutionary aspirations. For if one has mastery of that uniform cause he can move the world! Or so men have believed.

6. *The directionality of change.* On purely empirical grounds it is hard to prove that the claimed directionalities of development in society and culture lie elsewhere than in the beholder's eye. And the immense amount of variability one finds regarding claimed directionalities is perhaps further evidence in behalf of the belief that they have no other existence save in the beholder's eye. Still, there is at least the logical possibility that, variability of claims of directionality notwithstanding, there still lies ahead, yet to be discovered, the *true* direction that development is taking –

in democracy, in capitalism, in the modern university, in American or British civilization, or in human culture at large. It has to be said in further defence of the search for directionality that if change in a system, structure, or culture is indeed growth-like in character, does indeed exhibit immanence, continuity, necessity, and the incessant operation of uniform causes, then we have every right to expect in social change that final element of all genuine growth: directionality. The large amount of work known as futurology, on which Daniel Bell in the United States has written so informatively, suggests that, as the millennial year 2000 approaches, interest in the asserted directionality of change will increase. Interest in direction is, however, old.

I do not wish to suggest in the foregoing paragraphs that all sociologists are interested equally in all elements or aspects of change considered after the model of growth. Different times produce different emphases. As we know, the 19th century was keenly interested in the macrosociological, the panoramic vistas of change, with the well-known stage-theories of Comte, Marx, Spencer, and of many others the most spectacular result. There has been in this century much less interest in the panoramic vistas and in stages, though the recent works of Talcott Parsons and Robert Bellah, among others, reveal the perennial interest in the large-scale evolutionary view of things.

On the whole, though, sociologists of the present century have been more interested in the microsociological aspects of change. The so-called revolt against the theory of social evolution in ethnology and sociology during the present century was really not a revolt against the theory, or against the model of growth it contains, but, rather, against certain emphases, chiefly those of long-term stages. In clear fact, the doctrines of contemporary functionalists, and also the doctrines of substantial numbers of sociologists who do not necessarily label themselves either functionalists, structuralists, or systems-analysts, suggest the persistence of most of the essential elements of the metaphor of growth in the study of change. One may perhaps quibble over whether the political developmentalists, the sociological functionalists, and the economists who deal with economic growth, not to leave out the contemporary ethnologists, are "evolutionists", as this word is conventionally defined, usually with reference to the great stage-builders of the last century. But, labels aside, there does not seem much doubt but that the metaphor or model of growth continues to be what it has been for twenty-five hundred years in the West: the major source of our concepts and perspectives for dealing with change.

I shall come back to the model of growth shortly for the purpose of asking a few critical questions about it. First, however, let us look at another powerful metaphor in Western thought, the metaphor of *genealogy*, this one the prized possession of historians. What *change* has been to the social scientists, *events* have been to historians from earliest times – the central subject of inquiry. And just as the social scientists have employed the metaphor of growth to give explanation to change, so have historians employed the metaphor of genealogy to give perspective and unity to historical events.

The metaphor of genealogy

Genealogy, literally defined, is an account of the descent through time of an individual or family from remotest discoverable ancestors. When the idea first arose of using the visible linkage of generations, the linkage ritualized everywhere in birth, marriage, and death, as the model for human understanding of the vast unknown, we do not, of course, know. Very probably it is, like the metaphor of growth, universal in one degree or other in human society and has been for many thousands of years. All we know is that the metaphor of genealogy is to be found in the earliest existing works of literature and religion. Genealogy was the device used by the Jews to give the explanation of things that is to be found in the Old Testament, and probably no people has ever exceeded the Jews in their awareness of the event-character of human experience – and much other experience, including divine, as well. The Greeks were almost equally fascinated by events and by genealogical connections of events. It was the narrative and sequential method of genealogy that Homer used. A couple of centuries later Hesiod, in his *Theogony* especially but also in the remarkable *Works and Days*, made genealogy the structure of his account of the gods and the races of man. The *Theogony* is as rich in utilization of the images of sexual reproduction, of issue, and of the linkage of generations as the works of the earliest rationalists in Ionia were rich in the several images of growth.

Just as the metaphor of growth became rationalized and secularized in due time, so did the metaphor of genealogy. Hecataeus is a splendid example of a historian, in the late 6th century B.C., who was engaged in rationalizing history, in separating as best he could myth from reality, legend from fact. Herodotus went even farther in this direction. And, as every undergraduate in history knows, Thucydides went the farthest. Rightly he is to the long descent of historians what Aristotle is to the descent of social scientists. Even contemporary historians would be hard put to handle their data more rigorously, with greater respect for authenticity and objectivity, than did Thucydides. From the remarkable Athenian comes the line of historians through Tacitus, Orosius, Machiavelli, Gibbon, Michelet, Motley, Mommsen and so many others down to the countless individuals who today write for, or are reviewed in, such journals as the *American Historical Review*.

I am not suggesting there are not great differences among members of the line, or that an Orosius in the descent is as "good" as a Thucydides, a Maitland or a Mattingly. There are credulous and less credulous historians, patently partisan or subjective and, very different in motivation, the objective or dispassionate. But common to all is the basic framework or method. This method is the narrative method we call historiography. It is as distinctive in its utilization of events, time, human actions, and the *personae* of our records as the method of developmentalism is among social scientists who are concerned with change. And, as I have suggested, the historian's method is based upon the metaphor of genealogy. From Thucydides straight down to the Morisons and Mattinglys of our day the metaphor of genealogy is the means of giving unity and perspective to what would otherwise be a boundless mass of human experience.

The often-observed affinity between literature and history-writing, however objective the latter, comes directly from the fact that common to both literature – at least to novels, epics, sagas, and the like – and historiography is the structure of genealogy. To tell a story is to relate past and present, and sometimes future, genealogically, through the use of events, actions and persons. And this, allowing only for the differences of authoritativeness of record, of critical and "scientific" use of documents and records, is basically what history-writing is. It is not to be missed, irrespective of the differences of approach of the imaginative novelist and the document-rooted historian, that the praise we give each at his best is very nearly interchangeable. We properly laud those historical novels that set their plots and developments of character against a sound background of historical fact. And we properly laud those works of history which, as we are likely to say, fall into the category of great literature. The etymological affinity of "story" and "history" is fully supported by content and style that reign even today. Rightly did Aristotle place history among the arts, and rightly did he suggest that there is a level of truth belonging to art that science as such cannot hope to achieve.

Whether we are considering "good" history – that is, historiography constructed with maximum respect to documents and records, to what we call "the facts" – or "bad" history, certain consequences flow from the underlying genealogical framework just as surely as consequences flow from the sociologist's use of the framework of growth for his inquiry into change. I shall mention briefly a few of these consequences.

1. *The tyranny of time.* The historian as such cannot escape time either in the sense of the single crucial minute, hour, or day when something happened or in the sense of what we liken to the flow of time through past, present, and future. In this respect historiography differs significantly from the developmental constructions of those who, like Marx, Comte, Spencer, or the functionalists of our day, are less interested in the "whenness" of things, with their specificity in time, than they are with underlying, time-escaping, "natural" processes. If historians so commonly have thrown hands up in impatience at the social-evolutionary constructions of sociologists, the reason often lies in the fact that historians, like the poet Marvell, hear "time's winged chariot hurrying near." Ranke's famous words *wie es eigentlich gewesen ist* were uttered, we may assume, as much in indignation about the practices of time-omitting social evolutionists like Comte as about the liberties with time, place, and event taken by romantic historical novelists.

Genealogy requires full sense of the historicity of things, of their "whenness" as well as their "whereness" and "whatness". True, time is extraordinarily difficult to define or describe. With St. Augustine the historian can say "What is Time? If nobody asks me, I know; but if I were desirous of explaining it to one that should ask me, plainly I know not." I believe it was Trevelyan who caricatured the practices of certain of the more imaginative and literary historians with his mock words: "Men of the Middle Ages; you are about to begin the Hundred Years War." So deeply embedded in our consciousness today, however, are the utterly artificial, ethnocentric, and arbitrary divisions of time, "Ancient", "Medieval", and "Modern", that even a good historian can be forgiven

occasionally if he lapses into assumption that the unilinear and homogeneous scheme of time through which Western historians bind into one
genealogy the boundlessly diverse experiences, places, and time-sequences
of all who have ever inhabited the Eurasian promontory that is Western
Europe have a substantive reality.

That events and actions do indeed take place in time is beyond challenge. It is, however, the genealogical framework alone that demands the
fusing of all the diverse time-orders, time-bindings, and time-sequences
into the kind of "time" that the common narrative historical treatment of
a people or nation or civilization reveals. When Augustine wrote his *The
City of God* and Orosius his *Seven Books of History Against the Pagans*
there was no conspicuous problem in arraying the multiple peoples and
time-orders each dealt with into a single, unilinear time-order. For it was,
as both writers tirelessly made emphatic, God's time-order that was alone
real, the time-order that had begun some six thousand years before in the
Creation and that would, beyond all doubt, terminate within a few
hundred years for once and all. Everything, for Augustine and Orosius,
existed within the contemplation of God, which alone conferred reality
upon experience. If we are inclined today to smile at the liberties Orosius
took with his phases and sequences of events, peoples, and individuals,
all within a single lineal structure of time, look to the practices of our
contemporary historians of civilization who do not bother to hypothesize
God.

2. *The uniqueness of events.* As in any genealogy the loss of uniqueness of
identity of *personae* is fatal, so is loss of sense of uniqueness of events
generally held to be fatal by the conventional historian. In the same way
that the historian understandably looks skeptically or saturninely at the
sociologist's commonly event-less renderings of social reality, so does he
look with equal feeling on the philosopher's or scientist's neglect of the
particularity, the uniqueness of history's events, actions, and *personae*.
The historian's puny admission that in some slight degree events may be
compared shivers alongside the gigantic conviction that to compare,
classify, and categorize events is to mutilate them. Again Ranke's *wie es
eigentlich gewesen ist* may be taken as the proud motto of House of
History that stretches back to Herodotus and Thucydides. When Crane
Brinton wrote his *The Anatomy of Revolutions*, there were many to ap-
plaud, but not many of them historians. As one who, when that book

appeared, sat daily at lunch in the Faculty Club at Berkeley with historians, I have a vivid recollection indeed of the scorn that could attend
perception of a fellow-historian's betrayal of the fellowship. The task of
the historian is to identify in its existential uniqueness each action and
event that comes before his glass, set it in proper sequence with other
unique events, as in any sound genealogical series, and then pass on to the
inspection of another event, and another.

3. *Genetic continuity*. It is this, an inescapable consequence of the
genealogical framework, that saves historiography from being no more
than a museum of facts. Just as the sociologist has drawn from the metaphor of growth the momentous conclusion that changes beget changes in
continuous, and genetic, sequence, so the historian has always drawn the
conclusion from his metaphor of genealogy that events beget events, and
do so in an order that may be best rendered through unilinear narrative.
The asserted, dogmatic indeed, "continuity of history" or "seamless web
of history" are phrases which, on the face of it, are bizarre. For the raw
materials of historiography have been, until recent times when documents
and records have come in for wholesale and systematic consideration,
annals, diaries, and chronicles constructed by individuals for whom the
discontinuous, the irregular, the accidental and untypically catastrophic
were the sole objects of interest. It was precisely because events did *not*
seem continuous or directly emergent that chroniclers set them down.
There is, then, a slight element of humor in the fact that later historians,
following the genealogical principle of unbroken succession, would seize
upon the odd, disruptive, and spectacular events for construction of
narratives designed to show history as a seamless web. If we had before us,
through computer-magic, quite literally *every* event and action that has
ever taken place in human history, no doubt that utterly inconceivable
mass of material would reveal, at very least, continuity of some kind.
But the actions and events through which the alleged continuity of history
is proved by historians represent not only a tiny handful of grains of sand
from all the beaches and deserts of the world, each grain of sand has in
fact been chosen for its distinctive, even mutant character.

Despite protestations of many historians that they content themselves
with history *wie es eigentlich gewesen ist*, the very structure adopted for
retailing the facts selected suggests the contrary. For the narrative,
unilinear, genealogical mode of presentation is itself a massive, and by no

means unchallengeable, conclusion. When H. A. L. Fisher completed his fascinating and beautifully thought out history of modern Europe, he wrote: "One intellectual excitement has... been denied me. Men wiser and more learned than I have discovered in history a plot, a rhythm, a predetermined pattern. These harmonies have been concealed from me. I can see only one emergency following upon another, as wave follows upon wave, only one great fact with respect to which, since it is unique, there can be no generalizations... the play of the contingent and the unforeseen." But the very mode, the narrative-genealogical mode, Fisher adopted, accepted from his predecessors, for presentation of these emergencies, this play of the contingent and unforeseen, is itself a conclusion, a generalization, of highest order. For does not the genealogical metaphor state above all else that what precedes in time causes, gives birth or rise to, what follows?

4. *Causation.* In conventional thought about causation, there are, and always have been, three terms: an antecedent, an intervening state or process, and a consequent. This ancient conception of cause is the very cornerstone of conventional historiography. There is the antecedent event or act, there is the intervening condition, and the consequent. It is the intervening period, the second step, that is the real stuff of modern history-writing and the principal reason why historians, generation after generation, continue to rewrite the same "story" – of the fall of Athens or Rome, the rise of Venice or the Dutch Republic, or the American, the French, the Russian revolutions. It is easy enough to assent to, or stipulate, the first and third steps, the antecedent and the consequent. What is ever in doubt, and endlessly fascinating in contemplation, is the second step: how – through what motives, acts, events, generosities and basenesses – passage from the first to third was made. This is the step that keeps historians writing and books on a subject selling. And it always will as long as the genealogical mode of presentation, with its built-in, event-by-event, link-by-link, structure prevails.

It has been said by many historians of their discipline that history became scientific or objective when the practice of giving divine or demonological explanations of the second step ceased and historians turned instead to human motives as these could be deduced from documents. There is, of course, something in this. Science should not hypothesize gods and demons. But the more important fact seems to me to be that

while, from about the late 18th century on, divine interventions and dia-
bolic eruptions disappeared largely from European historiography, the
underlying framework of explanation continued. God was retreated to the
lumber room of history, but not God's wondrous ways. The historian,
in full humanist glory, took on the responsibilities of God.

For, there is this much truth in Marshall McLuhan's conclusions about
the post-Gutenbergian age in which we live: history – in the sense of what
is "out there" – is not merely interpreted by the historian; it is shaped, in
a large sense *created* by the historian; just as the "news" we get on the
6:00 evening television program is "given" us in every sense of that word
by individuals who, when they have survived as long as the Brinkleys,
Cronkites, and Howard K. Smiths, become themselves as much the
objects, the participants, of the "news" as they become the purveyors or
tellers of the news – *wie es eigentlich gewesen ist*, of course.

I hope it will be understood that in these remarks I am not emphasizing
the oft-emphasized subjectivity of human perception and selection; I am
not even emphasizing, here at least, the McLuhanesque envisagement of
the historian or news commentator as maker of news – of nationalism,
imperialism, or, as the case may be, of violence in the ghetto and on the
campus. I am willing to stipulate that even had no nationalistic school of
historians ever come into existence in the late 18th and the 19th centuries,
nationalism of a sort would have made its appearance anyhow. So too am
I willing to stipulate that even had no newspaper or television reports,
especially the latter, with their tedium-breaking instruments of sight and
sound, ever gone forth to tedium-saturated multitudes in the American
middle class, there would have been ghetto and campus revolts in the
1960s.

My concern here is neither subjectivity of perception nor the appetite
for "news" that has existed ever since "Omer smote 'is bloomin' lyre,"
but, rather, the method or structure of inquiry, the framework of presentation, by which the appetite for understanding of past and present is most
commonly satisfied. "How have things come to be as they are?" and
"How do things operate?" are both ancient and still insistent questions in
the minds of nearly all of us. Conventionalized structure of response to
these questions can become its own reason for being, just as surely as
institutions and organizations sometimes become their own reason for
being – above and beyond whatever may be the larger, external function
these satisfy.

It seems evident enough, still in reply to Professor Aron's question, that one reason, perhaps the chief reason, historians continue to tell the "story" of the French or Russian or other revolutions is only in small part because new data appear or new techniques of assembling the data may arise. It is hard to resist the conclusion that the ritual of convention-alized response creates its own needs and demands. One continues to tell the story because there is a story to be told and in historiography as in literature generally common subject matter does not derogate from distinctiveness of each of the artists involved. How, as one reflects on the matter, could a revolution – or any other signal event or act that is a part of cultural tradition – *not* continue to be told, just so long as there are artists to speculate endlessly on motives, connections, and patterns and also, not to be overlooked, to rise to the challenge that each fresh inter-pretation establishes in the minds of other artists? For at least twenty-five hundred years historians have been seeking to improve upon their predecessors just as poets and painters and musicians have; or, if not actually to improve upon, to deal nevertheless with like materials in a distinctive, impressive, and unforgettable way.

Beyond this artistic function of the metaphors I have been describing lies their undoubted social value. Dogma is required if there is to be a culture or community. Each of the metaphors serves, as I have suggested, a dogmatic function in our civilization. For most of us it would be difficult to live without the metaphors of growth and genealogy, applied to past, present, and future with respect to institutions, cultures, and peoples. Few would find it easy to live without the buoying-up effect of a metaphor that links events of past, present, and future genealogically, or the metaphor that sees irreversible processes of development, continuous, cumulative, self-engendered, in each institution or society. No doubt each metaphor is vital to our collective sense of identity in time, which may be in turn vital to our individual sense of identity.

A critique of pure metaphor

So much is true. But no matter how vital, how imperishable indeed, the two metaphors, each plainly presents serious difficulties to our under-standing of how things have come to be as they are, of how things operate in time. For, no matter how appealing and lulling each is when the objective is simply that of telling a "story", if we are to learn from our inquiries in such a way as to guide social policy it is clear that disadvantages, possibly fatal ones, lie in the two forms of inquiry I have been concerned with.

Thus, with respect to the first metaphor, that of growth, one is obliged to conclude, no matter how far he stretches the meanings of words, that social institutions, cultures, and societies do not really grow; do not follow paths of continuous, cumulative, necessary, and directional change over time; cannot in fact be understood, so far as changes are involved, through premises and concepts of endogenous, self-generating, and irreversible growth. We pretend it is all so, for words like growth and development are so universal in our consciousness, so imperious to all who listen, that a very great deal of "explanation" is accomplished through mere use of the words, through ringing of changes on the metaphor. But in blunt fact, the detailed record of a social institution or culture over a substantial period of time suggests that, not change, but inertia or persistence is the more common condition of human behavior; that change of any significant degree is likely to be the consequence of random events or other forces from the outside which cannot easily be subsumed within any pattern of asserted growth for the entity in question; that discontinuity rather than continuity is the more frequent attribute of the experience of any single people so far at least as change is involved.

Further, it is very difficult to find in fact that small changes of behavior within a structure have cumulative relation leading in time to larger changes *of* the structure in question. Or, putting the matter in reverse, it is very difficult to reduce the occasional large changes we find in history to simple, genetic accumulations of small changes which have taken place lineally beforehand. Efforts to find the "natural" pattern – be it trajectory or cycle – of change in some entity, a pattern that is made distinct from "artificial" or "accidental" changes, are notoriously unsuccessful. And, finally, there would seem to be an ineradicably subjective quality to all extrapolations of constructed "past" and "present" into the future. And it is by no means certain that the beguiling Leibnizian proposition, "the present is big with the future", has much if any substantive validity.

So too with the second metaphor, genealogy. Events do not clearly give birth to events despite the ease with which historians set forth their constructed linkages. Chronological continuity is not readily translated into the continuity of events and changes in time. Causality cannot be easily declared to lie in sequences and asserted linkages of events, motives, actions, and *personae*. For the historian as for the developmentalist directionality seems to lie in the eye of the beholder. Time is no more universal and absolute than it is homogeneous. There are as many "times" as there are places, peoples, and perceived genealogies.

In no way, it seems to me, are the inadequacies and deceptions of the two metaphors more vivid than when we come to the study of revolutions – be they political or other. For, whatever else a revolution is, it is, as I suggested at the outset of this paper, a major change or major event – if we prefer, a major complex of either changes or events. No one, obviously, wishes to settle for regarding a revolution as an act of God or an indecipherable eruption of the Unknown. That way lies passivity or superstition. But the alternative *need* not be reliance upon either growth or genealogy. No matter how dogmatically or tactically appealing the image of internal growth may be to the Marxist or the functionalist when he turns to the American, the French or the Russian revolution, seeking to find in 1775, or in 1789, or in 1917 the necessary or "natural" emergent of what Marx thought of as "tendencies working with iron necessity towards inevitable results" or what a contemporary functionalist might call "the continuous operation of the individual psyche, with its potential of unsatisfied desires... within the universe of its social system", we do not escape the realm of myth when we deal with revolutions in this wise. Nor do we when we turn from growth to genealogies of selected events, with selected acts and events intercalated for causal purposes by the artist-historian.

Despite the nearly sacred role of genealogy as ascribed causation, of growth as proffered explanation, there is a great deal, obviously, that historians and social scientists can do towards the explanations of revolution – and other forms of change, as well – by turning to other ways or frameworks of marshalling and giving meaning to data. To ask the empirical question, how did the French revolution come about? is in no way to be committed in advance to either the model of growth or genealogy, each with its implied premise of the unilinearity and homogeneity of time and circumstance.

Nor would I suggest for a moment that we lack for efforts along this line, though I think they are plainly few by comparison with all the efforts that have been lodged in the metaphor-drawn models I have been writing of. It has often seemed to me that Herodotus, for all his notorious technical faults of credulity and rumor-mongering, would make a more interesting study for methodological purposes than the great and more favored Thucydides. For Herodotus gives us the picture, not of history, in the singular, but, as his title implies, of *histories* in all their plurality. And as any reader of Herodotus knows, he was not very much interested in the strictness of chronology. Throughout he sees the experiences of others as a kind of vast laboratory of data making possible the kinds of questions he is ever asking himself and ever trying to provide hypotheses for, no matter how odd and credulous many of these are. But it was Thucydides, not Herodotus, who proved to be the true model of the long line of historians; Thucydides for whom the wrenching of any act or event from the seamless web of his own chronology would have seemed wanton violation of the uniqueness of each and every event.

There are others, past and present. The remarkable but still relatively little known (at least in the United States) Italian, Giovanni Battista Vico, is pertinent here. Again, as with Herodotus – or, for that matter, anyone who readily comes to mind – there are flaws. But in his profound opposition to Cartesianism Vico saw the dangers to any study of human behavior that tried to root itself in assumed natural laws of uniformity in time and space. Not for Vico any more than for Herodotus the "seamless web" of history, the unbroken continuity of history, either in the large or the small, least of all either genealogical or growth reconstructions – though it would be extreme to declare Vico free utterly of the premises of these reconstructions.

In France, the extraordinary Turgot, who seems to have read and been deeply influenced by Vico, showed the way toward a non-genealogical, non-developmental treatment of culture and society. I have reference here not to his well known *Discourse on the Successive Advances of the Human Mind*, although that contains some fascinating insights in the direction I have in mind here, but rather in his scarcely known *Researches into the Causes of the Progress and Decline of the Sciences and Arts* and also his incomplete but immensely original *Plan for a Work on Political Geography*. Nor, in this connection, should we fail to note what is in many ways the greatest single work of the French 18th century in the moral sciences, Montesquieu's *Spirit of the Laws*. Here too we have a master-historian, and also a master-sociologist, who chose to make his inquiries, and to set forth his results in non-developmental, non-genealogical presentation. In England, in the 19th century, was the vastly learned, and also imaginative, George Cornewall Lewis. His *Treatise on Methods of Observation and Reasoning in Politics* seems to me the most original and suggestive work in the social sciences in Europe until we come to Max Weber. No one more astutely and penetratingly exposed the pitfalls of developmentalism and genealogy alike in their application to past and present in society.

Perhaps above all, certainly in the late 19th and 20th centuries, was Max Weber. I would not declare him the only sociologist who is very nearly complete in his rejection of developmentalism and genealogy, yet at the same time avid in his concern with the problem of change, but he is beyond question the towering figure in the discipline. His comparative studies of religion and economic behavior, and of much else, come close to being the greatest works of social science we have.

There are still others; Frederick J. Teggart's *Processes of History*, and his *Rome and China: A Study in the Correlations Events*, Alfred L. Kroeber's *Configurations of Culture Growth*, Rushton Coulborn's *Feudalism in History*, done in collaboration with others but given splendid inspiration and guidance by the late Professor Coulborn, and Crane Brinton's *Anatomy of Revolution*, in many ways thin and inconclusive, but a bold start that, on the evidence, historians (and sociologists) have paid little attention to. Whatever the deficiencies of Brinton's book, at least revolutions are dealt with as a class of events in human experience and subject to the same kind of comparative investigation, with potentially verifiable hypotheses or propositions proffered.

In quick summary, and returning once again to Professor Aron's seminal questions: Apart from the kinds of data historians characteristically deal with – events, actions, *personae*, and among these the intrusions, impacts, migrations, invasions, "accidents", "catastrophes", and other externally-derived phenomena which in fact periodically and powerfully bear upon human experience in even the tightest and seemingly most autonomous of social systems – it seems unlikely that we shall ever reach a knowledge of how social changes, including revolutions, actually take place. But so long as historians choose to deal with these in the form of arbitrary genealogies, that is, in the structure of what is at bottom an art form, we shall go on and on with renderings of the "story" of the French Revolution (or whatever) with each new artist taking his departure from some real or imagined defect of ascribed motivation, or of genealogical succession, in the works of his artist-predecessors.

And sociologists, so long as they obey the siren-call of the growth-metaphor, seeking crucial causation, crucial sources, regarding the mechanisms of change within constructed social systems – be they "capitalism", "imperialism", "nationalism", a Parsonian generalized social system, or the French nation, or even one of Toynbee's or Spengler's "civilizations" – just so long will their allegedly natural and timeless conclusions regarding change be without signal use to historians and others concerned with the questions of how things actually operate and how things have actually come to be as they are.

Generalizations, conclusions, propositions, call them what we will, are indeed the objective of all inquiry that desires status of science, in contrast to art. But such propositions can have little if any value if they are rooted in metaphorically derived procedures which patently fly in the face of the historicity and multiplicity of human experience. It is generalisation *from* the empirical, the concrete, and the actual, not generalization achieved through their dismissal and the taking of refuge in timeless and eventless abstractions. Whatever the demands of a social theory, the first demands are those of social reality. All else is surely secondary.

NOTE

1. I have done that in my *Social Change and History: Aspects of the Western Theory of Development* (Oxford, 1969), though briefly and schematically.

Discussion

ROBERT NISBET: I would like to add some remarks. One cannot read contemporary philosophical, historical and social scientific writing without observing how the very idea of directionality still has deep roots. The search for a single theory that will account both for order and for change is surely as regnant in the sociology of Talcott Parsons as it was in the one of Auguste Comte. Few sociologists today have the audacity to deal with civilisations as Comte and Spencer and to some extent Marx did, although Professor Talcott Parsons tried it, a few years ago, in an utterly preposterous book called *Societies: Evolutionary and Comparative Perspectives*; but I take the absence of the promised second volume of that work as an excellent indication that Professor Parsons is not going to deal very much longer with sociology on the grand scale of Spencer and Comte. When sociologists do not deal with large-scale civilisation they have become as obsessed by something called a social system as ever a Spencer or Comte were obsessed by a civilisation. A social system is an adroit means whereby a unified theory of order and change can be written if not actually thought out, whereby one seeks to deduce change from social structure. I do believe it is absolutely impossible to deduce change from any form of social structure, or social system. I do not think it is possible to account for change except by reference, at least occasional reference, to the genius, the maniac, the prophet and the random event. The contemporary sociological theory is unable to achieve an eventless history as were the writers of the theoretical, conjectural and natural histories of the eighteenth century.

When one seeks to transfer the premises and insights of developmentalism to the concrete, one runs into a great deal of difficulty. Nevertheless I will accept developmentalism as probably one of the steel sinews of a civilisation that prizes its identity here. And I would say the same for narrative history: in its unilinear constructions, in its belief that there is a single time order, it performs a great dogmatic function and it is a lasting form of art. But there are other ways of approaching the past and present. One can liberate himself from the dogmas of the uniqueness of events and the unilinearity of time, disregard time and conceive the past in terms of classes of events: this is where the method of comparison really comes into existence. Something that was called, and I should add badly miscalled, "the comparative method," existed in the late eighteenth and in the nineteenth century, associated with the names of Comte and Spencer and others. But it was not a comparative method, it was an ingenious means whereby the supremacy and vanguard position of Western Europe in an evolutionary series could be reinforced by drawing examples from the cultures of the rest of the world arranged in an order of logical complexity. A genuine comparative treatment of the behaviour of human beings in past and present involves the willingness to arrange events and changes as well as structures, institutions, symbols and values into classes which permit comparative analysis. Revolution is an example. There is not one but a number of revolutions, and while admittedly there is something imperishably distinctive about the French Revolution that renders it forever unlike the revolution in Russia, each seems to me to possess a sufficient degree of identity as a revolution to make possible a comparative treatment about which questions can be asked and from which conclusions may be drawn.

Finally, I would like to say that in my study of philosophy as an undergraduate I never got beyond David Hume, and I will always regard his philosophy as the greatest single system that has ever existed, and I agree thoroughly with Bertrand Russell in regarding its response, *The Critique of Pure Reason*, as the greatest single disaster ever to befall human thought. I think David Hume said everything that can be said on the subject of explanation and causality. What we discover everyday in terms of common sense and ordinary experience are those more or less habitual, or highly probably relationships and correspondences. This permits a prediction of the past and a prediction of the present. We should modestly defer all efforts to predict the future until we have started the painful but vital labour of learning how to predict the past.

RAYMOND ARON: Mr. Nisbet, in your discussion of the so-called theory of development you bring together three different topics.

One is a criticism of the naïve conviction that the whole history of mankind converges in the end on the same more or less Western society; this was certainly a part of the primitive theory of development, and your criticism would be accepted by everybody today.

Your second point is your criticism of a theory of change as coming from inside the system. But, in this instance, I would ask where could the change come from if not from within the system? To have a general view of the system does not give us a theory of change. But even if you take the prophets as being the main instrument of change, they are inside the social system. So to have a theory of change coming from outside the social system seems to me self-contradictory. The functional structuralist theory is not a theory of change, it is only a description of the different elements of the system, and in each case you must find out where the point of change is.

Thirdly, you want to take historical phenomena outside the temporal sequence. Many historians would accept that in some cases, but I should say it would be rather difficult to understand the Russian Revolution completely if you forgot about the French Revolution, or the Federal Republic of Germany if you take it out of the temporal sequence of Hitler.

Does what sociologists and historians actually do correspond to Professor Nisbet's description? Are they really such prisoners of the image of unilinear development, either in the sociologists' sense of development, or in the sense of the genetic causality in historical narrative? Furthermore, is the comparative method he suggests fundamentally different from that which historians and sociologists actually use?

DANIEL BELL: Professor Nisbet has very boldly and very fearlessly in one stroke demolished all of nineteenth century sociology. In the process he has dug up some cadavers and created some scarecrows and taken the bones and thrown them to the winds, and taken a match and lit it to the straw and it burned brightly and fiercely. If he wants to make an *auto-da-fé*, I shall not join him in that endeavour. In reading his paper and in listening to him, I do not find one word I would regard as characteristic of the way in which sociologists today look at social change. His two expressions have been "change" and "growth." I know almost nobody in sociology today who uses the word growth. The word most used is complexity. The other terms are diffusion, change of scale, change in form. Even Marx and the Communists have talked of various kinds of development, never of unilinear evolution. Professor Parsons himself (whose second volume is in the press, incidentally) has chosen a scheme of complexity as a model around which to frame his analysis.

It may not be possible to produce change from social structure for Western society, but how would you account for changes in social structure? Huge changes are created simply by the additive role of millions of individuals who by their decision to have children shape the change of society. Are all these people geniuses, maniacs, prophets, that they create change in this particular way? Without this sense of demographic profile you have no sense of a society. Albania may be very aggressive and very Maoist but it's a very poor agency to take on all of world history, given its size and population.

Mr. Aron has raised the question "Why tell the story of the French Revolution?" Obviously, one doesn't tell its story over again because one has suddenly found new evidence and therefore has a new *éclaircissement*. There is an obsession with the French Revolution for a fundamental overriding reason: it has legitimated the idea of revolution. Since then, millions of people are now enabled, quite freely, within the norms of a society, to claim the right to make a revolution. Why was it so difficult to say something new on revolutions? The problem is not one of revolutions *per se*. Revolutions are usually the story of the victors; but there are many areas and times in history where people have failed. And yet those situations have been perhaps as important as when they have won. The problem is not really one of revolution but of revolutionary conditions, or of revolutionary situations; and this raises a very different kind of problem. Throughout history men have revolted against their times, when they felt a sense of helplessness and anger. But this was essentially a kind of Jacquerie. It was simply kicking at the pricks of fate. It was essentially an effort to strike out at what was going on. You have to some extent, symbolically at least, in the French Revolution, or in the beginning of the nineteenth century, a major change in consciousness. Injustice is no longer seen as a matter of God's will or of change; there is a new feeling that one can reorder society, that injustice is a matter of men's arrangements. Men had begun to understand nature and tried to master it. It was the same thing with society, when they began to understand it. But society maybe is too large, too complex, too differentiated to be mastered. And this is perhaps one of the reasons for the modern *hubris* about revolution.

RAYMOND ARON: I was extremely surprised to hear it said that Parsons wanted to deduce changes from the social system. He explicitly says the opposite, and the normal accusation against him was that he has a system so stable, so perfect in itself, that it could not change. What he wants to achieve, rightly or wrongly (leaving aside the question of whether he has succeeded or not), is a universal system of categories showing the different aspects of any society. It may be that these categories are so abstract that nobody can use them. And the book you mention as "preposterous" was just an effort to put a certain degree of content in the different parts of society which he has analysed and discriminated. The book is not very successful, but in itself it was not absurd, after having drawn a sort of general view of the social system in the abstract, to see how the different sub-systems did look in each concrete society.

ROBERT NISBET: What I most object to about Professor Parsons' book *Societies: Evolutionary and Comparative Perspectives* is a certain un-intended form of deception. We are told at the outset of the book that it is an effort to restore the dynamic evolutionary view of the study of society by drawing from contemporary biological and genetical studies of change. Alas, what happens in the book is that all too familiar lapse into nine-teenth-century social evolutionism complete with grand stages – read here primitive, intermediate and modern.

GEORGE NADEL: Mr. Nisbet's choice of Thucydides as a representative of the school of uniqueness does not seem to me very relevant because I'm not sure the absence of comparability can be imputed to Thucydides's history. He states that the value he puts on his work is the possibility of a recurrence of like events which will make his observations on the war he describes useful. It might also be said that his account of behaviour during the plague, and various other incidents like the Melos Dialogue, may be read not as explicitly as later commentators have done, but as *prima facie* evidence that Thucydides was dealing with kinds of questions which make it difficult to see him as a representative of uniqueness.

ALAN BULLOCK: Mr. Bell has referred on several occasions to a change of consciousness in the modern world. Historians have detected, or believed they have detected, such a change of consciousness in the past. I think of Paul Hazard's book on the late seventeenth century. Would the methods used by a sociologist to detect a change of consciousness today be very different from the perhaps impressionistic methods of historians like Hazard?

ROBERT NISBET: As far as Comte was concerned, he was referring in the positive philosophy to Civilisation with a capital C and when he thought of Western Europe as being in the vanguard of civilisation and looked back through time or across space to smaller societies, pointing out the dramatic notion of a single march of mankind in history. I cannot fault Comte for that: whenever anyone has the boldness to take all humanity for his subject, it is quite possible he will indeed wind up with something approximately analogous to what Comte or Spencer or Marx, of if I may say again Professor Parsons, has done. But the great danger, or rather the unintended consequence, of all this, is that concepts which were applied by Comte solely to this vast entity called civilisation have been utilised for entities, systems, structures and institutions which are much more concrete and whose actual history does not at all manifest developmental progress. Spencer said in his *Social Statics* and his *Principles of Sociology* that whereas progress for mankind as a whole is absolutely necessary, it is by no means inevitable or even probable for any given society. The unhappy mistake many of us have made in the last fifty years, particularly in sociology, is the utilisation of concepts fabricated in a much larger context, for the elucidation of, say, Dayton, Ohio, or London or whatever it may be.

A second point. As to the *social system*, I confess to incomprehension, frequent bewilderment, when the term is used. I do not know how to define or to locate a social system. Neither the city of New York, nor American society, nor Western society are self-contained social systems. One has to go to the entire world to find an entity that is sufficiently inclusive to permit explanations in terms of the interaction of immanent structures and events. I know of no way to account for the history of England or the history of any concrete people, society or culture except in terms of exogenous forces over the long run, and I will emphasise again that not change but fixity, persistence, inertia seem to me the most probable state of any given culture or community at any given time. While there may be minor changes, of course, what we tend to refer to as change turns out really to be motion, action, interaction, substitutionary behaviour, a great deal of which cancels itself out. A change of structure (like that in English society in the eleventh century) seems to me inseparable from a study of events, persons and circumstances which simply cannot entirely be drawn from within.

By taking phenomena outside the temporal sequence, I mean only that history is so multiple that its time does not lend itself to unilinear progression. I know that, from the point of view of many historians, it would be an act of mutilation of context to take Robespierre from the immediate cricumstances in which he was allegedly produced within France, and to compare him with given *personae* of another revolution.

DANIEL BELL: A change in consciousness alters the existential perception people have of the major problems of the world. Let me give you a few different examples. A change in the view of man's relation to the universe from an earth-centred view to a helio-centred view is a change in consciousness, brought about by the introduction of new knowledge in astronomy, which finally diffuses to the rest of society. Take another example which has literary sources: in the latter part of the eighteenth century, if you consider three books, Diderot's *Rameau's Nephew*, Rousseau's *Second Discourse*, and the first part of Goethe's *Werther*, you suddenly find an attack not on societies but on the idea of society. And once these three books have been summed up by Hegel in the last part of *The Phenomenology*, you have there the beginning of a change in consciousness, which begins to affect men's attitude towards society as a whole. Think of the Freudian revolution, of the discovery of the unconscious. People always had a sense that there was an underlying reality to the structure of the world. In Freud, you have this all suddenly applied to a person. Everyone suddenly realised that in his own single psyche there was a reality which he may not have been aware of before. To this extent this is a change in consciousness too.

ALAN BULLOCK: I can't see any difference between Mr. Bell's method and the one a historian would apply. He takes certain very powerful and original works, he is grouping similar ideas and then he uses (which is still very impressionistic) the word diffusion...

HUGH TREVOR-ROPER: I wonder whether the diffusion of anti-Semitic ideas in this century would be regarded as a change of consciousness over a wide area, a change which might have become permanent but for different political events. It arose from a mass of obscure literature circulated in bookstalls below the level of intellectual consciousness, not from any seminal work.

WOLFGANG J. MOMMESEN: If I may enlarge on the point which was raised by Mr. Trevor-Roper, the issue of anti-Semitism, it is very easy in this case to show that this was an ideology of groups which was a reflection of their feeling of being endangered by the process of industrialisation. There you have a kind of social history which adds to intellectual history, and I would expect the social scientists to ask the historians to do it.

Kostas Papaioannou: I am sorry the discussion hasn't centred on the only theory of change I know of that exists, in the strict sense of the term: the theory put forward by Hegel in *The Phenomenology of the Mind.* Hegel develops what seems to be a unilinear conception of history because his fundamental concept is that of experience. According to him, men want to experience themselves through history. This theory of experience immediately becomes a theory of change because it is impossible to experience oneself and remain unchanged. What is fundamentally lacking in sociological research today is this concept of experience. We shan't get at what is essential by referring to the social system or some Parsonian structure or other.

5 Political history in crisis

WOLFGANG J. MOMMSEN

On the position of political history within the social sciences

Political history can look back upon a great and time-honored tradition. The pioneers of modern historiography as a scientific discipline were all primarily political historians. Ranke, for one, was convinced that the great power states were the very elements of history, determining not only the course of events in international diplomacy, but also almost all domestic issues, and, in the last resort, the destinies of cultures. And John Seeley, following in Ranke's footsteps, defined history simply as "past politics". For more than a century the claim of political history to be the highest form of historical thinking remained almost undisputed, and it did not seem to be presumptuous if historians believed political history to be the very center of all social studies. In recent decades, however, the prestige of political history has suffered a great deal. Its claim to be the highest form of historical thinking, and at the same time to be the vital core of all disciplines related to the study of man in history, has been challenged from various quarters: by insiders, that is to say the professional historians, as well as by outsiders belonging to the wide range of social sciences which have developed alongside the historical disciplines since the middle of the 19th century.

In this paper I wish to discuss some of the aspects of the challenges thrown out to political history both by other branches of history and by political science and sociology. Secondly I should like to point out some possible responses to these challenges. This will imply drawing a rough outline of the role of political historiography within the context of the various social sciences devoted to the study of societies, and in particular the social institutions designed to guarantee a maximum of legal and social order.

The nature of the contribution of political history to the study of man in society can perhaps be demonstrated best by turning to marginal examples of political and social history – the revolutions. Therefore in the second part of this paper special attention will be given to the accomplishments of political historiography in regard to the analysis of revolutions, as well as to the limits inherent in this kind of approach. History is specifically devoted to the study of the causes and the particular nature of social change, though perhaps from a viewpoint quite different from that of the social scientist who is primarily concerned with the problem of whether it is possible to discover general rules or perhaps even laws of social change. Static cultures are, as a rule, not objects of historical research; and it may be added that static cultures in which social dynamics are reduced to a minimum and fundamental changes in the social, political or economic system are not likely to occur do not need historical reflection, though an antiquarian type of history, in Nietzsche's terminology, may still survive. It goes without saying that periods of rapid, or even violent change have always attracted the imagination of historians to a particularly large degree. We will have to explore the reasons for this phenomenon, and that may help us to define the future tasks as well as the limits of political history in a somewhat more precise way than has been done hitherto.

   S. T. Bindow recently argued that "there is every prospect that political history, whether local, national or supranational, will be strengthened rather than impoverished by the rise of other and newer kinds of history." This would seem to me to be a somewhat optimistic statement. There can be little doubt that political history, at least in its traditional form, is undergoing a severe crisis, and that, if it survives, as I for one believe, it will be no longer quite the same kind of history. One must not be deceived by the large and still growing appetite of the public at large for historical literature of a more or less popularized kind. Memoirs and autobiographies, as well as biographies of great men in politicaland cultural life, are still immensely popular, and the market for publications dealing with contemporary history is better than ever before; many publishing houses still make a fortune with items of this kind. Although the golden age of historiography, the 19th century during which the bourgeois class drew its ideological orientation from historical literature, is past, this trend is likely to continue at least in the forseeable future. However, historical literature of this kind is a transitory phenomenon; it is limited in scope and subject matter by the interests of the contemporary generation:

people like to know about and to read history that has some relevance to some sphere of their own experience. Moreover, it must be presented in a digestible form, that is, as a network of meaningful actions and interactions of individuals with whom the reader either can identify himself or whom he can admire as great men or even as heroes. This kind of history satisfies the needs of, as Alfred Heuss puts it, "primary reminiscence". This kind of historical consciousness, however, tends, under the conditions of modern industrial society, to lose momentum; moreover it bears no relationship to the actual social orientation and political activities of the consumers of this kind of historical literature. Its impact on the fundamental political decisions within a given political system is, as a rule, negligible.

Let us turn now to the more fundamental question of political history. Here the situation is much more serious. To begin with political history of the traditional type is suffering from its close association with a variety of concepts generally accepted throughout the 19th and earlier 20th century, but which now have been fundamentally called into question by more recent developments. At one time, for example, political history was associated with the idea of the state as the primary agency of all historical change, as "*realgestige Idee*" (Ranke), as the most prominent among the "ethical forces" in history (Droysen), or as the embodiment of national cultures (Treitschke). Admittedly this traditional attitude was strongest in German historiography under the influence of the philosophy of Hegel; yet the tendency to attribute to the state a kind of higher dignity, as compared with other social institutions exercising power, is deeply rooted also in the French, somewhat less in the Anglo-Saxon, tradition. It was modified, yet at the same time reenforced, by the rising tide of bourgeois nationalism. Throughout Europe the bourgeois classes identified themselves with the respective nation states, and eventually other sections of the population hastened to rally themselves around the national banner too. The traditional elites hoped that the nation state would protect their traditional privileges, while the working classes saw it as a means for breaking through the ring of political discrimination.

Admittedly national history cannot simply be discarded because the principle of nationality has been discredited; yet it must be realized that the great prestige of traditional political historiography depended to a large extent on its close association with the idea of the nation state. All the specific cultural and political values of a nation, so it was assumed, were handed down to forthcoming generations through the study of the nation's past, and therefore it was considered essential to do so. Nowadays this kind of legitimation of political history has lost ground, and the young generation, at least, finds it unacceptable. This is, however, by no means the whole story. For the nationalistic legitimation of political history as a master discipline within the realm of disciplines engaged in the study of society was commonly accompanied by two rather simplistic patterns of historical explanation. The first one was that "men make history"; that is to say, all historical processes can and ought to be traced back to the decisions and actions of particular individuals. These were, as a rule, the leading statesmen and, at times, their *entourage*. The second pattern of explanation may be epitomized as the ideological motivation concept, that is, the reduction of all relevant political actions throughout history to individual ideological attitudes or values, the most common ones being religious faiths or political ideologies.

This method of historical explanation assumed, as a rule in a rather naive way, that religious or political convictions were prime factors which had to be accepted without further inquiry; historians thus more or less unconsciously accepted the premises of idealism as a methodological principle. It is obvious that both these patterns of explanation were closely interrelated with one another, as the first one paved the way for the application of the second. It was a stock argument of historism (as different from Popper's historicism) that all historical phenomena have a specific character and must be interpreted by a kind of imaginative reconstruction which is applicable because there exists a certain degree of inter-subjective correspondance between the historian and his objects. Strictly speaking this particular relationship between subject and object was limited to the interpretation of the social activity of individual men, a factor which made it all the more advisable to write history in terms of what and why individual men did certain things at a given time and under certain conditions. It is obvious, however, that such an individualistic method of explanation could not be applied everywhere; complicated social institutions such as the state or modern parties could not be dealt with exclusively in this way. However, we discover that historicism from the very beginning found a way out of this dilemma by interpreting social institutions like the states as "individual totalities" (Troeltsch), obeying certain inherent principles like the "reason of state" or the principle of nationality. Modern historical literature is full of anthropomorphisms of this kind which allowed the extension of the operation called *"Verstehen"* to various complex social phenomena. The other way out of this dilemma consisted in interpreting social movements and parties largely, if not exclusively, in terms of their ideological orientation. The history of political parties was up to the recent past almost identical with the history of their ideological orientation, though Bryce's and Ostrogorsky's studies pointed already at the end of the century in a different direction. This method of historical explanation was, by the way, by no means restricted to the sphere of political history. The famous thesis of Max Weber on the origins of capitalism fits very well into this pattern; according to Weber it was specific "outer-worldly values" which induced the pioneers of modern industrial capitalism to burst through the fetters of a tradition-bound economy and to set in motion economic forces which eventually ended up in revolutionizing social systems everywhere in the world. The tendency to explain developments in the social sphere primarily in terms of specific religious or pseudo-religious values which motivated the respective social groups was in the early 20th century widespread and lost its great fascination only gradually.

The methodological outlook of traditional political historiography was heavily attacked by Marxism even at an early stage of its development. Already in the *Deutsche Ideologie* Marx wrote: "...we do not set out from what men say, imagine, conceive, nor from men as narrated, thought of, imagined, conceived". He gave primacy to the basic factors of social reproduction, *i.e.*, the economic system as such, and added: "This, as is notorious, the Germans have never done, and they have never, therefore, had an earthly basis for history and consequently they never had a historian? The French and the English, even if they viewed the relation of this fact with so-called history only in an extremely one-sided fashion – particularly as long as they remained captives of political ideology – have nevertheless made the first attempts to give the writing of history a materialistic base by being the first to write histories on civil society, of commerce and industry." Apart from the fact that for a long period historians did not pay much attention to Marxist philosophy, it must be pointed out that Marxism itself had so many political overtones that it could not seriously undermine the traditional political interpretation of history; even though Marx interpreted political developments as simple by-products of the patterns of production, he was himself convinced that the vital decisions fell in the political sphere. It was only the subsequent deterministic interpretation of Marxist theory by Kautsky which arrived at the conclusion that the collapse of the old order would come about automatically and that the politics of the Social Democrats, therefore, should be restricted to "revolutionizing the minds" of the workers while at the same time seeking a political *modus vivendi* with the class enemies for the time being. Leninist-Marxism revitalized the political aspects of Marxist theory by putting all emphasis on the revolutionary activity of the Communist party as the avant-garde of a future socialist society, anticipating rather than acting in accordance with the socio-economic laws of historical development as envisaged by Marx. The present conditions in the Marxist-Leninist camp would seem to corroborate the principle of the primacy of politics over the conditions of production. All the Communist states give priority to political goals rather than to the economic requirements of their societies, however much they may pay lip service to the need for increasing national production. The preservation of the present pattern of distribution of political power both against possible changes from within and against outside dangers is today obviously the dominant feature of Marxism-Leninism, and this fact explains its inherently conservative outlook.

These remarks should not, however, divert us from our main problem, the situation of political history. It would be erroneous to assume that any analysis of the conditions in the Communist part of the world can be used as a serious argument in defense of traditional political history against its critics from the Marxist camp. Actually, political history is challenged by no means only from this side, but from others also, which I consider to be much more serious. There is unanimous agreement at least on one point, namely that it is society differentiated by and composed of various classes and more or less organized groups, and not the state, as but one particular social institution, that is the decisive agent of social change, or, to put it in a more traditional way, of the historical process. Admittedly, the positions vary considerably as to the relative importance of these manifold social factors, yet few contemporaries are prepared to attribute to the state, as the formal political organization of society, even the rather cautiously circumscribed special role which Max Weber, for instance, ascribed to it. Weber defined the state as the agency of society having a monopoly on the right to use physical violence against subjects defying the rules and principles of the existing legal order. Even this narrow and very formalistic definition (compared with traditional definitions of the state) of the role of the state within society would seem nowadays to be an ideal-typical concept that attributes to the state a sovereignty of power that it does not, in fact, enjoy. To be sure, most people will admit today that the state plays a dominant role within the framework of the permanent struggle that is going on among different groups within modern dynamic societies; yet it seems evident that governments have more and more difficulty in seeing their policies through in the face of the hostility of numerous sections of society. The argument of Marcuse and others that the capitalist production process has emancipated itself completely from rational political control and therefore brings about more and more irrational results cannot be easily refuted.

Thus we may conclude that a main pillar of traditional political history, the concept of the state as a relatively autonomous political agency of society with preponderant power, has been seriously undermined. Accordingly, the concept that social change can be brought about primarily through the acquisition of political power and its exercise is more than ever before open to doubt. By implication, the traditional patterns of historical explanation in terms of individual actions of statesmen and their motivations have also lost much of their validity.

This situation affects historiography insofar as political history is everywhere challenged by other kinds of history, in particular social history. Social history is in vogue today: almost everybody declares himself in favor of it, though there are few who really know what form social history should take.

The most radical antithesis to traditional political history is represented by the school of the *Annales*. For many of its more radical followers, political history of the traditional mold lies within the sphere of the old-fashioned *histoire des événements* which, they say, must be superseded by a history of the fundamental social structures underlying and determining the events on the surface of historical formations. Long-term changes of socio-economic structures and population movements are in the forefront, and the actions of individual statesmen are sacrificed on the altar of a future *histoire de longue durée*.

Not quite as radical, but in its consequences perhaps even more far-reaching, is the socio-economic alternative to traditional political history, presented in varying forms by authors like Imlah, Rosenberg, Williams, La Feber, Wehler, and others. Here the recent achievements of economic history as regards patterns of economic growth are applied to the political systems as such; decisions are less the result of the political beliefs of statesmen than the inevitable response to economic crises, economic stagnation, or inflated growth. It is primarily the phenomenon of disproportionate growth which is held responsible for political conflicts and wars, while the ideological superstructure appears largely as a secondary phenomenon, much as in Marxist interpretations of history. The importance of these developments may be demonstrated by turning to the revived discussion on imperialism. While almost all historians in the West deny the validity of the standard Marxist-Leninist interpretation of Imperialism as the inevitable outcome of monopolistic capitalism, more and more people have come to believe that the imperialist expansion of the industrial states over the whole globe which took place in the second half of the 19th and the early 20th century was largely conditioned by the social problems that arose through rapid industrialization. The accumulation of aggressive energies in the industrial states of the West since the 1880s is not attributed solely to economic factors but rather to the social tensions created by the sudden and violent impact of industrialization and modernization on still largely tradition-bound societies. Imperialism and aggressive nationalism turn out to be not only two sides of the same coin, but also to be political strategies designed either to defend the privileges of tradiotional political and social elites, which came under pressure as a consequence of the process of democratization, or, on the contrary, to enforce the participation of the new middle class in the exercise of power. Both types had in common their enmity against an emancipation of the socialist working classes.

A third cast of social history tends to move even further away from traditional history, inasmuch as it devotes its energies to the study of social institutions long considered as being more or less outside the political sphere of action. Institutions like the family, the educational systems, the police, the prisons and the penal system, mental hospitals, attract the attention of historians who consider the well-being of the man in the street to be more relevant than the activities on the level of states and diplomatic relations.

It is at present difficult to say in which direction history will develop and in particular what the new social history will be like. Yet a completely new field of historical research has been opened up, guided by the premise that what really matters does not take place on the top level of states and societies, but rather in the lower and lowest echelons of society. Political history will have to take up the challenge thrown out to it here, or it will lose its sway over the historical profession sooner or later altogether.

Perhaps even more serious, in view of the traditional prestigious position of political history, is the fact that it has been challenged by political science as well as by empirical social science in a field in which it hitherto ruled sovereignly, the field of power politics and diplomacy. Political history is, of course, still accepted, or indeed required as a kind of introductory discipline, yet the trends point in another direction. Political factors enter into this, too, in particular the efforts of various politicians to foster a special discipline of peace research studying the causes of international conflicts and possible methods to reduce the likelihood of their arising. Political history is in this context degraded to a purely auxiliary science; it is considered more or less as a useful quarry where one will find examples and material which may be useful in testing more or less general theories of conflict and of power relationships. Both the individualistic approach of traditional political historians and their endeavours to detect behind events individual motivation structures are increasingly discarded in favour of general theories. Attempts like those of Carl W. Deutsch to introduce quantitative methods into political science may perhaps not yet lead to overwhelming new insights, yet they clearly abandon the traditional pattern of historical interpretation altogether.

So far the response of political historians to these developments has been ambiguous. While remaining sceptical about some of the new departures in neighboring disciplines, they tend to embrace freely most of these innovations, at least in principle. But in practice the possibilities of integrating the new research methods of social history and political and social science into their own research have been limited, if only because of the enormous communication difficulties between the different disciplines. Nonetheless this does appear to be a sensible approach, for political history can hold its own and perhaps enrich itself only by taking advantage of the findings of related disciplines. In this way political history may become once again the synonym of history in general. So far political history seems to possess an unlimited capacity for integration. Nonetheless it may be asked whether political history is not in danger of losing its identity if it goes on simply integrating new methods and new questions indiscriminately from wherever they come.

This leads to the fundamental issue of what political history actually stands for. I do not wish to intrude into the topic on which Professor Trevor-Roper is going to speak to us. However, a few basic observations are in order here.

History as a social science of relevance to contemporary society depends, in the first place, on the existence of an "open", a dynamic society, and, secondly, on the assumption that men are in some degree capable of shaping their future destinies in a rational manner. It furthermore assumes – and in this respect it stands on safe ground – that men are influenced in all their social actions by the conceptions which they have of their own past.

"*Geschichtsbilder*", if I may be allowed to switch for a moment into German, "*sind mächtig*", concepts of the past are powerful, they tend to influence the value systems of all groups in a given society considerably and are likely to affect their political and social attitudes more or less strongly. Concepts of the past as a rule do not have much in common with exact historical knowledge; they may have the shape of mere myths or, as is the rule in most post-Newtonian societies, of ideologies of various types. It must be conceded, as Daniel Bell has demonstrated, that holistic-type ideologies are today universally on the retreat. Yet other types of ideologies have replaced them. There are, on the one hand, those of a purely voluntaristic nature, as they do not claim to be based on a thorough scientific system, but justify themselves on moral grounds only. The romanticist anarchism of a section of the "New Left" is a particularly striking example for this. The other type of modern ideology wears an outwardly absolutely ahistorical gown. It presents its objectives as being in full accordance with the objective conditions and trends of a fully developed industrial system, in which, as is contended, the general course of events is determined by the technological process anyway, leaving space only for limited reforms and social "repairs". Economic and technological progress as such are presented as substitutes for all moral or cultural objectives. The conservative bias of such social ideologies is fairly evident, although its ideological character is hidden behind a mass of scientific as well as pseudo-scientific arguments. However unhistorical the industrial society may appear, in fact it is the most historical of all social foundations which history knows. And historical analysis may help to reveal the particular character of this society, indicating possible directions of more humane development.

It is at this point that history is capable of making an important contribution to the study of societies, insofar as it may help the empirical social sciences to overcome the limitations of a purely structural-functional approach, which without purpose tends to identify itself with the existing order instead of opening up new departures for a rational policy of reform.

If these premises are accepted, political history will have to play an important role in this context. For although the research methodology of social history will be needed to lay bare the historical foundations of industrial and post-industrial societies, its results must be integrated in a pattern of historical explanation which pays particular attention to the process of decision-making, including the attitudes and motivation structures of the various social groups directly or indirectly involved in it. The knowledge of how social change under given conditions actually occurs remains the very heart of all historical understanding. There is no question that thorough attention must be given to the conditioning factors, which involve numerous problems of a most complicated nature; yet they all must be brought somehow into direct connection with the process actually effecting social change of a relevant magnitude. Here political history as a special discipline within the sciences dedicated to the study of societies is in its legitimate sphere. Political history always asks when and where and how in a given society of a specific historical type decisions of historical relevance came about.

It will, of course, always remain a matter of dispute, in which spheres of the social process the vital decisions are located. Are they located in the political organisations exercising power in the narrow sense of the term, more or less legitimated by a legal system, or are they found in the economic sphere or perhaps even at a much more elementary level, involving, for example, biological factors such as population movement. Political history will have to pay attention to this question and will have to develop a new outlook to enable it to integrate these diverse aspects of social change in historical dimensions into its conceptual framework. On the other hand, not only political history, but all history depends on the assumption that in any given situation the historical process was "open" and that the future, at least to a certain degree, is given into the hands of purposeful, acting groups. The excitement which is evoked by any historical work of any distinction derives from the knowledge that there were alternatives for the acting groups concerned, and that the respective political courses decided upon had immense consequences, which affected indirectly or even directly our own social and political reality or our consciousness.

What is meant by this can perhaps be illustrated somewhat more clearly by turning to a historical phenomenon of outstanding relevance to our own historical-consciousness revolutions, especially political revo- lutions. The term "revolution" nowadays is used by historians, social scientists, and the general public as well with the most diverse meanings. Economic historians speak of the "industrial revolution", or even of "the first" and "the second industrial revolution", in view of the secular changes brought about by the irrevocable process of industrialization; Marxists tend to bring whole periods in which a change from one type of organization of the means of production to another takes place under the heading of revolution. There is much justification for this, as the term implies in its strict meaning a period of both rapid and fundamental change within a given social system. Yet I will restrict myself here, in order to stick to my argument, to the analysis of political revolutions in the accepted sense, that is to say more or less violent upheavals of a particular system of political rule, involving more or less substantial changes in the social structure, in particular as regards social stratifi- cation. In this sense it is justified to call the events in France from 1787 to 1795, or in Russia from February to October 1917, or the upheaval in Germany right after the First World War, revolutions, while it may remain a matter of some dispute whether the so-called "National Socialist revolu- tion" in 1933/34 deserves such a relatively honorable denomination.

It goes without saying that the revolutions of modern times, or, to be more precise, the conceptions which the various social groups in our own time have of these events, play an important role in their overall ideological orientations. The catchword "revolution" is likely to divide people up into various political camps, and this is especially true if individual revolutions, as like those mentioned above, are taken into consideration. For the majority of the peoples of the highly industrialized West, the French Revolution of 1789 ranks high in the hierarchy of sentimental memories, since it paved the way for modern democratic constitution- alism. The antimodernist counterattack of Fascism was, as many of its exponents confessed openly, among other things directed against the decisions of 1789, against liberal individualism and a pluralistic society. The Marxist camp argues that the bourgeois revolutions initiated by the

French Revolution were but a first step on the road towards a socialist society and therefore have to be followed up by a second wave of revolutions which was opened up by the so-called "Great October Revolution". They clearly consider the socialist revolutions to be the last ones in the world historical process, and tend to magnify the October Revolution into a gigantic myth of largely religious dimensions. The "New Left" in the West on the other hand welcomes revolutionary developments almost offhand as any leap forward which tends to break up the supposedly solidified political structures; it views them as being morally good, whatever the consequences. Attitudes as regards particular revolutions constitute, as it were, always a kind of crossroads in day-to-day political strife. These few remarks may indicate already the relevance of a rational historical analysis of revolutionary processes, applying all the methods and techniques of a critical research discipline available for a society which cares to solve its conflicts primarily by rational means.

In describing and analysing revolutions historians virtually put all the major political positions of our day on trial, a trial which ought to be in principle rational and methodologically controlled at every stage of the argument. Were the American and French Revolutions and the other revolutions related to them "democratic revolutions" in the broadest meaning of the term, as Palmer would have it? Or were they the breakthrough of bourgeois class society, as the Marxists argue? Or were they perhaps largely a myth, with little relevance to the social stratification and the social order as such, an interpretation put forward by Cobban. Each of these answers implies conclusions which will be of considerable relevance to the political consciousness of present-day societies.

A similar conclusion presents itself if our attention is turned to the interpretation of the Russian Revolution of 1917. Did it signal the triumph of a new social order over imperialist capitalism and the advent of a superior socialist system, or was it perhaps little more than a fatal cataclysm which was the result of the complete breakdown of the social system of Tsarist Russia? Was it the harbinger of a new age for mankind, or was it rather the painful process of establishing a dictatorship designed to overcome the economic, cultural and social backwardness of Russia by force? The high esteem in which Peter the Great is held once more in Russia by historians and authorities alike throws an interesting sidelight on this issue. And, last but not least, the question could be raised whether after all the stature of Russia as an autocratic and imperialist power did not remain much the same despite the October Revolution and all that followed it?

Let us take yet another example. Was it a good thing that the German Majority Democrats stopped the German Revolution of 1918/19 in its initial stage in order to save as much as possible of the German Empire? This is a question traditionally answered in the affirmative by all but the Communists, if only because this action prevented a possible Bolshevik rise to power in Germany. Historians nowadays take as a rule a different stand on this issue, and this is by no means because they have sympathies with the extreme left. With some justification they argue that the democratic potential of the "Soldiers' and Workers' Councils" could have been utilized in the interests of the democratization of German Society. Understandably this view has contributed a great deal to the revived debate about the parliamentary system.

Equally passionate debates emerge when the question is raised whether the nationalist rise to power in 1933 and 1934 ought to be described as a revolution. In many ways it was a revolution, indeed, provided that one does not prefer to call it a counter-revolution (a distinction between revolutions and counter-revolutions from an ideological point of view would seem to me to be arbitrary; I do not see why revolutions which may be called "progressive" are more revolutionary than those that are not).

As Schoenbaum has demonstrated the social fabric of Germany underwent considerable changes under National Socialist rule, though not in the direction which was indicated by National Socialist petit bourgeois propaganda, nor in accordance with the view of Marxism-Leninism that fascism was but an extreme form of the rule of monopolistic capitalism.

In raising questions of this kind and in trying to find answers substantiated by historical evidence, the primary objectives of political history come to the fore. Political historians aim at influencing the political convictions and attitudes of the particular groups with which they identify themselves. Actual opinions about the character of the political and social order are being modified, or perhaps corroborated by a critical analysis of the historical dimensions involved. Historians help the individuals and groups for which they write to identify their own ideological position more correctly by placing it in its relevant historical context; this, in many cases, will induce them to reflect on their own respective positions, something which might enable them to react in a more rational way to the political challenges of the day.

In order to achieve anything of this kind the political historian must do above all two things. Firstly he has to analyse carefully the historical processes concerned, something which requires the close scrutiny of all relevant sources of information. Secondly he must integrate his findings into a general historical context which includes, explicitly or implicitly, the present day and his own particular relationship to it. It is obvious that this holds true, in principle, for all kinds of political history, though the interrelationship of historical interpretations of revolutions with present-day political positions is particularly striking.

From the aforesaid it follows, furthermore, that the numerous attempts of historians and social scientists alike to develop, by means of a comparative analysis, a general theory of revolutions or at least a set of fairly general rules in regard to the typical course of revolutions, will be considered by political historians as of only secondary importance, however successful such undertakings may be. For political historians the imperative question will always be what message is embodied in the revolutionary process which they reconstruct carefully and often at great pains. The question of whether there are more or less general laws governing the typical course and the different stages of any given revolution, or of how much and at what points in the revolutionary process violence will of necessity occur, these are questions of subordinate importance. This does not mean, however, that historians are not interested in generalisations of this kind. On the contrary, they are very much so, and in explaining the course of events they always take refuge in theoretical statements of more or less general character, though as a rule implicitly, and furthermore as a rule in a hypothetical way.

They would be happy if the social scientists would supply them with suitable middle-range theories about social attitudes of groups and individuals under specific conditions. Even so they would apply them only as hypothetical models of social behavior used as a kind of scale which makes it possible to describe the extent to which social actions and attitudes of the individuals concerned deviate from the norm.

Yet it must be said that until now the results of the various attempts to arrive at more or less general theories on the character and the course of revolutions, on the basis of historical or of structural-functional analysis, are anything but encouraging. Rosenstock-Huessy's *Die Europäischen Revolutionen* is a most stimulating book, yet its argumentation is nowhere less stringent than in the part in which he tries to generalize about revolutions. Somewhat more substantial are the attempts of Lynford Edwards and Crane Brinton, though they both employ rather traditional interpretative techniques. It is revealing that Brinton warns his readers from the start that they should not expect too much as far as general laws and regulations are concerned. The first and the second of Brinton's six generalizations as to the causes and the nature of revolutions will possibly be accepted by most historians. It is indeed true that revolutions in the sense which I stated above, namely rapid and violent changes within a given political system, require as a first prerequisite a certain degree of dynamism in the social fabric as such; otherwise the political and social energies which come to a sudden eruption during the revolutionary process could not have accumulated at all in a relevant magnitude. The thesis of Griewank and Arendt that revolutions are specific phenomena of modern times is supported not only by the etymology of the term "revolution", but also by historical experience.

In more or less static societies revolutions are unlikely to occur. It is this observation which induced Max Weber to assume that in the bureaucratic society of the future – the "iron cage of serfdom" – which he envisaged as being already in its initial stage, successful revolutions were no longer possible and would be replaced by *coups d'État*. (Weber was convinced that for this very reason the Bolshevik revolution was bound to fail.) The question may indeed be raised whether in highly industrialized societies with a fairly rigid social structure and only limited economic growth the likelihood of revolutionary outbreaks might be smaller than in previous historical formations, though I, for one, tend to be reluctant in regard to such presumptions. A certain degree of dynamics, either upwards (as Brinton believes) or downwards seems indeed to be a precondition for revolutionary developments, and also – this refers to the second of Brinton's generalizations – of the development not so much of sharp class distinctions, but of an intense class-consciousness, which admittedly plays a distinct role in most revolutionary processes. But the four others – the defection of the intellectuals, the failure of the administrative machinery, the breakdown of public finance, and the loss of self-confidence on behalf of the ruling elites – these points concern only symptoms, and it will be difficult to verify them in general if one picks a really representative sample of revolutions. Apart from this Brinton's deductions are by no means altogether impartial; they show a distinct bias against revolutions. He tends to observe revolutions more or less with the eye of a member of the old ruling elites giving advice on how they might have avoided the disaster which, as is said, almost always leads to a more rigid and more authoritarian government than before – something which surely was not the case in France in 1830, or in Germany 1918/19. Other literary attempts to generalize about revolutions are even less satisfying, at least from our special point of view, as, for instance, Hannah Arendt's otherwise most interesting study *On Revolution*, which contains some highly erroneous statements as, for instance, that all revolutions started as restorations. In this respect, Gottschalk is far more cautious, and up to a point right, in pointing out that the first cause of a revolution (that is to say the initiating factor) is always a provocation, often of an economic nature.

It will have to be admitted that there have been made and, indeed, can be made, fairly general observations as to specific features of modern revolutionary processes; yet their applicability to individual cases appears to be restricted. They will certainly be useful in sharpening the eyes of a historian or a social scientist who is studying a particular revolution. He will be put by them on rewarding tracks, but otherwise their value is limited. They definitely will not be sufficiently trustworthy as to support any theory of even middle range validity. In this respect Palmer's skeptical comments contain much truth:

> Of any concrete and particular social and human situation, historical, currently political, or other, I doubt whether any significant generalization can be shown by evidence to be wholly valid or wholly invalid. To put it another way, a generalization to be accepted would have to be encumbered by so many *ifs*, *ands*, and *buts* as to lose some of its hoped-for scientific precision (in Gottschalk, *Generalizations in the Writing of History*, Chicago 1963, p. 75).

It would seem that comparative social science, at least so far – there are but very few relevant studies in the field – is even less successful in its attempts to arrive at fairly general theories when dealing with revolutionary periods. One might perhaps agree with J. C. Davies' finding that most revolutionary upheavals occur in a situation in which there exists a considerable gap between the rising social aspirations of the population at large and the social achievements of the political system, although it does not at all fit the Russian example (which is put forward as the main evidence). And in many but by no means all cases (as for instance the German Revolution of 1918/19), we observe an economic recession after a period of more or less constant growth immediately before the actual outbreak of a revolution. But these are at best necessary preconditions for revolutions. Criteria like the aforesaid ones by no means explain why a given political order suddenly collapses under the impact of a revolutionary upheaval at a particular junction of the social process, nor can they be considered as reliable indicators for the possibility or even the likelihood of revolutionary eruptions. Tanter and Midlarsky, who attempted to verify the hypotheses of Davies on a more universal plane, arrive, on the basis of a sample of revolutions between 1955 and 1960, at the conclusion that the lower the level of intellectual training in the pre-revolutionary period, the longer and the more violent the revolution will be. This may be true for the particular short period they examined, but a historian who has in his mind a vivid picture of the French Revolution of 1789 feels irritated, or at least frustrated.

It may well be that social scientists, by refining their theoretical instruments and applying much more sophisticated techniques in the utilization of empirical material, may be able to find correlations of more general value and validity. It seems doubtful, however, that revolutions can sufficiently be isolated from the general historical context for examination by comparative structural-functional analysis. Most scholars engaged in research of this kind concede that it is extremely difficult to define exactly the starting point as well as the end of a revolutionary process. Nor is the degree of violence a reliable guide as to the intensity of a revolutionary process. It would seem to me that social science is much more successful in dealing with periods of relative social stability (which may include relatively stable economic growth) than in dealing with revolutionary periods where it runs into almost insurmountable difficulties: it must pay attention to an unlimited number of variables, which moreover tend to have a different relevance at different stages of the revolutionary process. At best social scientists are capable of coming to terms fairly well with the preliminary stages of revolutions.

It is perhaps possible to set forth through a comparative analysis which combines the research methods of the ordinary political historian with those of the empirical sociologist some of the preconditions for the outbreak of revolutions with a fair degree of validity, as for instance:
- A solidified political structure no longer in line with the dynamic processes within the society;
- A decline of economic growth or at least a deterioration of the condi-

tions of substantial sections of the population after a period of fairly steady growth;

- A widening gap between "rising social aspirations" and the social achievements of the existing social fabric;
- A utopian ideology, articulated and supported by sufficiently large groups of the intelligentsia, the access of the latter to the leading elites being limited.

Yet if we turn to the actual course of revolutions, the ordinary research methods of the political historian promise more concrete results than any kind of quantitative analyses. This is due to the particular character of such periods of very rapid social change. A revolution is always associated with, or rather caused by, a sudden collapse of what is called by Max Weber the *"Legitimitätseinverständnis"* on behalf of the governed, sometimes only partially, sometimes completely. This is always the typical starting point for a revolutionary process, which by the way should not be mixed up with the issue of "domestic war" – successful revolutions may well get along with an absolute minimum of violence. Consequently a variety of political and social forces, with a more or less institutionalized basis, are set free which hitherto were more or less under control of the respective authorities. All depends on particular conditions: whether the clash between these various political forces, which may or may not be organized on class lines, will be extremely violent or not; whether the reaction will be so strong as to unleash further political or social forces which under normal conditions might perhaps not have made themselves felt at all. It seems to me that for this very reason it is impossible to predict what the eventual outcome of a revolution will be; at best the direction of events can be distinguished up to a point. Yet whether the old order will be restored again (as in Germany and in Austria in 1849), or a thoroughly new order established (as in France in 1791 or in Russia in October 1917), or perhaps a compromise arrived at (as in France in 1830 or in Germany in 1918/19), depends so much on the individual conditions in any given case that any general theory is bound to fail.

The main reason why generalizations on a quantitative basis have small chances of being valid must be sought in the fact that in revolutionary situations comparatively small minorities often play a decisive role, a role entirely out of proportion with their relative importance in the society as a whole. This is just as true of mass revolutions as of so-called palace revolutions and the like. In a revolutionary situation the internal balance of power is more or less out of order and may allow for the most extra-ordinary developments. Much the same is true with regard to public opinion which is extremely confused and easily fascinated by sensational schemes which under regular conditions it would not tolerate. And last but not least the role of particular individuals in such periods may be extremely great, something which almost entirely escapes a quantitative approach. Alfred Cobban writes with regard to the French Revolution of 1789:

> At any point the course of the Revolution could be diverted by a change happening or an individual decision determined by a freak of personal character.

This is not a matter of rejoicing for the political historian. In stressing the factor of individuality I do not wish to withdraw into the camp of histori-cism which stressed the individual character of all historical events and the acts of individual personalities. Yet whether this is justified or not, historical figures like Robespierre, Lenin or Hitler are not easily dismissed. Their personal impact on the course of events was enormous, even if we concede that they acted like Hegel's *"weltgeschichtliche Individuen"* – that is, that they acted in accordance with the objective conditions of the time. For this reason it seems to be indispensable to interpret their actions and motivations with the traditional philological techniques of historio-graphy. Content analysis will not do the job, for it can bring to the fore only statistical, that is average, results. Nor will social psychology supply more than additional information and partial explanations. The role of individuals in revolutionary processes must, of course, be interpreted within the social context which creates the opportunity for them to realize their maximum potential. There is a distinct correlation between the structure of social systems and the chances for individuals to rise to dominant positions: unstable political systems offer and augment the opportunity for particular individuals to achieve their arbitrary goals, and systems already in the process of revolutionary changes are even more propitious in this respect, even if the results may not always be of a permanent character.

It is at this point that the political historian is in his proper field of research, even though he still will have to rely heavily on the assistance of his colleagues from the other social sciences to supply him with supple-mentary information to throw new light on a specific problem. Similarly, even if his primary interest is not in general theories of social action, the political historian will, in turn, be able to supply social scientists engaged in formulating and testing such theories with valuable information. It is to be hoped that in the future a much greater degree of give-and-take will develop between historians and sociologists than has been the case hitherto.

It should be understood, however, that the main object of the work of political history lies elsewhere, although in the final analysis both the historian and the sociologist seek to develop methods of rational orientation in our world.

Even if the political historians could do their work boldly using only the research methods of structural-functional analysis and comparartive interpretation of quantitative data, they would hardly find this satisfactory. This does not mean that they are content to write narrative history in the traditional way; they seek to describe revolutionary processes neither from the viewpoint of how the revolutionaries or their counter-revolutionary adversaries saw themselves, nor even less from the viewpoint of their present-day heirs. They rather examine the validity of the current notions about revolutionary phenomena, comparing them with available data on the degree of social and economic change actually effected. Sometimes their findings are not flattering for the revolutionary cause and the social myths surrounding it; the counterrevolutionary forces usually come off even worse.

Political revolutions, despite the constant advances and retreats within a revolutionized society, despite the fact that most of the revolutionary achievements are lost again in the aftermath of the revolution, nonetheless highlight innovations in political institutions and in the social structures. While many of the principles and ideas put forward for the first time are forgotten in time, even if the revolution itself was successful, they tend to be revived again in more or less different guise at later junctures of the historical process. And the patterns of political or social organization tried for the first time under the extraordinary conditions created by revolutionary upheavals often find a revival even generations later. These violent convulsions of societies reveal both the possibilities and limitations of men to shape the political and social order in altogether different ways. It is worthwhile recording such extraordinary events not simply because they make fascinating reading, but because it enables the present generation to learn about the unmeasurable possibilities as well as the enormous risks and pitfalls which are associated with a policy of a thorough reshaping of political and social structures in present-day societies.

Here I would like to take up again the point I made at the beginning of this paper, namely that political history's contribution to the understanding of present-day societies can be meaningful only in dynamic societies which are willing to determine their own future rationally. Political history draws all its vital energies from the assumption that an unknown future lies ahead with unlimited possibilities of development and possible solutions to social and political problems. We look back into the past because we want to know more about ourselves and about the particular character of the society in which we live.

I should like to conclude this paper with one additional remark. If the dreams of some social scientists to determine a perfectly reliable method of predicting revolutions came true (which I, for one, am skeptical about), there would be no more revolutions. For the implication would be that the dynamic energies of modern societies could be measured in quantitative terms at every point. Yet this could be done only in societies in which all spheres of social change are subjected to rational control by bureaucratic agencies of every kind. Under such conditions, however, the social and political energies necessary to bring about a radical breakup of the fetters of the established order could hardly accumulate to a sufficient degree. To put it in another way, it would mean that the nightmare of Max Weber's dreams, the "iron cage of serfdom," had become reality. I suppose that things will never come to that, at least not in the forseeable future, and for this very reason I sincerely believe that political history will remain an exciting subject for all who stand for an open society.

Discussion

WOLFGANG J. MOMMSEN: In my paper I rely largely on the experience of an historian primarily concerned with the nineteenth and twentieth centuries, and this may explain some of my shortcomings.

I have a feeling that history, and especially political history, is right now in a situation of crisis, that challenges have been thrown out to it both by historians and by social scientists. Political history is in a kind of crisis for reasons which are themselves historical. I believe the traditional preoccupation with what happened within the state on the level of political decisions is partly due to the fact that for ideological reasons the state was considered a predominant agency of social change in the last two centuries. The state has had a predominant position in political history since Ranke. This way of describing history is connected with other concepts of explanation, as for instance the idea that it is men who make history, mainly statesmen. Nowadays the assumption that social change is primarily brought about via the state, and via the political institutions within a given social system, seems to be undermined. Mr. Bell, as well as Mr. Wiles, agreed upon the relative degree of autonomy of a political sphere within a society. But I must confess that amongst younger historians, at least in Germany, this is a thing which is not accepted anymore. We have to define the interaction between the political sphere and the social sphere much more than has been done hitherto, and for this very reason the old political history is under sharp criticism. There are, of course, many other types of history, like social history in its many versions. I describe briefly in my paper social economic history dealing with patterns of economic growth. On a different level, there are attempts by the political sciences to arrive at systematic explanations of decision-making processes, which are very far from what the historian traditionally used to do. At last, there is the structural-functional approach to history, which tries to arrive at generalisations as to the course of history which do not necessarily take into account the individual motivations of persons or groups concerned. This is, to put it briefly, the present situation.

What does political history actually stand for? I would say it is a social science of relevance to contemporary society, but only if one accepts that the society is an open and dynamic one. There is another assumption: that men are in some degree capable of shaping their future destinies in a rational manner. There is the assumption, too, that their consciousness, or their ideas of what society is like, shapes their decisions at least to a certain degree. The conceptions which they have of the past seem to be powerful in this context, and this justifies why the political historians are concerned with past events. Of course, the concept of a historical event is a rather difficult one. There are no events as such. All events, in the proper sense, are related to a rather general concept of what historical processes are. The political historian can do two things; firstly he can make visible the motivation structures which guide groups of individuals; secondly, he must find out about the conditioning factors (and this has been largely neglected by political historians just relying on the evidence of what happened in decisive political institutions). I should say that in this field a considerable change has to take place if political history wants to survive as a discipline of some weight. I would even go as far as to say that all quantitative history ultimately depends on this kind of political history, if you consider its interest for our own society.

I should like to turn to the example of political revolutions because the word revolution is now so fashionable that it is applied to almost every process in society. Our time is more interested in events representing discontinuity than in those representing continuity; at these junctures, the different forces and the ideological concepts which guide political and historical processes come to the fore most prominently. The question whether the French Revolution is a democratic revolution or simply a first step in a process of revolutions which leads up to a completely socialist society, or whether it is perhaps just a superficial thing which didn't change the social structure very much, is likely to influence our present-day consciousness to a very large extent. This is one side of the problem. The other side is whether we can find out general laws or simply generalities about such processes of social change. Political historians are less interested in such generalisations than in the message embodied in revolutions. Mr. Crane Brinton's book has already been mentioned here. But as soon as a revolution is actually under way, it seems that generalisations don't work very well any more, and in this situation the more or less traditional techniques of political historians are indispensable for a variety of reasons. One reason is this: the typical thing which characterises a revolution is that the *Legitimitätseinverständniss*, which acted as stabilising factor before, all of a sudden disappears. You have a rapid process of exchange of political positions and of social solutions, and it is very difficult to generalise upon the eventual outcome of this – in my opinion almost impossible. However, it is very interesting to see that in such processes the possibilities of shaping a society more or less rationally come to the fore; that the French Revolution, to take an example, brought about different concepts as to how society in the modern world should be organised. The other thing is that it seems to be very difficult to generalise in a revolutionary situation because we always find that marginal groups, or even individuals, have a decisive influence on what goes on.

RAYMOND ARON: Why should there be a crisis in political history in a century where politics have been so terrifying, in a century where a so-called revolution made in the name of a theory of economic predominance has become a political régime where political considerations have a determining voice?

PETER WILES: Indeed, there should be no crisis at all. What we have is the justified bewilderment of everybody at the human condition, which has never been more political than today. In our general despair, we look for disguised words for "causation" and "explanation"; we find out less demanding definitions of what "causation" and "explanation" might mean. At one time we used the concept of "dialectics"; there is a lot of "genetical causation" in this discussion (I still haven't understood what it means). I've heard the word "interpretation," which would appear to be nothing else than "explanation," and I have even heard that you can explain things without being able to predict them! This is a very natural reaction to the fact that political history is extremely important and extremely difficult. I will go further and make a really shocking statement – Toynbee's methodology is exactly right, and I recommend it to all political historians. What is wrong with Toynbee is something completely different from methodology: it is lack of talent.

We are discussing the possibility that it may be wise to generalise about revolutions. I will give you three generalisations which don't seem to me to be absolutely unimportant or absurd about revolutions. I thought about this, of course, in the context of the student revolution: I was able to make predictions to my students on the basis of having read a little about the French and Russian revolutions, and indeed about the English civil war, and these predictions to some extent came out right. One, there were the more extreme groups playing a greater role at a later date during the revolution than at the beginning. And two, the revolution is going to eat its own, whether it is the moderates that eat the extremists or vice versa; there won't be a compromise. And thirdly, the past is going to survive, whether the moderates or the extremists win, or, indeed, if the revolution is defeated. These are absolutely commonplace observations and this is why we are frightened to make them and to put them in books! But after all my students didn't know them...

HUGH TREVOR-ROPER: I think that Toynbee's methodology is wrong, although he has considerable talent in expressing it. His methodology consists in selecting examples which seem to support the conclusions and not testing them against the possibility of the examples which point in the other direction. I suspect Professor Wiles of being consistent and using the same methodology himself.

PETER WILES: I do agree that the way in which he uses his methodology expresses his lack of talent. He does not stick to the rules, the very simple rules which he lays down and this is indeed my great criticism against him.

HUGH TREVOR-ROPER: But how do you distinguish a methodology from the way you are using it?

ALAN BULLOCK: Many years ago, wondering what I should do to startle the world with the originality of my historical talents, I formed the idea of writing a comparative study of revolutions, and I laid out in rough the history of half a dozen revolutions: I wanted to see how far I could conduct a comparative study of them. I found that I was faced with this very simple fact: if you start to make a comparative study of revolution, either you turn into a sociologist and then begin to enunciate generalisations about revolution as such and try to make them more and more precise, or, as most people do, you seize on one and try to push the others into the pattern of it. This is what strikes me very much with Crane Brinton, and also with Toynbee, who began as a classical historian of the ancient world of the Mediterranean and was always looking for parallels elsewhere. Dealing with the Russian and the French revolutions, what should I do? Try and make out that the Jacobins played the role of the Bolsheviks, and the Girondins played the role of the Mensheviks, or try and make out that the Bolsheviks played the role of the Jacobins and the Mensheviks played the role of the Girondins? My difficulty there was that I didn't want to be a sociologist, to elaborate a model of revolution, because my interest, if not in the unique, is in the particular, the here and now. Of course, the particular can be repetitive, and no historian of quality would have thought he was writing a word of history if he did not attempt what Mr. Wiles calls the "lower level generalisations." Think of Tocqueville describing the revolution of 1848 and saying: "Revolution always repeats itself." Marx borrowed it from him and added "that first of all it repeats itself as tragedy and then as farce." The historian is always interested in picking up splendid generalisations, but he is not prone to develop them himself. There is a difference of temperament here between the historian and the sociologist, far more important than a difference of method; a different cast of mind between those who are bound to make use of every generalisation, of every extension of thought and concept available, and those who are bound to be sceptical until they have tried out these things against the actual events they are seeking to describe. Let me conclude with giving one illustration: a great deal has been issued about psycho-history. I would have thought it would be splendid to use the findings, shaky though they may be, of psycho-analysis for historical biography – or even further, for the understanding of certain selected phenomena. But so far the results are not impressive: The only book I know which is always referred to with great respect – Erickson's study of the young Luther – seems to me to be extremely hypothetical and to give less information about Luther than most books I have read about him. No historian should close his mind to the possibility of new forms of investigation, but before we turn over to highly esoteric forms we want to see a number of successful applications.

DANIEL BELL: In some sense, I don't believe there can be such a thing as "comparative history." Comparative history is a pitfall which any historian enters into at his own risk. By the very definition of Mr. Bullock, history is particular, concrete, manifold. How do you compare particulars to particulars? You cannot. What has to be done is to interpose analytical categories which necessarily violate the particular. If I want to compare, for example, the political system of the United States, France and England, one has a president, the other a prime minister, the third a president, yet it is inadmissible to use the terms president, prime minister and president, because they are very different in each of the systems. So I have to find a higher order of abstraction to deal with them, and I find the word executive. But if I use the word executive, and if I want to compare that kind of person to a tribal chief, who is not really an executive, I have to retreat to a higher order of abstraction called "super-ordinate role". Any good sociologist knows that these analytical categories will violate the particular. If you want to know "is the Jacobin a Bolshevik or the Bolshevik a Jacobin?", in Mr. Wiles' terms they are both extremists. Extremist here is a higher order of abstraction which, to a certain extent, violates the particularity of Jacobin or Bolshevik. Churchill and Hitler are extraordinarily different kinds of persons, and yet a sociologist, with some violence to their personalities, could call them both charismatic leaders, a term which would override important ideological particularities but would point attention to a different phenomenon: their relationship to the masses.

There can be no such thing as comparative history; there can only be either history or sociology.

RAYMOND ARON: Do you believe that what you call the crisis in political history is determined mainly by the conflict between different historical schools, by the mood of a society which has more interest in economic matters, or by the superiority in scientific value of non-political history?

WOLFGANG J. MOMMSEN: We are no longer sure that the vital innovations, the decisive changes, take place on the level of political institutions. A study of the history of the nineteenth and twentieth centuries shows that most important decisions took place very often on a much lower and more complicated level. What Bismarck decided upon and his motives are perhaps just half of the story: people are more or less bound to do certain things because of the pressure of a society.

RAYMOND ARON: Do you believe that what you say is entirely true of Soviet Russia?

WOLFGANG J. MOMMSEN: Indeed, Communist Russia is an example of a situation in which the state may be considered to be the primary agent of social change. So this is an example in favour of "old-fashioned" political history. But in the West the situation is rather different, and quantitative history and social history are legitimate.

RAYMOND ARON: It's not only that. The main question is: does quantitative history explain what is happening in the political field?

ALAN BULLOCK: In the end, I am afraid Mr. Mommsen is going to say that everything is related to everything else and before you can arrive at any suggestion about political decisions you will have to bring in the history of education and a great many things which are only marginally related. I am sure this is right. But, if you do it, you are in fact validating political history as one of the best organising principles for the presentation of history!

I would like to say something else. A great deal of the revolt against political history is a revolt against politics. As people shouldn't be able to make decisions, as there shouldn't be men like Stalin and Hitler, we'll pretend they don't exist and that, in the end, decisions are taken by great anonymous forces, which is much more acceptable to us than this intolerable thing, the influence of individuals on particular decisions.

KOSTAS PAPAIOANNOU: The case of Soviet Russia provides an excellent illustration of the crisis in traditional political historiography. Perpetual paradox is the keynote of the story there. A régime based on the economic conception of history arrives, after two years in power, at Lenin's famous phrase, "Whoever doesn't know that politics is paramount over economics doesn't know the first thing about Marxism." But in this society there is apparently no political history. Unanimity is the rule, the details of political action are unknown, we know nothing of what happens at Politburo meetings, and so on. It is impossible to understand the recent history of Russia without taking into account certain phenomena which do not come into traditional political historiography; in particular, ideology. Collectivisation remains completely mysterious if one leaves out of account the eschatological faith of the special group constituted by the Bolsheviks, the diabolisation of the kulak, and personal conflicts inside the Central Committee.

KARL D. BRACHER: The discussion between Professor Mommsen and Professor Bullock can be illustrated very well by looking at the interpretations of Nazi Germany. There is a strong tendency to describe the history of Germany in the twenties and thirties in terms of purely social and economic development. This goes so far that in the work of some German historians the personality of Hitler completely disappears, as well as the political process. All events are explained by conflicts of industrial interests. This kind of historical description doesn't really

Political history in crisis

function. You will find out that some of Hitler's aims were quite irrational and could not be explained in terms of usefulness. What you have called a crisis in political history could be defined as a crisis in the measures by which you determine the weight of certain factors in certain situations. This is not a new problem. It happened in the twenties as well. Most of the historical literature produced in the twenties in Germany led to a complete misunderstanding of what was really going on in the country.

6 In praise of history

HUGH TREVOR-ROPER

What is historical knowledge for us today?

This is a question which, in one form or another, I often put to myself.
Any scholar, I believe, must ask himself the purpose of his own study, and
keep reminding himself of his answer, in order that he may be conscious
of his purpose in pursuing it. Otherwise his work may well disperse itself
in irrelevancy or triviality, or sink into pedantry. When I ask myself this
question, I always find it accompanied by another, its corollary. That
corollary is, what would our life be without a knowledge of history? And
I try to envisage an intellectual world from which the study of history is
removed; a world in which, outside the natural and applied sciences,
only "modern subjects" – politics, sociology, economics – and languages
and literature are academically studied. I admit that when I envisage such
a world, my heart shrinks.

Life without history, and a sense of history, would be, to me, a sorry
affair. Of this I feel certain. How could one move through the world in
one dimension only, taking for granted all the graduated deposit of time
and human achievement which we see around us? I would find such a life
impoverished, thin, vulgar. It would be vulgar because of its implied
immodesty. To take the world as we have inherited it, to assume that it
is all ours, to acknowledge no debt to our predecessors, to please ourselves with the arrogant assumption that the labour and genius and
suffering of the past is of no significance to us and that every mechanical
invention that we use, every art that we acquire, every opportunity which
we enjoy, is ours by mere right of birth, seems to be unbearably immodest,
aggressive, complacent, and I find myself morally revolted by such an
attitude when I encounter it.

And we do encounter it. No doubt, in some societies, or classes of
society, it is natural, unreflective, innocent. History, after all, is itself an

acquired art. It had to be invented or discovered. For long periods, men were content to remember only what they had been told by eye-witnesses: all else was "time out of mind; the dark backward and abysm of time", through which no continuous path was to be found. Only occasional, half mythical figures, transmogrified beyond recognition, still stared, isolated, larger than life, through the distorting haze: Alexander the Great, whose romantic conquests were narrated in the distant East; Alcibiades whom François Villon would include in his catalogue of fair women whose beauty had dissolved like last year's snow.

Even today, when the mist is dispelled and all the paths – or nearly all of them – are cut, paved and signposted, there are people who are totally indifferent to history. Sometimes, when I visit some place of tourism, some temple or palace or villa or amphitheatre, I watch the movements or overhear the remarks of the other visitors, and I realise that history is to them a complete blank. Behind the last frontier of living memory, one century is to them quite indistinguishable from another, and if they are told (as I have heard them told by an unhistorical workman) that an 18th century college quadrangle was built "thousands of years ago", they are content with the answer. They walk through a gothic cathedral or a Palladian courtyard as a man walks through a picture gallery who knows nothing of art, who cannot distinguish a Primitive from an Impressionist, a Rembrandt from a Goya. If one has no concept of the past, no guiding lines through it, no sense of graduated change, how can one do otherwise? All centuries are the same in time that has dissolved into timelessness, "time out of mind".

We may feel pity for those who lack this dimension of time. We may think them unfortunate, deprived of the opportunity to enrich their lives, forced by urgent daily mechanical pressures to forego these luxuries of the mind. But there are today educated people who (as it seems) positively wish to join them, who look upon history, and even the sense of history, as an impediment to human progress, and who wish to see mankind emancipated from these constricting tentacles of the past. Marx believed that the historical process which he had himself studied so profoundly would lead, ultimately, to the end of history; and he wished to bring it to an end. The revolution, of which he hoped to be the midwife, was to introduce a society in which that painful process, the brutal contest of economic forces now rendered obsolete, would have ceased – just as the Christian revolutionaries of earlier ages had looked forward to a static millennium as the culmination of their worldly endeavours and doctrinal fidelity. And some of our modern sociologists take pleasure in informing us of their contempt for history; history which, perhaps, they define in terms which we, as historians, would not accept.

Faced by this revolt against history, this formidable alliance between mere philistinism on one hand and self-styled "progress" on the other, I find myself a "conservationist". Why, I ask, should a few aggressive "developers", aided by the apathy and indifference of the public, drive their unnecessary turnpike road through my ancient estate, demolish my historic house, root up my long planted avenue of living trees, in order to build over its desolate ruins, their stinking modern petrol-station and their noisy road-house? But this, I soon realise, is too personal, too selfish an argument. It will hardly convert the floating voter to my side. Therefore, if only for technical reasons, I must contain my emotion and deploy instead my reason. I must give a rational defence of my property, showing that it is not only my own interest that I am defending but the interest of society: that historical study is not merely a luxury or a pleasure, the enrichment of a private life, but an essential intellectual discipline – indeed, more essential than the new disciplines which threaten to undermine it.

I recognise that this is not the view of everyone, or even of all historians. In the past, history has been defended, at the highest level, on other grounds. The men of the Renaissance looked to it for moral examples. The Romantics saw it as an escape from the present. The great German historians of the 19th century saw it as an end in itself, an undeviating fidelity to indispensable fact. But whatever we may owe to the work of these men, I cannot share their philosophy. Moral examples, as Sir Philip Sidney wrote, can be found more purely in literature than in history: Spenser's *Faerie Queen* is more edifying than the *Lives of the Popes*. Romantic historiography can be a travesty of truth which numbs the understanding of history; what damage was done to medieval history by the example of Sir Walter Scott! The Great Germans of the 19th century have been followed by the less great Germans of the 20th century who have nearly killed history by their kindness to the dispensable facts.

Among my own colleagues I find historical study defended on what seem to me most unstable ground. On one side, I am assured, by a well-known and very able English historian, that history has no meaning, no lessons: its only function is to amuse. On another, I hear a somewhat shrill voice pouring contempt on all those of us who ask historical questions: history, he insists, is not the asking of questions (he is clearly no Greek scholar) but the relation of stories, in vigorous personal style and patriotic narrative form. And the most learned of all my English colleagues will recognise no historian who is readable, no historian who seeks to interpret evidence except for its own sake. To him, it seems, it is the technique that matters, and the highest praise that he will allow to a historian is that he is an expert, praised by other experts, for his documentary expertise.

I am afraid that I dissent from all these views. To me history has lessons: I would find it hard to be interested in it otherwise. I simply cannot read history for amusement only, as so many people can. Equally, I find myself impatient of mere expertise, the expertise of Schoolmen exhibiting their own professional virtuosity without leading the layman to any interesting suggestion or conclusion. To me history is an intellectual pursuit, which entails the constant asking of questions. Of course the answers to those questions are provisional, not dogmatic, for the science is empirical, not deductive; and I regard interpretation as an inseparable part of the exercise. Philosophically, I find myself most sympathetic, in theory at least, to the "philosophic historians" of the 18th century – or at least to the best of them-for admittedly their philosophy, being sometimes insufficiently ballasted with fact, could run away with them. I admire erudition and enjoy penetrating to the evidence of history; but always it is with interpretation in mind. Historians who are not always aware of the questions which they should be answering, or of the laymen for whom they should be answering them, have little to say to me.

But I am not here concerned to weigh historians or identify myself with a particular historical philosophy. I am concerned to state the reasons why I believe that the study of history is not only a form of entertainment, at least to the writers, but also a necessary intellectual discipline, why I think that it should be not left as a private pleasure to those who have leisure to indulge it, but taught as an essential academic subject.

Briefly, I think that the study of history is a necessary intellectual discipline for two reasons. First, it is a necessary ingredient in other disciplines; secondly, it is, in itself, an intellectually stabilising force. These two reasons are connected, and it is difficult to separate them in explanation. Nor shall I try artificially to separate them; I shall try to express my own conception of historical study and thereby allow them to disengage themselves.

For what is historical study in itself? I think that all historians would agree that it is not now (as it was in earlier times) a mere narrative of public events. Nor is it merely (as the Romantic writers treated it) a narrative of public events decorated and brought nearer to us by social illustration. It is an attempt to perceive the objective reality of a previous period, and to perceive it as part of a *continuum* which includes the present. Renaissance historians, for their moral purposes, selected from the surface of the past: great individual figures, or heroic episodes, or noble examples were isolated from their trivial context of petty fact and temporary circumstance and seen all the more vividly in that isolation. Romantic historians made an artificial gulf between past and present in order that the one might provide an escape from the other. But a modern historian, whatever permanent lessons he may have learned and retained from his predecessors (and it would be a cheap form of modernity in any historian to refuse such lessons), does not seek such isolation or such escape. He sees any historical period as a totality. The politics of the past, to him, are real politics, like those of the present, taking place in a partic- ular context – a social, economic, intellectual context – and that context is both glutinous and, in spite of all circumstantial differences, recognis- able: glutinous in the sense that particular persons or episodes cannot be seen correctly if detached from it, and recognisable in the sense that it is the context of a real world, comparable with the real world about us. Of course in many ways it may be very different from our modern world, but the modern historian tries to recognise its differences as well as its simi- larities; indeed it is only by recognising its differences that he can define and hope to understand the degree of its similarity and make compar- isons.

The difference, of course, is that in dealing with the present we take the context for granted whereas in dealing with the past we have to discover it intellectually. But the recognition that we cannot take it for granted, that we have to discover it, is one of the most important changes which have taken place in the study of history in the last century. In the Middle Ages, in the century of the Renaissance, there was no such sense of the past: the context of century after century was seen as a permanent theatre in which only the actors constantly changed. Just as the artists of the Quattrocento painted the life of Christ against a modern background of Tuscan or Umbrian villages, populated by the stirring coloured peasant life of 15th century Italy, just as Shakespeare's actors represented scenes

of Caesar's Rome or of Macbeth's Scotland in the ruffs and doublets of
Jacobean England, so even the boldest and most modern of Renaissance
historians – even Machiavelli and his disciples – would see the political
lessons of Antiquity, the political maxims of Tacitus, as directly transfer-
able to their own times. Even the great historians of the Enlightenment,
even Gibbon himself, who certainly studied society in depth, seem to us,
too often, insensibly to place the events of the past in a modern, 18th
century context; and in 1834 Macaulay could write, with his invariable
confidence, as one enunciating a truism, that "a Christian of the 5th
century with a Bible is neither better nor worse situated than a Christian
of the 19th century with a Bible... the absurdity of the literal interpretation was as great and as obvious in the 16th century as it is now."[1] On
which one is tempted to exclaim with that great Dutch historian, the late
Pieter Geyl, "An extraordinary statement indeed! How can a man who
expects the early Christians and the Protestants in the first flush of their
fervour to read in the Bible what he, son of the Enlightenment and of
Utilitarianism, finds there – how can such a man penetrate into the spirit
of the past?"[2]

No historian today, not even the boldest and rashest, would dare to
echo the words of Macaulay. In our less confident age – precisely because
we live in a less confident age – we recognise the relativity of ideas, even of
axioms. To us the liberal certitudes of the 19th century, the rational
certitudes of the 18th century, are relative. They may contain permanent
truths, but we are not sure. They are the assumptions of one age and, as
such, they do but prolong, in another form, the timeless assumptions of
the Renaissance. What a world of difference there is between the Middle
Ages of Augustin Thierry and the Middle Ages of Marc Bloch, between
the Renaissance of Jules Michelet or even of Jacob Burckhardt and the
Renaissance whose intellectual climate has been reconstructed in our own
time by scholars like Fritz Saxl, Eugenio Garin, Frances Yates!

To me this sense of the past, this sense of a constantly changing social
context and a constantly changing set of intellectual assumptions, within
which historical events, *l'histoire événementielle*, takes place, and by
which apparent similarities may be turned into real differences, is one of
the rewards of historical study. But it is also, I believe, part of the objective value of history; and it is at this point that I can begin to divide my
argument into its two related strands. For first, the study of history is, I
believe, relevant to the present: it is not a mere academic exercise, or an

enjoyable luxury; and because it is relevant, we cannot afford to take risks; it is important that we should appreciate its full depth and complexity. And secondly, the historical context, as I have tried to describe it, is not exclusive to history. Other disciplines also partake, far more than our ancestors thought – far more than the specialists in those disciplines often seem to think – of the same context.

Let us consider first the relevance of the past to the present. This is an old theme on which scholars and statesmen have played many variations. But it is nevertheless true. The modern anti-historians speak and write as if our own age was post-historical, sufficient to itself, or at least as if industrialisation of the last half-century had so transformed society, even humanity, that no useful comparisions could be made with pre-industrial society, no useful lessons, drawn from it. To this I would answer that, on the contrary, in all subjects, the most useful comparisons are precisely those which are made across a contextual frontier, for it is only by comparing what is not exactly comparable that we can isolate the variable elements and come to tested conclusions. If I were considering (for instance) the ways in which small heretical movements can grow into political forces, I would not wish to study only the Communist or Fascist parties of the 20th century. The common background being taken for granted, we might too easily fail to notice some distinguishing reason. I would wish to study also the Calvinists of the 16th century, the Christians of the Roman Empire. By comparing movements thus separated in time, movements whose very different contexts have to be separately and intellectually apprehended, we would be more likely to isolate the determining forces, less likely to be satisfied with superficial generalisations. In other words, we would be more likely to understand.

Again, circumstances change and sometimes, when they change, no contemporary experience can provide a parallel, or a key, to the new events. For what is historically possible in one century is not historically possible in another. As Voltaire wrote, in his *Lettres philosophiques* (and the remark was taken over by Gibbon as "an obvious truth")[3], a Cardinal de Retz, in the 18th century, would not have roused ten women of Paris to riot, and a Cromwell would have been a mere merchant of London. Who could have imagined a Hitler or a Stalin in 19th century Europe? When they emerged, in 20th century Europe, the men of the 19th century, who still ruled in the West, could not recognise them. They had known nothing like them in their own time, and so, through ignorance of history, because their range of human examples was limited to their own time, they translated them into their own language. Sidney and Beatrice Webb, those great Panjandrums of Fabian Socialism, so insufferable in their omniscience and self-conceit – how they remind me of some of our more modern sociologists! – went to communist Russia in the 1930s and came back to complete a huge work on the subject, in which they assured the faithful that Stalin was not a tyrant, not a dictator, not even a monarch, but only a conscientious Fabian bureaucrat, the secretary of a committee, the Sidney Webb of the liberal social democracy of all the Russias.[4] Neville Chamberlain, that no less obstinate, no less well-meaning man, equally confident that all useful knowledge was contained in the experience of the present – of his present, of late 19th century Birmingham – was just as convinced that he understood Hitler. Were they not both men of the industrial age, realists who, in spite of some differences of opportunity and upbringing, must have the same fundamental ideas? "With the mentality of a business-man" writes Sir John Wheeler-Bennett,[5] "he was used to striking a bargain by which, though the shareholders in some subsidiary company might suffer temporarily, the corporation as a whole would benefit in the long run"; and he assumed that Hitler, behind all the vulgarity and the rodomontade, had a similar mentality. It would have been better for humanity if these well-meaning men had been less confident; if they had recognised that Hitler and Stalin were phenomena whose like were not to be found in their own limited life span, but must be sought where they would be found, in remoter history.

To make historical parallels is a dangerous game, and to suppose that the past provides an easy key to the present is a vulgar error. No historical situation ever recurs exactly; only the crudest historical autodidact would defend the study of history by so naive an assumption. The historian knows that no moment of history ever returns, that the determining forces of any situation are too many, too complex, that they are largely intangible, often unobserved, dependent as much upon elusive moral forces as upon calculable facts, and that it is inconceivable that the exact mixture and the exact balance should ever be repeated. But this does not mean that we should study history less; rather we should study it more, or more carefully, in order that we may be more aware of this subtlety and this complexity, that we may recognise the wide range of human behaviour and not be surprised by the sudden contrast between that range and our up-to-date but rootless parochialism.

The difficulty is, the layman wants quick answers. He has been told, by the pundits, that history is a science, and so he asks for exact answers. What, precisely, are the "lessons" of history? What does it predict in this or that situation? We know, of course, that there are no such tabloid answers. History is a means of understanding, not a set of formulae. Those who claim more from it, claim too much. In the same way, we are often asked, about the great historians, what was their historical philosophy, and we are expected to give quick answers, or our critics will be dissatisfied either with us or with them. But the very complexity of history, which prevents it from giving short answers to the one question, disqualifies the other also. The historical philosophy of some historians can no doubt be expressed simply, but those are the system-mongers whose work seldom lasts long or provides a reliable guide. The great historians have always been those who have not sought either to extract too positive answers from historical evidence or to supply too systematic a philosophy. And yet, what is history if it is not always looking for answers, tentative though they may have to be? Historical truth is not worth cultivating for its own sake; there are too many unimportant truths, and if truth once becomes secondary, we might as well read historical novels or poetry. *The Iliad, Don Quixote, War and Peace* are a thousand times better than mere historical finality.

Therefore I will insist on historical philosophy. A work of history that is inspired by no philosophy, that despairs of answering any general question, that resigns itself to being a mere narrative, that buries itself in the ritual cult of its own documentation seems to me a barren exercise. In this I agree with Polybius, the most inquisitive and philosophical of the ancient historians: "Take away from History the questions Why, How and to what end things have been done, and whether the event corresponded to the intention, and what is left is a mere pageant, not a useful lesson; it may please us for a while but it leaves no lasting profit."[6] The first of English "philosophical historians," the founder of the chair at Oxford recently held by our modern Polybius, Sir Ronald Syme, made these words the epigraph of his most famous work of history[7]; and their sense was recapitulated, over a century later, by Gibbon, in a footnote on the historians of the Ottoman Turks: "Dr. Johnson praises Knolles as the first of historians, unhappy only in the choice of his subject. Yet I much doubt whether a partial and verbose compilation from Latin writers, 1300 folio pages of speeches and battles, can either instruct or amuse an en-

lightened age, which requires from the historian some tincture of philosophy and criticism."[8]

So, if I were to summarise my first reason for the study of history, I
would say that it provides a necessary extension of the evidence for the
social sciences. Such an extension is not only necessary in order to widen
the range of evidence in a complex subject which its over-confident prac-
titioners are too ready to simplify; it is also perhaps even more necessary
in order to supply the movement which is an essential element in social
equations. For history is sociology in movement, the empirical evidence
of societies in action, and tested by action over a long period of time. I
sometimes think that our modern sociologists see their social models as
static constructions and that the dynamic of time is needed in order to
show how those models actually work – and whether they actually
work. But this dimension of time, which alone shows us society in actual
operation, is only ascertainable through the study of history; and as I
cannot conceive of any useful historical study which does not include a
study of the social context, so I cannot conceive of any useful sociological
study which does not include an illustration of the model in action, subject to the driving force and obstruction of ideas, events, individual free
will, human error: in other words, history.

But is is time to come to my second reason. It is a reason which stems
from the same general conviction as the first, *viz:* my belief that the study
of history is today more complex than it has been thought to be in the past
and that this complexity is due to what I have called its context; by which
I mean, especially, the social and intellectual world which, at any given
time, is taken for granted by those who live in it but which later historians
must seek to reconstruct intellectually because it supplies both the conditions and, in part, the explanation of those public events with which alone
the older historians were concerned. My second reason for regarding the
study of history as a necessary intellectual discipline, and not merely a
luxury, is that without such a study, as I envisage it, the study of art,
literature, ideas is incomplete and barren.

I am afraid that this may be thought an aggressive attitude. A few
years ago, perhaps, I would not have expressed it thus. But I now believe
that the specialisation of studies has developed so far, and has been so
exaggerated and distorted by external causes – by academic proliferation
and pressure to publish – that only a greater deference to historical study
can hold those studies together and prevent them from dispersal into

irrelevance. And I think that historical studies can so hold them together precisely because historical studies have that "glutinous" context which I have described. But I shall try to explain myself a little less metaphorically.

It is a commonplace saying today – it has been a commonplace since Herder – that all the intellectual or artistic activities of men are rooted in the culture of their societies. This, to me, is an absolute truth. To me, also, as I have made clear, the history of men is the history of their societies and therefore of their culture. It therefore follows that, for me, the development in time of ideas, or of art, or of literature, is, to a large extent, not autonomous. Ideas do not breed ideas, nor art art, nor literature literature. The development of each is part of the development of society, *i.e.*, it is part of history. To give a crude example, in order to understand how the classical poetry of the 18th century gave way to the romantic poetry of the 19th century, it is not enough to study the poetry of those two centuries, for the change was not purely internal to poetry: it was the reflexion, in poetry, of a change in society, a historical change, and therefore it is there, in history (as I have defined it), that the change must be studied, and its true motor found.

Having written that last paragraph, I feel almost ashamed of such banality. Surely this is a vulgar truism, hardly worth expression. And yet, it seems to me, it is a truism more often uttered than applied. Professors of literature write about literature and its history as if it were an entirely autonomous subject; they trace the pedigree of language and style as if Herder had never lived, as if Ennius begat Lucretius and Lucretius begat Vergil and Vergil begat Lucan and Lucan begat Statius in a pure and insulated Republic of Letters without any reference to the great social changes which were taking place in, and overturning, the Republic of Rome. Similarly "historians of science" write about the scientific revolution of the 17th century as if one discovery, or machine, bred another in similar insulation, without reference to the wider intellectual revolution of which, to us, that scientific revolution is an integral part; and "historians of ideas" ascribe a similarly self-contained intellectual pedigree to ideas themselves: the idea of the decay of nature, or the plurality of worlds, or the mixed constitution, or the social contract is pursued in a rarefied intellectual world of academic parthenogenesis.

Of course I exaggerate. Of course there are some wonderful works of scholarship which disprove my jaundiced assertions. Joseph Needham's work on Chinese science (however contested by warring sinologues), Marcel Bataillon's incomparable work on Erasmianism in Spain, the writings on Spanish literature of Americo Castro, Erich Haase's posthumous work on the literature of the Huguenot Diaspora, the art-historical writings of Emile Mâle... it would be easy to compile a long list of books which have given new significance to the study of literature and art, science and thought, by re-annexing them to the historical context with which they were organically connected. But such a list, I think, would only prove my point that it is the historical dimension which gives that significance and makes those subjects live.

But let us not be too historicocentric. The formula can also be reversed. History too can become detached from that cultural context which it shares with other humane studies and by that separation dwindle into insignificance. We have seen this happen in the past, and we have also seen the process reversed. Medieval studies, which seemed so prosperous in England a generation ago, have declined steeply since; and they have declined, I believe, precisely because they have become thus insulated, whereas in France they have been revived largely through the great work of Marc Bloch, who reunited them with the major and continuing problems of society and culture. Detached from those human problems, history, like any other form of study, will always wilt; re-attached to them, it can always, I think, revive.

And I think that it is a duty, not merely a pleasure, to revive it and keep it alive. The study of history is, after all, the only study we have which effectively articulates the passage of humanity through time. Before history begins, we have no sense of time; and the future, I believe, is unpredictable except in the most tentative and conditional manner. Of its duration we cannot speak, and although we may make limited predictions for the next century at most, which are likely to be wrong (who could ever have predicted the events of the 20th century?), we certainly cannot go beyond that. Therefore the few thousand years of history are the only period during which we can study, empirically, the forms and limits of the social behaviour of man. We talk easily about the future. The anti-historians wish to sacrifice the past to the future, knowledge about the past to speculations about the future. But how can we guide ourselves through the future without the stabilising experience of the past? Perhaps we shall not have a future. In that case past history will be the sum of human experience. But I prefer to agree with Bertrand Russell that "it is not too late to hope that mankind will have a future as well as a past. I believe that if men are to feel this hope with sufficient vividness to give it dynamic power, the awareness of history is one of the greatest forces of which the beneficent appeal must be felt."[9]

NOTES

1. Macaulay, *Essays*, "Ranke's History of the Popes."
2. Pieter Geyl, *Debates with Historians*, Groningen and The Hague, 1955, p. 24.
3. Voltaire, *Lettres philosophiques*, 7ème lettre. Gibbon, *Decline and Fall of the Roman Empire*, ch. LXX.
4. Sidney and Beatrice Webb, *Soviet Communism, a New Civilisation*, 1935.
5. Sir John W. Wheeler-Bennett, *Munich, Prologue to Tragedy*, 1948, p. 40.
6. Polybius, *History*.
7. W. Camden, *Annales rerum Anglicarum et Hibernicarum, regnante Elizabetha* (1615) *Praetatio*.
8. Gibbon, *Decline and Fall of the Roman Empire*, ch. LXIV.
9. Bertrand Russell, *Portraits from Memory and Other Essays*, 1956, p. 193.

Discussion

HUGH TREVOR-ROPER: In this discussion of the position of the historian between the ethnologist and the futurologist, the historians have been hard-pressed. Sociologists tend to use the device of ideal types, which can easily become caricatures; we have been told that historians have insufficient contact with sociology and anthropology, that they do not make comparisons, that history is unilinear and that our profession consists merely of adding fact to fact.

Giving my own views, I mustn't claim to represent more than myself, but I think that some of my opinions are the common property of most modern historians. I believe that anthropology is very useful to historians but that its usefulness is limited. It is true that, in the remote past, historians didn't much trouble about anthropology. They divided the world as it were into Greeks and Barbarians and didn't bother about the Barbarians. But from a very early stage in the study of history, anthropology came into it. Look at the great historians of the eighteenth century. It was they who systematically brought anthropology into history. They read the accounts of the Barbarians, the famous *Histoires édifiantes et curieuses* of the Jesuit missionaries; they studied the behaviour of hitherto unknown tribes in America and East Asia in order to discover more about history. Through the philosophical writings of Montesquieu and others, relativism came into history. All great changes in historical study tend to come from outside. The specialists in any discipline follow each other, refine upon each other and keep within the same limits as their predecessors. In order to make a change of direction, the impulse comes generally from outside, from philosophy as in the eighteenth century, from literature as in the nineteenth century. All the great eighteenth-century historians who wrote under the influence of Montesquieu, Gibbon being the greatest, did use anthropology in order to study history and their own past. Like most modern historians, I have read the great anthropological classics – with pleasure, because they are readable, unlike sociological books. The effect of this no doubt amateur study of anthropology on the historian must be a certain humility. From anthropology we recognise the autonomy of distinct societies. We recognise that their whole working, even their basic rules of thought, even their definition of what we regard as reason, rationality, may be quite legitimately different from our own. But this recognition does not come to us only from anthropologists but also from historians themselves. When Ranke said he wished to study history *"wie es eigentlich gewesen ist"* he did not mean that he wished merely to reconstruct a narrative of facts, he meant that he recognised the autonomy of different societies, not in space, as the anthropologists do, but in time. He recognised that the men of the thirteenth century, for instance, had a perfect right to exist autonomously and independently: they were not to be judged by the rules and canons of the nineteenth century.

Historians today are much more aware of the existence of separate societies in space and time. I would like to refer here to a whole area of history which has not been mentioned in the course of this discussion: the history of art. People who have studied the artistic and intellectual culture of society have been perhaps the first among historians to appreciate the completeness of the difference of intellectual climate between one period and another. Since they have to interpret iconography, they see, as it were, the world picture in its totality – visibly, sensibly, directly. They have brought us to recognise that the entire world picture of a period which we used to think so rational, so akin to ours as the sixteenth century, was in fact governed by norms, by rules of thought, by attitudes of mind totally distinct from ours, so that the very concept even of the word "reason" meant something different to them from what it means to us. This fact became very apparent to me when I was working on the subject of belief in witches, on how an age so like our own, according to rational, secular, modern historians, could in fact not only take this belief seriously but increase its intensity over a hundred years. Belief in witchcraft did not creep along at the bottom, as a peasant superstition surviving from a more enlightened age. When one studies the sixteenth century and the early seventeenth, one finds that it positively grew in the highest and most educated classes and was deliberately propagated by the most influential thinkers of the time. This is a problem which cannot be faced in the old terms of supposing a gradual, linear progression from darkness to light, from superstition to enlightenment. We have to take the period autonomously, against its proper background, to investigate the whole structure of thought of the time, and then we discover that reason itself proved the existence of all these superstitions which we regard as being now totally dispelled by the growth of reason.

There have recently been some historians who have been very active in telling us that we ought to introduce more anthropology into our study of history and that we would understand the activities of men in, let us say, seventeenth-century England, better if we knew a little more about the behaviour of Sudanese or Bantu Tribes. This, I think, is going too far. I agree that historians should study anthropology and draw lessons from it, but I would insist that these lessons are simple and general; there is no need for historians of Europe to bury themselves in the details of the endogamous or exogamous practises of Polynesian tribes. So much for the anthropologists.

Now I turn to the futurologists. I am, I must admit, more skeptical of the debt which historians ought to pay to them. When I was an undergraduate I remember attending a class given by a distinguished tutor of my college who was then a Marxist and who attempted to recommend us the Marxist key to history. He explained it by saying that proof of the pudding is in the eating, that if any system of history is right in the past then it will prove its validity by correctly prophesying the future... and he prophesied a good deal of the past in terms of the future. My first attempt to take him seriously was to enquire to what extent the rise of Fascism, which was clear at that time, had been prophesied by the Marxists. I found that this was apparently left out of the formula. It was explained afterwards as being the last convulsions of dying capitalism, a phenomenon so unimportant that it had not been thought necessary to mention it explicitly. This may be so, but later, when Fascism nearly conquered the world – because I really think that but for certain isolatable and in themselves trivial events Fascism might have conquered the world – I felt that this phenomenon was too important to be dismissed as a mere irrelevant and expendable footnote to the progress of the Marxist theory. Since then, I have often wondered whether any historical system, any set of historical beliefs, however undogmatic they may seem, can prophesy the future. Let us consider a few instances. I cast myself back to the height of the prosperity of the Roman Empire, in the reigns of Trajan and Hadrian, the time when Pliny and Tacitus were writing. Both authors were aware of the Christians and refer to them. Did it occur to Pliny or Tacitus, or to any other pagan writer, that the future would be with this despised Jewish sect living in conventicles?... Even if Mr. Bell had been the most highly paid rhetorician of the court of Trajan, or Hadrian, I rather doubt whether with all his present resources of futurological science he would have been able to predict that particular event of the future. Or leap forward 600 years to the seventh century. Could anyone have prophesied, until it had actually happened, the rise and conquest of Muhammadanism in Asia? Further forward, let us suppose that in 1571 there was a Commission for the year 1600. Could anyone have supposed that the Catholic Church would in fact recover the greater part of its losses, that by 1630 the question would be not the survival of Catholicism but the survival of Protestantism? This formula could be repeated again and again. There are living among us people who were alive and flourishing in 1900, or 1910, 1912. I wonder whether any of them, however much advantage they might theoretically have had of proto-futurology, could conceivably have prophesied, or could be blamed for not having prophesied, the extraordinary events which have happened in the world since 1900. Admittedly, there have been successful prophets. Have they been sociologists? (The futurologists haven't yet had time to prove themselves – that, I allow.) In the 1520s Erasmus prophesied the counter-Reformation in remarkably accurate terms. In the 1840s, when the German Liberals were prophesying the liberal conquest of Germany, Heinrich Heine prophesied something remarkably like the Nazi ideology. Mention has been made of the remarkable prophecies made by Jacob Burckhardt in the 1890s which look forward so clearly to the establishment of Fascism in Europe. But when we think of it, none of these men used sociological concepts or dogmas, they merely used imagination. Erasmus was a scholar, Heine a poet, Burckhardt a historian. Whereas our modern futurologists sometimes seem to suggest that one can predict the future on the basis of a very narrow band of historical experience, merely the one of industrial society, Burckhardt based his profound historical observations and prophecies on a study of history from the age of Constantine the Great to his own time. The difficulty of the whole sociological attempt to prophesy is that it is based on assumptions of continuity which are not always true. Nearly all changes come out of society, but they often come out of groups which, at the time, are ignored. Nazism had appeared in the world before anyone knew about its origins. Something similar can be said of all kinds of historical and ideological movements: they seem to spring up from nowhere and it takes a good deal of historical research to discover their origin. So, for the historian, there is only one method: the empirical one. All historical thought that isn't irremediably obsolete has been based on experience. The sociologist proceeds from dogma: he is elaborating mere models and the proof of a model is how it works. These events which are so despised by some sociologists, and stuffed into the footnotes of their works, leave a deposit on the structure; they may even form the structure if their impact is sufficiently strong or if they are themselves sufficiently repeated. Let me give some instances. The social structure of Spain was created in the Middle Ages by the fact that Christian Spain was a society organised for war. By the sixteenth century, the golden century of Spain, the actual structure was fixed and could not be entirely transformed even by events so enormous as the discovery of America and all its wealth. The military structure, created by the events of the Middle Ages, remained the social structure. Something very similar can be said, I suppose, of Prussian history: think of the events which occurred between 1864 and 1870. In that time, Prussia won three Blitzkriegs. In 1914, the German Imperial government believed that it could win a quick war by another Blitzkrieg. We know that it failed, that the war lasted four years, but that was an accident. When Hitler came to power, he thought that he was going to make Blitzkriegs which would work. So powerful was the memory of the successful Blitzkriegs that even the failure of 1914 did not deter Hitler and those who supported him, who were after all quite a large proportion of the élite, from trying again. We know from the study of German war production in the Second World War that the German economy had not even been organised in 1939 for a real total war, but only for a succession of Blitzkriegs, against Poland, then against France; and they succeeded. But there were some others which didn't. So, events of the 1860s were still very effective in the 1930s.

I must confess that, in spite of the claims which have been made by sister disciplines, I remain a historical imperialist. History, among all the sciences, is, it seems to me, the one which is most purely empirical. Whenever any part of it becomes hardened into dogma, that part is willingly abandoned by historians to sociologists, to whom we give our coherent systems in return for their spare parts. I would willingly give them Toynbee in exchange for the term "charisma," although as a matter of fact we could have got on quite happily using the word "prophet," as we had before. I believe that history must not only include anthropology and sociology but also dominate them, to test them and to keep them empirical. And in history thus seen I include political history. We've been told there is a crisis in political history. It may be an unfashionable subject of study today, but it remains essential. In the nineteenth century many historians, not only English ones, believed that the reason why England did not have a bloody revolution in the eighteenth century was that it had a bloodless revolution in the seventeenth century, in 1688. This may be an over-simplification, but the fact remains that the difference between bloody and bloodless revolutions lies often in political history.

RAYMOND ARON: I have never doubted that an essential part of what might be called the political structure of France, or "the rules of the game of politics in France," is the French Revolution. No French sociologist would deny that the memory, the trauma, the legend, the transfiguration, and the presence of the French Revolution is a truly essential part of the way the French conceive of and practice politics. The last time they demonstrated it was in May 1968, a totally incomprehensible event for anyone unfamiliar with certain other events which have left an indelible mark on the French unconscious. Between May 27 and 30, most government officials had left their ministries pending the arrival of the new masters – where else in Western Europe could this have happened except in France, where the tradition of changing governments or régimes by means of riots in the streets is an integral part of the nation's political consciousness?

I agree with you that the highest *Wissenschaft* is history, and the best expert the historian – on condition, I would add, that he is at the same time an anthropologist, a sociologist, and a philosopher. If he has all these virtues and is also a good historian, then he is above the rest. But maybe that is talking about history as it should be written rather than as it is.

DANIEL BELL: I know nobody, within my specific kin, who said that you can predict events. No one makes that claim. One minimises some very simple understandable facts about human society if one just deals with events, on the one hand, or social structure on the other. For example, I will make a prediction which may seem to be a little trivial: in the next five years, there'll be at least one election in England. If you look at the fact that out of 160 nations in the world within the last twenty years, only about thirty have had regular elections, I'm making a prediction statistically very powerful. There is a stability in the institutional life of Great Britain which permits that kind of prediction.

I am not interested in the long-range predictions because they tend to be of a very general nature and involve usually a philosophy of history. Indeed, I could play the game of Tocqueville, Burckhardt or Weber, on a methodological principle. I would make a prediction, for example, that within the next twenty-five years you will have a considerable further decentralisation in the Soviet system. (I make it on a sociological proposition that you cannot organise a complex society on the basis of a simple command economy.) Or, that after the death of Mao, there will be in China a greater return to bureaucratisation and the rise of a more rationalised type of society. (Again on the basis of a theoretical proposition that a large-scale complex society cannot be organised on the basis of enthusiasm.) I will make the prediction that, in the twenty-first century, colour may become the most important political problem because of the gap between rich and poor nations. And I would say that in the twenty-first century the major political confrontation probably will be between Japan and China. But I'm not interested, as I say, in making such predictions because I think it's a mug's game. What interests me is to identify problems, constraints, and alternatives, even if I don't know which alternative will be chosen. This derives from an image of a society based upon a hypothetical-deductive model, in my case of the post-industrial society, which is relatively short-run, I mean here fifteen or twenty years. For example, I will make two kinds of forecasts along this way. I will predict decreasing productivity in most of the Western societies because of the expansion of tertiary sectors, and this raises the problem of the standard of living. I predict a continued demand for women's rights, not simply because women are now fundamentally more aggressive than before, on a basis of some kind of ideological tremor, but because there is a change in the social position of women which for the first time gives them a platform to make these kinds of demands. I would say that the Women's Liberation Movement has a substantial basis and a continuing interest which the Youth Movement has not.

These are not predictions of events, in Mr. Trevor-Roper's sense, but predictions based upon changing patterns of a social structure.

HUGH TREVOR-ROPER: Mr. Bell predicts that in Great Britain in the next five years there will be a general election; he is just predicting that the British Constitution will last for another five years.

DANIEL BELL: Exactly. In some countries they obey the law and in some they don't.

HUGH TREVOR-ROPER: I'm not going to dispute that. You make distinctions between predictions of events and predictions which I understand to be based on a sociological scientific basis. I cannot make this distinction between events and social structure. The rise of Christianity in the Roman Empire and then in Europe has been regarded by every writer since Gibbon as being a social revolution. It was also, I believe, unpredictable. Anyway, those predictions which are alleged to be sociologically based seem to me predictions which anyone could have made without having the benefit of the science of futurology. Any historian might predict that there would be a decrease of productivity in Western society without this new science.

DANIEL BELL: I'm not saying that I'm reading entrails in any respect but simply that I can give a better reason why I make that prediction. A lot of people can predict the weather to some extent on the basis of their bones and rheumatism. They may not have reasons for understanding the general movements of clouds in this way.

ROBERT NISBET: I would like to say once again that it is difficult for me to see the impact of either psychology, anthropology, sociology or economics upon the strict discipline of historiography before the First World War.

Besides, does Mr. Trevor-Roper think that history is peculiarly fitted, in a way that sociology is not, for such ventures into the future, or does he really think that history, like other disciplines, should leave futurology all alone? It is also important to ask whether his skepticism on futurology rests upon a belief that the present did not lie in the past, and that the future does not lie in the present, or whether it is rooted in a surmise that the intellectual faculties of human beings will never be able to make these predictions. As for Burckhardt, who indeed made impressive predictions, he tells us in his letters that it was not in his role as a historian but as a reader of the philosophical conservations and in relation to his own moral philosophy that he slipped into pessimism.

Finally, I was pleased, but somewhat thunderstruck, to hear a historian in the year 1971 speaking of historical method as being irremediably empirical. I dare say the magnificent work of the philosopher F. H. Bradley, *The Presuppositions of a Critical History*, written some three-quarters of a century ago, made it clear once and for all that the historian is not an irremediable empiricist, for he is dealing with the facts within a genealogical framework, which is in itself a profound conclusion.

HUGH TREVOR-ROPER: In the nineteenth century, the most profound influence on historical study was, I believe, the writings of Sir Walter Scott. Even Ranke admitted that in his historical studies he was bowled over by them. Mr. Nisbet said that Freud had no influence. But Sir Louis Namier had this statement: "It is not Marx, it is Freud who enables us to understand history." To analyse the motives which made men go into an English Parliament in the eighteenth century, for instance, it was not enough to study their public statements in Parliament as had been done before: one had to use the Freudian discovery of the subconscious and look beyond these publicly avowed reasons. And considering that there are Marxist historians in the world who are presumably influenced by Marx (who was not primarily a historian), I'm staggered by Professor Nisbet's statement.

Are historians better than sociologists at prophesying? I must admit that they prophesy a great deal less. They are much more cautious. Historians have seen the working out of events, the change of social structures, the coming of revolutions over a very long period in time; they don't start their studies in 1900 and therefore they are to that extent more chary. Mr. Nisbet said that Burckhardt made his interesting pro-phecies as a pessimist, not as a historian. I can't divide the human mind to this extent. If a man is a historian, he uses his historical experience even when he may be expressing himself as a pessimist. As for Mr. Nisbet's last point about history being irremediably empirical, I'm afraid that is just what I believe. I do not think that any useful historical understanding was provided by F. H. Bradley.

PETER WILES: I believe that futurology as prediction of the predictable future is a very useful activity. We should not make people shy because they like to practice it. In fact we want to know what the political future will be.

I think that Professor Trevor-Roper has been very unfair to futurology in saying: "Could Tacitus have predicted the victory of Christianity?" It is the most unhistorical question on your part because the victory of Christianity was – am I not right? – two centuries away at that point of time. You are just demanding too much.

DANIEL BELL: Futurology should obviously be a cooperative effort. It should include economists, science-fiction people, who for some reason have been excluded from the Commission on the Year 2000; it should certainly include poets, like Heine, novelists such as Dostoevsky and surely historians such as Trevor-Roper.

WOLFGANG J. MOMMSEN: I think the role of Burckhardt as a futurologist should be explored. It seems to me impossible to believe that Burckhardt's prediction meant that the Bismarckian nationalist state would lead straight away to a Fascist dictatorship of the militarist type. His prophecy was formulated in vague, almost empty, formulas; you can easily read into it afterwards what you feel yourself. As regards Max Weber's famous concept of *bureaucratisation*, I think it works as a very useful hypothesis and as a guideline for the interpretation of modern history just as much as for empirical social studies, but it is no more than that. Weber didn't give any definite time limit, but if you study his work more precisely you will discover that he expected the process of bureaucratisation to go on much faster and the end of a dynamic society like ours to be reached much earlier.

HUGH TREVOR-ROPER: The social scientists – I may do them an injustice – seem to suggest that society has so changed in the last century that if we are to recognise ourselves we had better not go back beyond 1900. We could deduce everything that is likely to happen in industrial or post-industrial society from the facts of industrial society. This is an attitude of mind which I really contest.

Humanity is the unifying force of historical studies. As Marc Bloch wrote in his *Métier d'historien*, the historian is like the ogre, wherever he smells human flesh there he goes. No school of contemporary historians has so influenced me as the *Annales* as represented by Marc Bloch, Lucien Febvre and Fernand Braudel. Nevertheless, I think that there is a moment when the *Ecole des Annales* seems to have forgotten the remark of Marc Bloch. The emphasis on quantitative history, on the subordination of man to the dogma of economic fact and statistical tables, has perhaps gone too far. The essential centre of history is man. What is history? Is it the luxury of rich nations, or has it a function? Of course, in a sense, it is a luxury of rich nations. When one walks through life, one is surrounded by the deposit of history. I object to those who refuse to recognise this. The first objection is almost a moral one: I find it insufferably arrogant to assume that we owe nothing to the past, that the genius and labour of the past can all be taken for granted, that we have an absolute right to the inheritance. Another reason is that it is so much more interesting, when one walks through life, to be able to recognise things, to distinguish the architecture of a period from the one of another, to identify a deposit left by certain precise social or political circumstances, not just to walk through as one might through a picture gallery if one didn't know the difference between a primitive and a Goya. I realise that people can answer me there: "This is a very complacent attitude; this is decorative learning; you enjoy being educated and superior." There may be perhaps some grain of truth in that, and it is not on this basis that I would attempt to defend the teaching of history over many centuries. More profoundly, it has to be continued if we want to understand man, to become tolerant, to distinguish truth and falsehood, to recognise that ideas which are heretical at one time can become truth at another. The whole concept of the relativity of human behaviour is illustrated in history.

ALAN BULLOCK: I might go back to the original issue which was bothering me when we first threw this off in discussion. I was concerned with a situation in which young people coming to University seemed less inclined to accept history as a relevant or necessary part of the discipline of human discovery and saw history as being superseded by the social sciences. The dimension in which the social sciences incontestably have their strongest claim is in our understanding of the present. Historians, even contemporary ones, would not venture within a certain area of the present; the older school of historians thought that history stopped a long time ago. It was inevitable, especially as the impact of change became more marked in all our lives, that certain disciplines should develop in an attempt to describe and then to understand what was going on. This seems to me the great work of social science; there is a vast amount which social science has added to our stock of human knowledge by its observation and attempted analysis and interpretation of what is going on around us. What worries me is that, if you confine yourself entirely to the present, you heighten the sense of its uniqueness. The historian, who is slow in moving, takes a longer perspective and is perhaps more inclined to be skeptical about the uniqueness of a period. This is a most valuable corrective to a study which is wholly concentrated upon the present.

Social science, like history, has an empirical subject, is concerned with what it can observe, with hypotheses which it throws up. But back of it is always the belief that this is only the first stage in the development of the social sciences along the line of the natural sciences, and that one day we shall, by developing these methods, be able to provide a shortcut which will no longer require examination by reference to events because we shall have a model which is not just a hypothesis but will provide us with a sure, safe shortcut to our understanding of the present. However much the social scientists, when we discuss with them, say to us: "This is an empirical study and our models are only to be taken as hypotheses and so on," this is misunderstood by many people, especially amongst the young, who believe that the study of social science can in the end supersede history.

RAYMOND ARON: Like Professor Trevor-Roper, I am convinced that historical knowledge is an indispensable element in any culture worthy of the name because it is an indispensable instrument of the knowledge of man by man, or of the knowledge by man of his own extraordinary diversity. What is new and perhaps unique in our situation is that we experience this diversity without knowing "if there is a good life and what it is." Never have societies been so powerful, so proud of their power, and yet so unconscious of their aims.

7 New historical method

FRANÇOIS FURET

History and primitive man

In the so-called classical age in Europe, history and ethnology emerged
as two disciplines at once related and opposed, their interconnections
deriving from two parent categories: For while both contributed towards
the description of the human universe, history scanned space, ethnology
time. In bibliographies drawn up in Europe at the time of Bacon, travel
books, with their descriptions of foreign, and in particular exotic, lands,
are classified as a sub-section of "history". A traveller who told of the
customs of distant peoples was not merely exploiting the picturesqueness
of the difference between them and his readers: He was bringing back
from contemporary space an image of the past. The primitive was the
infancy of the civilised. Two basically different ways of looking at man
were thus brought together.

Perhaps it is too much to say they were actually brought together.
Ethnology and history were already separated by the idea of nationality,
which played a decisive part in the shaping – and in the isolation – of
history as a branch of knowledge. The process began in the sixteenth
century, with the secularisation of time in relation to the old apocalyptic
chronology of the four kingdoms, which according to the prophet David
were to follow one another in order of decreasing degeneracy. In this
context the Roman Empire was the interminably prolonged end of human
history, surviving on into the Holy Roman Empire of medieval Christendom. But the Old Testament account yielded first to the pressure of
humanism, then to Protestantism, and finally to the rise of the nation
state. Humanist philosophy was too fascinated by antiquity to have room
for a historicist view of the past, but at least it laid down the intellectual
foundations for it by inventing scholarship and distinguishing between
"true" history and "fable". Religious schism distorted the meaning of the

scriptures, ousting their account of the Beginning as well as their prediction of the End. But if the deciphering of the past parted company from
the Church and the apocalypse, it was only to project onto the State instead its sense of irreversibility and its obsession with origins. At the same
time as it became secular, history became national. France presents clear
examples in Jean Bodin, Le Popelinière and Pasquier: It was in reaction
against "Italian" humanism, conceived of as a two-fold Roman imperialism
owing allegiance both to antiquity and to the Pope, that the French jurists
founded the Gallican school of history, with the object of justifying the
power of the king, especially against the extremists of the *Ligue*.[1]

So from the sixteenth century to the Enlightenment, history – secular
history, since sacred history was kept carefully distinct – was above all the
history of nations, *i.e.*, of the peoples and states of Europe. Even Voltaire,
who tried to go beyond this restricted view of things, makes implicit
reference in his universal history to the State of Louis XIV, the culminat-
ing point of civilisation. The nation-state marked human progress; the
new subject of anthropology was restricted to primitive groups.

Thus also in the eighteenth century when the description of "primitive"
peoples became a more or less systematic branch of learning, the study of
them in time was accorded the dignity of a scale of values, but not the
study of them in geographical space. The national groups explored by the
historian were seen as what those described by the traveller ought to be.

The nineteenth century probably increased the antagonism between the
two disciplines by doing away with their complementary. The imaginary
line through time and space joining the two universal figures, man in his
infancy and man the adult, primitive society and civilised society, was
broken and superseded by the rise of the indefinable and the particular:
The nation-state ceased to represent the collective progress of mankind
and became the battleground *par excellence* of the antagonisms and differences between man. History, instead of having a fixed frame of reference
showing the stages of human development, was torn by conflicting claims
and a balance of forces perpetually changing. The ideology of progress
somewhat hastily extrapolated from human activities in general the ex-
ceptional rhythms of economic change and turned time into a kind of
indefinite drift subject to the pull of competing nationalisms. Progress
became a means to and an object of power, an area in which the various
national histories confronted one another. Henceforward history concerned only a few countries – those which produced, those which changed;

in other words, those that mattered. The rest of human space was relegated to historical non-existence, and travel incidentally lost its bibliographical and scientific status. Ethnology developed as a kind of subsidiary science, defined negatively, by what was not included in European or North American history. That it was regarded as something minor and secondary, a vague by-product of European expansion, a mixture of blindness and guilty conscience, may be seen not only in the works of the great liberal economists and historians of the nineteenth century, but also in the strange European-centredness of Marx. The historian having transformed the exception into a model, ethnology was left to reign over the reverse of history, a field at once vast and marginal. It became the separate domain of the unwritten as against the written, the unmoving as against change, the primitive as against progress.

The dichotomy has continued into our own day in which it has become more and more untenable. It has been seriously challenged by two series of contemporary events, one external and the other due to the evolution of the social sciences themselves.

The idea of progress has been called in question by many major events in contemporary history. Neither the Hitlerite nightmare, nor the transformation of the Russian Revolution into a bureaucratic and ideological Terror, fits easily into a picture of the human race marching steadily towards reason and liberty. Although the power of man over nature is now growing at an unprecedented rate, there are also an increasing number of insoluble problems, historical dead-ends, and outbursts of social violence. Technical and economic progress is accompanied by political unreason and universal disorder. This throws doubt on the idea of a comprehensive history in which development takes place at all levels at the same pace and according to one dimension of time. A major factor in the abolition of the traditional opposition between ethnology and history is probably the fact that human space has become homogeneous at the same moment as time has ceased to be so.

Human space has not only been explored, inventoried, covered. In the last few decades it has also been, largely because of decolonialisation, taken over by the idea of nationalism – by the irresistible extension of the European political model.

So the whole world has been promoted to the dignity of having a national history, and the countries of what for economic reasons we call the Third World are all feverishly examining and exalting their own origins, hoping to find in them their identity. They have stopped thinking of themselves as set apart in space in order to assert their difference in terms of history. When the West tries to resist this levelling, the only clear distinction it can offer is one taken from economic history, such as Rostow's take-off. This is perhaps no more than a devious way for the West to put itself forward once more as an example: In a linear pattern such as that proposed, "post-industrial" society becomes the direction in which mankind is moving. This does at least bring the whole of mankind back into history.

So space is historicised but at the cost of splitting up time. For history, as it becomes less European-centred and includes the whole of humanity, comes up against the ethnological challenge of the plurality of societies and cultures. This undermines the notion of a homogeneous time: Not only do different societies evolve at different rhythms, but even within one society the constituent levels of reality do not all obey one general homogeneous temporality. "Change" has become a concept measurable, in its various aspects, in economic terms; but it has also brought to light instances of resistance to change. "Take-off", "modernisation", the universalisation of material progress and economic growth are thought of as being the basic direction of contemporary history, but they come into conflict with tradition, legacies from the past, the whole complex of socio-cultural inertias. So, by stretching out to cover the whole of the human world, history discovers itself to be non-history also: Change reveals the unchanging. The great nineteenth-century school of history, Manchester and Marxist, assuming a general progress based on economic development, thus finds itself doubly called in question: By the crises of the contemporary world, and by the extension of its own hypotheses outside Europe. It is not surprising that history should simultaneously try to save its imperialism as being the medium of "modernisation" and turn once more to ethnology to remedy some of its own defects. A second, perhaps less obvious, set of modifications in the relations between history and ethnology arises from history's own evolution as a branch of learning in the last thirty or forty years. I refer to what is called in France, rather vaguely and negatively, the replacement of "narrative" by "non-narrative" history.

It is worth trying to define these terms, setting aside the fruitless controversy to which they have given rise. "Narrative" history seems to me to be at once a type of description of the past and a type of selection of facts. Based on the desire to reconstruct "what happened" and then to relate it by means of a story, it chooses its materials accordingly. In other words, the famous "events" are selected and organised along a time axis in such a way as to foster the development of a story. That being so, the event contains the change, and the chain of events is designed to give a meaning to the succession of changes. This is why this type of history is characterised simultaneously, though contradictorily, by the short term and by teleology: As an event, which is the sudden irruption of the unique and the new into the concatenation of time, cannot be compared with anything that precedes it, the only way to incorporate it into history is to endow it with a finality. And since history has come to be a way of interiorising and conceptualising the idea of progress, the "event" is usually a stage in the advent of something, whether that something be a republic, liberty, democracy or reason. The historical "fact" may be reconstructed with infinite patience according to the strictest rules of scholarship, but it still derives its meaning only from a general history arrived at quite separately and independently. Time, in this kind of history, is made up of a series of discontinuities described as if they were continuous: The classic definition of a story.

"Non-narrative" history rejects the story – at least in this literary form – insofar as it begins by defining problems. It has made important borrowings from contemporary social sciences (demography, geography, sociology, etc.) and revived historical curiosity by making it specific. Its first move is to break down the different levels of historical reality, retaining only one, or a group, and describing that as systematically as possible, *i.e.*, in isolation. That is why the historical "facts" it constructs are different in two ways from those of "narrative" history: First, they usually have nothing to do with the traditional field of great political change, and second, they are selected not for their uniqueness but for their comparability with other facts that precede and follow them. A "fact" is no longer an event chosen because it marks a high point in a history whose "meaning" has been established beforehand; it is a phenomenon selected and construed in terms of the repetitive nature that makes it comparable with others over a given area of time. Documents, "facts", exist no longer for their own sake but in relation to the series which precedes and follows them: It is their relative value which becomes objective instead of their relation to some indefinable "reality". The result is a renovation both of historical curiosity and of historical method. The raw material of history is now by definition so diverse that the historian can use it according to his own preference and ability – as an economist, a demographer, a sociologist, an ethnologist, or a linguist.

But every methodology has its faults. The sort of historian we have been speaking of changes the nature of the problems regarded as traditional to history. But this methodology cannot deal with the unique and the non-comparable, and the expert in intellectual biography cannot be accommodated by it. The same is true of the historian of antiquity, who lacks and probably always will lack the series of data necessary for systematic quantification. But, more than this, history based on serial data accords a privileged position to a certain type of source, a certain type of problem, and above all a certain type of time. Its sources must be either numerical or reducible to homogeneous and comparable units. This at once restricts and extends the field: For while the "hapax" is no longer usable, a part of the vast mass of the unwritten, hitherto used so cautiously, can be organised into series. Iconography, aerial photographs, to name only two examples, can provide historical evidence more weighty than that of the eternal writings of the eternal eye-witness. It is also natural that these kinds of sources should lend themselves to researches and hypotheses which are economic or ethnological rather than actually political, since they imply the equalisation of individuals in terms of their roles as economic or socio-cultural agents. In this way, through a misunderstanding, a kind of history which aimed at being more "scientific" intersected another which aimed at being more "democratic", the latter wishing to rehabilitate the anonymous "little man" hitherto crowded out by the great political heroes who could never have existed without him.

Serial history is a history of the long term, as has been demonstrated above all by Fernand Braudel in his books and in one epoch-making article. Serial history is made up of the description of repetitions and regularities and is only worthwhile when it brings out developments long enough to indicate trends and dimensions. Is the growth of the agrarian economy in the first two-thirds of the sixteenth century shown up by various different indicators, a definite take-off, or merely the recovery from the great crisis which lasted from 1350 to 1450? The only way we can answer that question is by analysing a longer period covering before and after. Thus the choice of identical indicators over a long period of time enables the historian to identify the different periodicities – brief crises and longer recessions, cycles and trends – and to incorporate them into a general interpretation. But at the same time it gives preference to the conservative elements in any system rather than to the factors affecting qualitative change. A historian belonging to this school rediscovers the long economic states of permanence and the social and cultural inertias which have long characterised the societies of the ethnologist: To use Lévi-Strauss's expression, he too now has his "cold societies".

Ethnology might draw up an inventory of history's borrowings in which the first column would list the methodological changes – the systematic use of unwritten sources; the growing use, in the case of written documents, of statistical or pre-statistical evidence; "structural" textual analysis, whether on a linguistic or psychoanalytical model, or one derived from content analysis. The second column would list history's new subjects of interest: Anonymous man instead of great men; non-development instead of change; the rudiments of culture instead of "great" literature and so on. The inventory would in fact cover the major part of contemporary historiography, in France and elsewhere.

The line dividing history and ethnology has never really been based on epistemological criteria but rather on the external conditions governing the development of the two branches of knowledge and on a sort of custom separating two academic finds. Now, like so many others, this distinction is fading, though the new set of relationships is no easier to define than the old disciplines they replace.

NOTE

1. See especially Kelly, *Foundations of Modern Historical Scholarship*, New York, Columbia University Press, 1970.

The historian and the common man

JACQUES LE GOFF

History and ethnology became separate subjects only in the middle of the nineteenth century, when, even before Darwin, the advance of evolutionism had separated the study of advanced societies from that of so-called primitive ones. Until then history had included all societies, though wherever there was a sense of progress, history was restricted to the sections of mankind that were capable of rapid change. The rest were relegated either to *mirabilia* in which primitive men were bracketed with monsters; to travellers' tales in which the natives were just one variety of animal life; at best to geography, in which men were a mere element in the landscape; or at worst to oblivion.

Herodotus, the "father of history", is also the father of ethnography. The second book of his *Histories*, for which he chose Euterpe as patron, is about Egypt. The first half is the work of an ethnologist not content with merely describing manners and customs; it also points out what the Greeks borrowed from the Egyptians, thus showing that the Hellenes were not completely uninfluenced by the Barbarians. The second part of the book is written by a diachronical historian who traces the dynasties one after the other, often reducing history to no more than a collection of anecdotes.

The ethnographical view takes on a different aspect in Tacitus. Foreshadowing Rousseau, he contrasts the corruption of civilisation, of which Rome is the prime example, with the wholesomeness of "noble savages" like the Bretons and the Germans. Here is his description of his father-in-law Agricola's attempts to civilise the former:

> To accustom these men, scattered and ignorant and therefore prone to war, to the pleasures of tranquillity and peace, he encouraged them privately and helped them officially to build temples, markets

and houses, praising the most active and reproaching those who hung back... And he had the children of the leading citizens instructed in the liberal arts... so that those who recently would have none even of the Romans' language might now aspire to their eloquence. Hence even our clothes came into favour, and the toga became the fashion; and gradually they slipped into the trappings of vice – porticoes, public baths, elegant banquets. The naïve called all this civilisation: it was really but an aspect of servitude.

Yet even here Roman history tended to crowd out other nations from the historical writings of the later Empire. The Christians inherited this prejudice. Salvianus, in the middle of the fifth century, was practically the only one to think and say that the simple but honest Barbarians were better than the sinful Romans.

And then only the Christians had a right to history. Pagans were excluded – and not only pagans proper, but also "infidels", and, at least at first, peasants. True, for a long while the prevailing notion was not of progress but of decline. *Mundus senescit* – the world grows old. Mankind had entered in life's sixth and last phase: Old age. But even this progress in reverse was another unilinear process favouring societies which changed, even though the change was for the worse. And when medieval Christianity annexed pagan antiquity, it was only to extol the singular merits of the Roman Empire and draw a new line of progress from Rome to Jerusalem. As Augustin Renaudet observed, Dante "proudly repeats old Anchises' prophecy: *Tu regere imperio populos, Romane, memento.*" Virgil and the Sybil foretell Christ according to a teleology which leaves out of the advance towards salvation all who are not the heirs of Rome.

Yet the universality of Christianity's claim was in principle favourable to ethnology. As all history was universal history, all nations were called to belong to it, even though in fact the only peoples who were interesting were those which changed quickly.

Sometimes a medieval clerk would mix time and place, history and geography, and be an ethnologist without knowing it. Gervais of Tilbury's *Otia Imperialia*, a collection of *mirabilia* made for the Emperor Otto of Brunswick (ca. 1212), begins by tracing the history of man, according to Genesis, up to the Flood, but then goes on first to a ragbag of geographical, historical and ethnographical observations, then to an account of rites, legends and miracles found in the various places where the author had lived: England, the Kingdom of the Two Sicilies, and Provence.

The Middle Ages also prepared all that was necessary to pave the way for a "noble savage": a millenarianism, which expected the return of the golden age, and a belief that historical progress, if it existed, was made up of rebirths, returns to an innocent primitivism. But the men of the Middle Ages lacked a content to give substance to this myth. Some looked to the East: The belief in Prester John helped them to work out an anthropological model in the form of the "pious Brahmin". But Marco Polo was not taken seriously. Others discovered the "wild man" or "*homme sauvage*" and turned Merlin into a hermit. Then suddenly the discovery of America provided Europe with "noble savages".

The Renaissance kept up both lines and both attitudes. On the one hand, "official" history concerned itself with political progress, that of princes and cities, the two rising forces being royal bureaucracy and the urban bourgeoisie, both of which sought their justification in history. On the other hand, the curiosity of scholars led them to explore the field of ethnography. The literary genius and erudition of Rabelais, to take one example, exercised themselves in an imaginary ethnography which was nonetheless close, very often, to its peasant inspiration. As George Huppert has said:

> There are certainly other epochs, less fortunate in this respect than antiquity, whose history had not been written. The Turks or the Americans, lacking a literary tradition of their own, certainly presented an inviting target for a modern Herodotus.

They were waiting for Herodotus, but it was Livy who came. Etienne Pasquier's *Researches* made him the ethnographer of the past and laid down the "origins" of that science.

But the coexistence of historian and ethnographer was not to last. The rationalism of the classical age, followed by that of the Enlightenment, was to restrict history to nations enamoured of progress. R. C. Collingwood was right when he said: "In the sense in which Gibbon and Mommsen were historians, there was no such thing as a historian before the eighteenth century."

Now, after a divorce of over two centuries, historians and ethnologists are beginning to draw closer again. The new history, at first sociological, tends to become ethnological. What, then, does the ethnological point of view reveal to the historian about history?

In the first place, ethnology modifies the chronological perspectives of history. It leads to a sweeping rejection of the event, and thus to the ideal of a non-narrative history. More precisely, it puts forward a history made up of repeated or expected events, feast-days of the religious calendar, events linked to biological and family history – birth, marriage and death.

It makes it necessary to distinguish between the different times in history, and to give special attention to the sphere of the long term, to that almost motionless time described in Fernand Braudel's celebrated article.

The historian who looks with an ethnological eye on the societies he studies has a better understanding of the "liturgical" element in a historical society. A study of the "calendar" in its secularised and vestigial forms (very visible in industrial societies in the way Christianity took over the ancient religious cycles of Easter and Christmas, the seven-day week, etc.), or in such modern forms as the calendar of sporting events, reveals the surviving influence of ancestral rites and periodic rhythms on so-called advanced societies. But here more than ever we see the necessity for the historical and the ethnological points of view to work together. A "historical" examination of feasts might throw definitive light on the structures and transformations of societies, especially those called "transitional," such as the perhaps rightly named Middle Ages. A study of that kind would enable us to follow the evolution of the carnival as feast and psychodrama of the urban community, coming into being in the late Middle Ages and fading out in the nineteenth and twentieth centuries under the impact of the industrial revolution.

Emmanuel Le Roy Ladurie has made a brilliant analysis of the bloody Carnival at Romans in 1580 – "a tragedy-*cum*-ballet, in which the participants acted and danced their revolt instead of setting it out at length in manifestoes." But that year the annual game was transformed into a unique event. The significance of a feast is usually to be seen through the rite rather than through the act itself. Louis Dumont has shown, in an exemplary study of the ceremonies of the Tarasque, the magical and religious meaning of the rites by which the people of Tarascon, from the thirteenth to the eighteenth centuries, tried to win the good will of an ambiguous monster which had become the "eponymous beast," the "palladium of the community." "The chief feast at Whitsun," says M. Dumont, "linked this figure to the great local parade of the guilds." There is a parallel to this in London, at least since the sixteenth century, where the floats in the Lord Mayor's procession were got up by the various corporations. Thus, in an urban society, new social groups play a similar role in community rites to that played by the young in traditional rural societies, a transformation which brings us down to the majorettes and the hippy festivals of today. Liturgy and feasts are to be found in every society; are they especially linked to archaic or primitive societies? Evans-Pritchard seems to think so: "An anthropological training, including field work, would be especially valuable in the investigations of earlier periods of history in which institutions and modes of thought resemble in many respects those of the simpler peoples we study." But were the men of the Western Middle Ages – Evans-Pritchard stops at the Carolingian era – primitive? And are we not primitive, too, with our strange sects and horoscopes and flying saucers and pools? Can medieval society be described as a liturgical and ludic society?

As against the historian of volatile societies, of urban men swept by fashion, the ethnologist will urge the claim of the fabric that binds history together – the conservative rural societies (though these, as Marc Bloch pointed out, are not so conservative as has been thought). Hence has come about a ruralisation of history. Perhaps, as a medievalist, I may be allowed to cite some examples from my own period. To the urban and bourgeois Middle Ages proposed by nineteenth-century historians, from Augustin Thierry to Henri Pirenne, have succeeded what seem to me to be the truer, rural Middle Ages of Marc Bloch, Michael Postan, Léopold Génicot, and Georges Duby.

After this conversion to the common man, historical ethnology leads naturally to the study of states of mind, mental outlooks, considered as "that which changes least" in historical evolution. Thus, in the very heart of industrial societies, the primitive rears its head as soon as one examines collective psychology and behaviour. This difference of mental phase forces the historian to become an ethnologist. But the mental elements concerned are not lost in the mists of time. Mental systems are historically datable, even though they bear the flotsam of archaeo-civilisations beloved of André Varagnac.

So ethnology leads the historian to bring out certain social structures more or less obliterated in "historical" societies, and to make his vision more complex by taking in the social dynamic, the class struggle.

The notions of class, group, category, stratum, etc., need to be reconsidered after the insertion, into the social structure and its workings, of fundamental realities and concepts which have been thrust aside by post-Marxist sociology:

a) The family, and kinship structures. The introduction of these into the historian's *problématique* could lead, for example, to a new periodisation of European history in terms of the evolution of family structures. Thus, Pierre Chaunu and the Centre for Quantitative Historical Research at Caen define the great unchanging datum in the dialectic between man and space as "the existence of *communities of residents* (which coincide only 80% with parishes)" from the twelfth and thirteenth centuries to the end of the eighteenth, throughout that traditional peasant civilisation, all of a piece, existing in the long term. An ethnological as well as legal study of lineage and the community, of the extended and the nuclear family, should revitalise the foundations of comparative studies of yesterday and today, Europe and the other continents, especially with reference to such subjects as feudalism.

b) The sexes. A study of this subject should lead to the de-masculinisation of history. How many roads in Western medieval history alone lead to woman! In many respects, the history of heresy is that of woman in society and in religion. And if the Middle Ages can be credited with anything new in sensibility, it is courtly love, constructed around the image of a woman. When he sought to identify the spirit of the Middle Ages, Michelet, who always seized the essential, lit on the diabolical beauty of the witch, and the lowly and therefore divine purity of Joan of Arc. And who will find out the truth about the most important phenomenon in the "spiritual" (in Michelin's sense) history of the Middle Ages – the astonishing rise of the cult of the Virgin in the twelfth century?

c) Class, and the village communities. Marc Bloch recognised the importance of these in medieval Christendom, and the Marxists continued an analysis which, if it could be freed of dogmatism, would help to renew social history. And here we see one of the possible – and paradoxical – consequences of an ethnological regeneration of the *problématique* of history. In the past, history was content with an episodic and fictionalised evocation of events linked to certain classic structures in "historical" societies, as for example those of the Middle Ages. But the history of the feudal wars needs to be revised in the light of a study of private war and vendetta. This history of family, urban and dynastic factions also needs to be revised in the same light: Removed from the anecdotage of narrative history, from which they were among the worst sufferers, Guelphs and

Ghibellines, Montagues and Capulets, Armagnacs and Burgundians, Yorkists and Lancastrians, could be restored to relevance and scientific dignity in a comparative ethnological history.

Ethnological history also involves a revaluation of the role in history of magical elements, charismas.

First, dynastic charismas. The recognition of these would make it possible, for example, to "rehabilitate" feudal monarchy, which has long been regarded as being of a different nature from all other institutions. Marc Bloch, with his work on the "*rois thaumaturges*", and Percy Ernst Schramm, with his study of the insignia of power, were pioneers in a line of research which ought to aim at the very centre of medieval monarchy instead of its survivals and magical signs. The ethnographical attitude should transform the value of such evidence on divine right in the medieval West as is offered by the life of Robert the Pious of Helgaud, Giraldus Cambrensis's diabolical genealogy of the Plantagenets, and Charles the Bold's attempt to break through this magic barrier.

Then there are professional and occupational charismas. To remain in the Middle Ages, one thinks here of the prestige, from the fifth century on, of the smith and the goldsmith, whose magical image was recorded in the sagas and the *chansons de geste*. The recent discovery in Normandy of the extraordinary tomb 10 in the Merovingian cemetery at Hérouvillette has revived the magical craftsman of the Early Middle Ages, buried with the arms of the aristocratic warrior and with the mechanic's tool-bag, and whose place in society can only be understood through a combination of the study of technology, sociological analysis, and ethnography. And we ought to trace, in our own societies, the evolution of the doctor and the surgeon, both heirs of the sorcerer. The "intellectuals" of the Middle Ages, the academics, cornered the charismatic paraphernalia which the "mandarins" have made good use of right down to our own day: the professorial chair, the gown, the vellum document – all signs that are more than signs. By these means the most renowned of the mandarins join the "stars" of society, from the gladiators down to the modern idols. But the wiliest and greatest of the intellectuals, from Abelard to Sartre, have contented themselves with their charismatic power alone, without recourse to signs.

Individual charismas, which enable us to reconsider the role in history of the "great man," not entirely explained by the sociological reduction.

To take yet another example from the Middle Ages, the transition from dynastic to individual charisma is shown by St. Louis, who ceased to be a sacred king only to become a royal saint. Secularisation and canonisation went together; what was gained on the swings was lost on the roundabouts. And one cannot help suspecting how much a study of charismas in history might enlarge our understanding of a phenomenon of the twentieth century which is certainly not a minor one – the cult of personality.

Finally there are all the eschatological beliefs, all the millenarianisms which characterise the return of the supernatural into all sections of societies and civilisations. Far from being confined to archaic or "primitive" societies, these are signs of failure to adapt, or to be resigned, in societies caught up in the ethnological rush. Norman Cohn has described what these apocalyptic waves were like in the Middle Ages and the Renaissance. The success today of religious sectarianism, astrology and betting shows the permanence, in precise historical situations, of those who make "*il gran rifiuto*." While François Furet dealt mainly with the "uncivilised" aspect of history looked at from the ethnological point of view, I place the emphasis mainly on the common man.

What ethnology brings to history is first and foremost a higher evaluation of material civilisation or culture, though historians have been somewhat cautious about this. In Poland, for example, where enormous strides have been made in this field since 1945, encouraged by national and "materialist" motives, not to mention epistemological misunderstandings, hard-line Marxists have feared that material inertia might encroach on the social dynamic. In the West, the great work of Fernand Braudel, *Civilisation matérielle et capitalisme (XIVe-XVIIIe siècle)* did not allow the new point of view to operate in the field of history without submitting it to the specifically historical phenomenon of capitalism.

Out of all this vast new sphere for the curiosity and imagination of the historian, I should like to select three points:

1. The emphasis on techniques. Here the most interesting question is the way in which ethnology obliges the historian to reconsider the ideas of invention and the inventor. Marc Bloch began to approach the problem in relation to medieval "inventions." Here again we find, to use the terminology of Lévi-Strauss, the contrast between hot and cold societies, or rather between hot and cold areas within one society. The debate about the building of Milan Cathedral in the fourteenth century, with its conflict between architects and masons, brought out the opposition between science

and technique. "*Ars sine scientia nihil est*," said the learned French architects. "*Scientia sine arte nihil est*," replied the Lombard masons, equally learned in another system. Interest in this aspect of things has begun to call forth a history of substances and raw materials, even humble ones like salt and wood.

2. The entry of the body into history. Michelet had called for this in the 1869 preface to his *History of France*, deploring the fact that history took too little interest in food and many other physical and physiological circumstances. His wish is now beginning to be fulfilled. In the case of this history of food, this is largely due to such periodicals and centres of research as the *Annales-Economies, Sociétés, Civilisations*, of which Fernand Braudel is co-director; the *Zeitschrift für Agrargeschichte und Agrasoziologie*, under Wilhelm Abel at Göttingen; and the *Afdeling Agrarische Geschiedenis* under Slicher van Bath at the Landbouwhogeschool at Wageningen.

Biological history is also making a beginning. A special number of the *Annales-ESC* in 1970 indicates lines to be followed, and François Jacob's great book, *La logique du vivant*, the history of heredity by a biologist turned historian, shows how the rapprochement can be arrived at from both sides.

To return to the ethnological field proper, it is to be hoped that historians will pursue the path which Marcel Mauss pioneered in his famous article on *the techniques of the body*; a knowledge of these, put into a historical perspective, could be decisive for the description and differentiation of societies and civilisations.

3. Housing and clothing should provide the ethnological historian with an excellent example of dialogue between immobility and change. The essential problems of taste and fashion can only be treated by means of interdisciplinary collaboration, bringing in not only the historian and the ethnologist but also the aesthetician, the semiologist, and the art historian. Here again researches like those of Françoise Piponnier and Jacques Heers show the historians' readiness to root their work in the already proven richness of economic and social history.

4. Finally, historians and ethnologists ought to get together to study the phenomenon which is cardinal to them both: Tradition. Particularly enlightening among recent studies here is the work of Jean-Michel Guilcher, an ethnologist who is an expert on popular dance.

I shall not dwell on the fact that the ethnological point of view involves a new type of historical documentation. The ethnologist does not despise written records, far from it, but he encounters them so rarely that he has developed methods independent of them.

Here the historian has to stand side by side with the ordinary man, who does not or did not bother with papers, in a universe without texts and without writing.

Here he will encounter first of all archaeology, not the traditional archaelogy of monument and object, closely bound up with the history of art, but the archaeology of everyday, of material existence. This has had much light thrown on it by the excavations of Maurice Beresford in the "lost villages" of England; of Witold Hensel and his team in the ancient Slavic *grody* in Poland; and of French and Polish members of the VIth Section of the École Pratique des Hautes Études in various medieval French villages.

Then there is iconography, but here again it is a question not so much of this history of traditional art, linked to aesthetic forms and ideas, as that of gesture, utilitarian forms, and perishable objects not thought worthy of written record. A beginning has been made with the iconography of material culture, but the equally necessary but difficult iconography of mental outlooks still waits to be called into being, It must be implicitly present though in, for example, the card-indexes of the Department of Art and Archeology of the University of Princeton.

The ethnological historian also comes up against the formidable problems of oral tradition. How is one to seize the oral element in the past? Is oral the same as popular? What has "popular culture" meant in the various historical societies? What have been the relationships between élite and popular culture?

I shall be even briefer on certain self-evident aspects of the influence of ethnology on history.

Ethnology strengthens certain current trends in history. For example, it suggests the generalisation of the comparative and regressive methods and hastens the relinquishing of the European-centred point of view.

I shall close by stressing the limits to collaboration between ethnology and history, with reference to certain problems arising from the relationship between them and certain dangers to the study of historical societies which could arise from the substitution, pure and simple, of an ethnological for a historical point of view.

Special attention needs to be paid to areas and periods in which there has been contact between societies and culture and where one side belongs traditionally to history and the other to ethnology. In other words, the study of *acculturations* should make it possible to distinguish more clearly between the ethnological and the historical. Here the historian will be chiefly concerned with finding out to what degree and on what conditions the vocabulary and method of acculturation between societies can be applied to the study of acculturations within a single society: Between popular and élite culture, regional and national culture, North and South, and so on. And how, in this context, is one to regard the problem of the "two cultures", of hierarchy and struggle between them?

The vocabulary will have to be made more precise, and this may eliminate some misleading comparisons. I suspect that the idea of the *diachronical*, which Claude Lévi-Strauss borrowed from Saussure and Jakobson and introduced with good effect into ethnology, is very different from the idea of the *historical* with which there is a tendency to confuse it, in the hope and belief that it may provide a tool in common between linguistics and the human sciences in general. I wonder myself whether the diachronical worked out by Saussure in order to give back a dynamic dimension to language, which he had turned into an abstract object, does not operate according to abstract transformation systems very different from the evolutionary schemas by which the historian tries to understand the development of concrete societies. In saying this I do not mean to repeat what I take to be a false distinction between ethnology as a science which directly observes living phenomena and history as a science which reconstructs dead ones. All science consists of abstraction, and both the ethnologist and the historian find themselves face to face with the *other* and under the necessity of identifying with him.

Is there not also a danger that the historian-ethnologist, having once erred by favoring that which was rapid and changed, may go to the other extreme and pay too much attention to that which is slow and changes little if at all? There is a risk that he may stick too close to the ethnologist's antitheses between structure and context, structure and event, and come out on the side of structure, when current historical method really needs to go beyond these false dilemmas.

The historian ought rather to take note of a critical attitude towards the idea of the unchanging which is spreading in the human sciences, ethnology included. At a time when ethnology is re-historicising itself, when Georges Balandier is showing that there are no societies without history and that the idea of unchanging societies is an illusion, is it wise for the historian to fling himself into an ethnology outside time? Or, to use Lévi-Strauss's terms, if there are not so much hot and cold societies but rather societies more or less hot or cold, is it legitimate to treat hot societies in the same way as cold ones? And what about those that are "lukewarm"?

While ethnology does help the historian to strip himself of the illusions of linear progress, the problems of evolutionism still remain. To take the neighbouring discipline of pre-history, which also concerns itself with societies without writing, is the historian to go on thinking of it as pre-history, or is it really just history of another kind?

If one stays too close to ethnology, how is one to explain *growth*, an essential phenomenon in the societies studied by the historian and an insidious modern form of progress which needs to be debunked (as Pierre Vilar has done in revealing the ideological presuppositions of Rostovian take-off), but which is nevertheless a reality that must be accounted for?

Moreover, should we not distinguish between several different kinds of ethnology? That which is concerned with Europe may not be the same as those which deal with more or less preserved societies like the Amerindian, the African, and those of the South Seas.

The historian, who is an expert on change, must be careful not to become insensitive to it (in dealing with *transformation*, he will eventually find himself on common ground with the ethnologist, so long as he does not resort to the *diachronical*). His problem is not so much to find a way from the primitive to the historical, or to reduce the historical to the primitive, as to explain the coexistence and the interaction, within one society, of phenomena or groups belonging to different times and different lines of evolution. It is a problem of differences of level and phase. As for the way in which the historian may learn from the ethnologist how to recognise, and to respect, the *other*, this is a lesson ethnology is unfortunately not in the best possible position to teach, since its own current controversies show that the denial and destruction of the *other* is not an activity confined to just one of the human sciences.

GEORGES DUBY

History of systems of values

1. In this connection a study of a more current history would probably have been more enlightening. I specialise in a distant history, that of the medieval West, which has quite a different tempo from that followed by the present trends of our civilization. Above all, its sources permit only a very restricted application of statistical methods, and it therefore has only a limited bearing on an essential point in our discussion: What are the limits and the dangers of extrapolation? So my readers should be warned that my observations and examples will be cautious ones, based on this limited experience.

2. The global history of a civilization results from changes taking place at different stages, at the level of ecology, of demography, of techniques of production and mechanisms of exchange, changes in the distribution of power and in the situation of the decision makers, changes finally in mental attitudes, collective behaviour, and in that vision of the world which governs these attitudes and rules this behaviour. Narrow correlations unite these diverse movements, but each one of them follows its course in a relatively autonomous way, according to a particular pace. One can observe at certain levels, especially in political relations, modifications that are, at times, very rapid. My personal experience urges me to think that the history of systems of value, which constitutes the precise object of this debate, takes no account of abrupt changes.

a) At times this history may be disturbed by phenomena of acculturation. One culture can, at a particular stage of its evolution, find itself dominated, invaded and penetrated by a foreign culture, either by a traumatic effect of a political origin, such as invasion or colonization, or by an insidious infiltrating action, the occurrence of attraction or of conversion, ensuing with unequal vigour, conditioned by unequal stages of development, unequal degrees of seduction of the civilizations thus confronted. But even in this case, modifications always seem slow and partial. Cultures, no matter how primitive they be, react stubbornly to aggression and for some time resist effectively the intrusion of foreign elements.

It is striking, for instance, how slowly Christianity (which is only one element among many borrowed from Roman culture) spread among the tribes brought into closer contact with a less primitive civilization by the great migrations of the Middle Ages. Archeology reveals that Christian symbols penetrated very slowly the tombs of German burial grounds; and pagan beliefs, under the superficial clothing of rites, of gestures and formulas imposed by force on the whole tribe by the converted chieftains, survived for a very long time; the prelates of the eleventh century were still bent on extirpating them; this was not completely accomplished by the end of the Middle Ages, even in the Christian provinces where the Church was firmly established. Furthermore, the latter had been forced to give room to a number of these beliefs, the most tenacious and no doubt the most essential ones, such as the belief in a mysterious survival of the soul of the deceased during the period between the funeral and the resurrection of the dead. Likewise, with the military expansion of western Christianity in the last years of the eleventh century, the scholars who accompanied the warriors discovered, at Toledo, in the Campagna and at Palermo, the staggering riches of Jewish and Greco-Arab science and rushed forward to take advantage of such treasures. However, for many decades the system of values which these intellectuals represented prevented them from borrowing more than a few techniques connected with the art of reasoning, or with the measurement of things, or with the care of the body. Without a doubt, repressive measures emanating from ecclesiastic authorities came very quickly into play to prevent them from also appropriating the philosophic and moral content of the translated works. But these prohibitions were always evaded; the thirteenth century totalitarian Church was unable to prevent reading and commentary of the New Aristotle in any of the great centers of research. And yet the corrosive power of this doctrinal body had not managed, two centuries later, to open any breaches of consequence in the coherence of Christian thought.

b) Movements which cause systems of value to change are slower yet when sheltered from external influence. Tendencies for growth or regression of economic activity (in this field the medievalist has the advantage of being able to observe mechanisms of prolonged stagnation and of recession), themselves closely connected with the graph of demographic curve and with the modification of techniques, naturally determined changes in the ordering of production relations and in the distribution of wealth at the different levels of the social structure. But these changes seemed to have occurred over longer periods of time than the economic transformations that caused them, and one discovers that these delays and slowdowns were in part caused by the weight of ideological factors. In fact these changes were produced within a cultural framework which adapted itself to incorporate them but which was slower to modify its own structure. This cultural framework was in fact constructed on a network of traditions, transmitted from generation to generation under multiple forms by the various education systems and solidly supported by language, rites and social conventions.

To tell the truth, the capacity of resistance to innovation within the various cultural milieux that interpenetrate in the midst of any society differs considerably. Yet, in most of these milieux the strongest inclination by far is toward conservation. The conservative spirit is particularly strong in peasant societies, whose survival long depended on the extremely precarious equilibrium of a coherent mass of agrarian practices, patiently tested, which it seemed foolhardy to upset; their survival depended on rigorous respect for all custom and on a certain wisdom transmitted by the Ancients. But this spirit is no doubt just as strong with all social elites seemingly open to new ideas, new aesthetics and styles, but in fact subconsciously tormented by the fear of less superficial changes that threaten the authority they exercise. More than anywhere else perhaps, this spirit thrived among the clergy, entrusted with safeguarding the concepts and moral precepts on which the influence they exercised and the privileges they enjoyed were based. Furthermore, such resistance was naturally reinforced by a general tendency towards a progressive vulgarisation of cultural models, constructed according to the interests and tastes of the ruling strata. The attraction elicited by these models and their diffusion among the lower ranks of the social structure sustained the vitality of certain mental attitudes and practices and maintained, below the fasade of modernism in which the elite find their satisfaction, a solid layer of traditions which support conservative aspirations.

Nevertheless, the fact of the matter is that these conservative aspirations

were at times thwarted when the more rapid evolution of material structures made fissures in the inner and outer barriers and favoured communication and osmosis, whether through the weakening of the family,
opening out to other cultures, or the loosening of hierarchies. Other more
direct changes affected political structures, as for example when a new
power relationship was connected with a deliberate attempt to modify
educational systems. It was at this stage that a sudden event, such as
war, revolution, institutional change, could prove to be somewhat
disturbing. It is important, therefore, to discern, at the core of any society,
the groups of individuals who, by virtue of their profession or political
position, their age bracket, are less hidebound by traditions and more
likely to oppose them; it is also imperative to measure the power which
these agents of innovation possess effectively. But regardless of their importance or their capacity for subversion, the cultural system opposes a
very structured resistance to their action.

At various junctures of the system, cracks appear leading to the gradual
disintegration and then to the breaking up of the body, but the disintegration is an insidious one: The final collapse comes about only after a very
long period of erosion, and even then indelible vestiges of the past always
persist.

3. In support of these general remarks, let us view a milieu which is
extremely receptive to innovation, that of men of learning who gathered
in Paris at the height of the Middle Ages. Their meeting place was one of
the main crossroads of the world – an urban agglomeration undergoing
continual growth. Its population, more than that of any other city, was
exposed to economic trends and, in the heart of the greatest state in the
West, to the influence of political action. It was also the meeting place of
all those who, from one end of Latin Christendom to the other, were
driven by burning thirst for knowledge. Their occupation, teaching, in
itself for a great part steeped in routine, was even more so at that time,
since it was aimed to form eminent members of the clergy. Nevertheless,
teachers were brought face to face with younger people whose demands
urged them onward (a case expressed very clearly by one of these teachers,
Abelard: "My students demanded human and philosophical reasons;
they had to have intelligible explanations more than just affirmations").
Finally, it was a pedagogy based on dialogue, debate, free discussion, on a
competitive spirit comparable to that which, in tournaments of the day,

animated the knights and induced the same spirit of recklessness, a spirit
rooted therefore in contesting established ideas. Let us try as much as
possible (the advantage of historical observation is that it can develop
over a long period, but it is, on the other hand, limited by gaps of information which, for the early period, leave a great number of questions
unanswered) to restore the system of values such as it was accepted on the
one hand around 1125 by Abelard's contemporaries and, on the other,
around 1275 by those of Jean de Meung.

One hundred and fifty years apart, years filled with prodigious activity.
A moment of dilatation, comparable in intensity and impact to the one
we are now living through and – in my eyes – just as earth-shaking. Some
radical transformations took place at the level of infrastructures: In
Abelard's time, towns were just emerging from the rural environment;
though money circulation had been recently revived, real wealth was still
represented by land; the only work was in the fields, no matter how important handicrafts production had become, stimulated by a propensity
for ostentatious luxury on the part of an aristrocracy whose stark conditions had been mitigated for a century by the growth of agriculture; for all
men an existence completely ruled by the rhythms and pressures set by
nature. At the time when Jean de Meung undertook to write the second
part of the *Roman de la Rose*, the population had no doubt tripled; the
rural countrysides had finally been settled but were henceforth, economically and politically, under the town; within the walls of the latter developed a type of life free of nature's tyranny, escaping the oppression of
hunger, cold and darkness; money, which had become the main agent of
power, the incentive for social promotion, had, thanks to its circulation,
enriched beyond all measure, in the Rue des Lombards next to the schools,
businessmen from Italy. Changes were just as important at the level of
political relations. At the beginning of the twelfth century, these were
maintained completely within the framework of feudalism, which for the
working masses meant complete subjection to the castle lords and village
heads. For the richer ones it meant military service, booty from plundering
expeditions, refusal to accept all constraints, except those flowing from
homage, from feudal concession and submission leading to the feudal
lords. One hundred and fifty years later, a genuine State, established on an
administrative network that had been so improved as to allow the rebirth
of an abstract notion of authority and the sovereign's personality to be
effaced behind that of his servants; a decrease in violence, which had made

a ritual of the art of war and made combats look like sporting contests; juridical rules fixed in writing and processed by law clerks; the practice of discussions; a sense of liberty reinforced by associations based on equality and all those mutual interest groups at the different levels of society strong enough, in certain areas adjacent to the towns, to stir up the first strikes. A century and a half that saw the development and failure of the Crusades, the plundering in Spain, Sicily, and Constantinople of superior cultures whose brilliance scorned the simplicity of the Carolingian civilization, an astonishing rolling back of the frontiers of the universe, the sweeping invasions of Mongol Asia, the march of Marco Polo towards Peking, the penetration of the frontiers of Africa and Asia, no longer by men of war but by merchants and missionaries who learned to speak other languages and use other methods. A century and a half which witnessed the development of heresy in many forms, which saw it finally contained and dismantled by the repressive grid which the Church managed to lay over the whole of Christendom, a heresy that was strangled, reduced, partially assimilated by orthodox tradition, at the price of all kinds of misrepresentations as shown in the fate of the Franciscan message. A century and a half, finally, which saw aesthetics follow a road leading from the tympanum of Autun to Cimabue and the pulpit of Pisa, from the vaults of Vezelay to those of the Sainte Chapelle, from the Gregorian plain-chant to the polyphony of Notre-Dame.

Now, in a cultural milieu like this one, so penetrated by a demand for truth, a thirst for knowledge, and a taste for the modern, it did not appear that such upheavals led to any significant change in the system of values. No doubt the primary of reason was, around 1275, exalted more pointedly, and in particular – we know with what insistence – in the second *Roman de la Rose*. But two generations before Abelard, Bérenger de Tours proclaimed "the honor of man" to lie with reason; and the clear vision of things which, through the application of reason, the contemporaries of Jean de Meung tried to attain, proceeded in fact from the patient use of the organs of logic which the teachers of the Paris schools learned to employ in the first years of the twelfth century, in order to clear up the ambiguity between signs of truth found in the sacred books and those seen in the visible world; meanwhile, these processes became more subtle and more effective, but they changed neither in nature nor in purpose. No doubt in 1275 the critical spirit attacked boldly what the intellectuals of the period called the empty façade of display: Hypocritical acts of devotion, submission of "sanctimonious hypocrites" to papal authorities, privileges of born aristocrats (the latter had never been questioned by Abelard, himself perfectly integrated in this category, which he never renounced), licentiousness in the game of courtesy (which the same Abelard had forced himself to practice as best he could) and the sophistications of wordly ethics. But, there again, one guesses that a similar attitude, a similar inclination for contestation, a similar aspiration for honesty and measure in life already influenced Paris teachers in the first quarter of the twelfth century; their aims were not the same, but this was only because the problems raised by the social, political and moral environment were not worded in the same terms. As for the more unremitting attention given nature, that "work of God", in the last third of the thirteenth century, determination to discover its laws, to understand clearly the natural order "from which flow the ways of truth" and thus to succeed in laying a solid foundation for ethics and faith, one can already strongly feel this attention and determination (more timid, less assured, still lacking weapons for conquest but busy at forging them) in the minds of those who, a century and a half earlier, at the time of Louis VI and Suger, were writing commentaries on Scripture, observing the course of the stars, and studying how the sun's rays spread. Thus, there was no evidence during this period that beliefs were seriously affected. Dante alluded to the disciples of Epicurus, who preached that the soul dies with the body, and he said they were numerous. Such ideas had to remain clandestine of course, and those who shared them, when not caught, escaped the historian's eye. In Paris, however, how many intellectuals were moved by a critical spirit and anguish beyond the stage of zestful irony? Those I mention seem to adhere without effort and quite openly to the essentials of Christian dogma. No doubt their Christianity was of a new type; compared to 150 years earlier, it was much more independent of the prostrating and ritual aspects of religion, henceforth oriented toward a suffering, fraternal God, with whom man could attempt to dialogue; many then, along with Bonaventure, turned towards mysticism, a direction which Bernard de Clairvaux had for the most part traced; Abelard had already studied the Gospel enough to declare that sin lay in the intention and not in the act, and Anselm of Canterbury had, before him, concentrated his study on the question of incarnation. What appeared most clearly, in all these areas, was in fact certain lasting achievements: A technique for analysis, a desire to understand whetted by methods and objectives of a certain pedagogy, moral requirements dictated by a particular situation in the midst of society, a vision of a natural and supernatural world based on texts better and better interpreted.

The only notable changes to be seen are at two levels. In the first place they are due to an awareness of relativity-that of time, first of all. At the end of the thirteenth century time was no longer conceived as a homogeneous unit in which past and future would adhere closely to the present maintaining with it a mystical relationship. When the Dominican Humbert de Romans meditated on the recent history of Christianity, he sought an explanation in a chain of natural causes. His knowledge, based on personal experience, of the failures of the Church, the lowering of imperial dignity and the collapse of Latin institutions in the Orient prevented him from still believing that the history of God's people was marked by unity and necessity. At the same time the gradual discovery of the immensity, the diversity, the complexity of creation, the new awareness that the world is full of men who refuse to listen to the message of Christ obliged the more lucid minds to think that Christianity was not perhaps the center of the world, or at least that Christianity took up only a limited section of the world. They also came to realize that Christian thought was incapable of absorbing or breaking up the coherent system of Aristotelian thought. In the second place, many men mentioned here accepted without reservations the new feeling for earthly happiness, which, according to Jean de Meung, had been offered man on the day of his creation: A *joie de vivre* which the retreat of Nature and Reason before the onslaught of Pious Cant had managed to compromise, but which it was now the duty of philosophers to restore. These intellectuals pushed aside resolutely all exhortation to a *contemptus mundi* and all examples of renunciation and withdrawal, which the monks had propagated triumphantly for a long time, and until but recently.

Consequently, modifications at the level of ideology were clearly less defined than those which, during the same period of history, affected economic activity, demography and power struggles. Systems of values were not static; their foundations were upset by transformations in the material, political and social structures, causing them to change. However, this evolution continued without haste, smoothly, even in the avant-garde cultural milieux, the function of which was to work out an adjustment of these systems. Beneath the turbulence created by controversies, diatribes and condemnations, these systems yielded gradually and with flexibility, in the eyes of the historian.

4. Concerning the major problem, that of the capacity to predict these changes, I shall venture only a few remarks.

a) The historian's task is to offer explanations *ex post facto*, that is, to give order to the events which he is dealing with, to link them together and thus to introduce a logical sequence in the unfolding of a linear time. This very undertaking should make him at first more attentive to innovations which he detects and then, in order to throw light on them, extract them artificially from the great currents of habits and routines submerging them in the stream of life. Furthermore, when seeking to report on these innovations, and more especially when the latter are at the level, not of the event but of structures, he is induced to favour necessity rather than change. Between the affirmation, at the end of the thirteenth century, of the concepts conveyed at the time by the words Nature and Reason, the expansion of the *joie de vivre*, the discovery of relativity and, on the other hand, the rise of urban prosperity, the expanding horizon of Western Europe, the rise of certain social groups, the gradual fading of the celestial Jerusalem and the perfecting of the syllogistic tool – between all these factors the historian finally reaches satisfactory correlations. In the same way, he succeeds in attributing to environmental changes the passage from a religion based on the monastery of Moissac's eternal abstract God to a religion based on a vision of the suffering Christ. In such a way, consciously or not, the historian provides arguments for all systems of aspirations, all conceptions which attribute the successive stages in the historical process to a chain of determing causes, thus claiming to predict the future, working hard to construct on past experience trends which supposedly must extend into the future.

b) Eleventh century monks based their beliefs, for example, on an interpretation of history. The periodic processions were meant to symbolize the march of man toward the eternal light, just as the Eternal Gospel of Joachim de Fiore which established 1260 as the exact date for the coming of the kingdom of the Spirit. Marxist thought is also based on an interpretation of history and adopts, concerning the ability to foretell, a position which one must consider with deep attention. "Predictive lessons derived from history," writes for instance Antonio Labriola, "which are at the heart of the doctrine behind the *Manifesto*... imply neither a chronological time, nor a forecast of another social pattern. It is the whole society which, at a moment of its evolution, discovers the cause of its fatal march and, at a salient point of its evolutionary journey, itself sheds light to clarify the law of its own movement. [This forecast] derives neither from chronology, nor from foreshadowing, nor from promises; it is 'morphological' to explain it in one word which, I believe, expresses everything."[1] Let us be clear about one thing: what may be predicted is the progress of society toward new forms; this phenomenon can be foreseen insofar as the repetitive character of certain relations and the fact that they are subordinated regularly to set laws are firmly established. However, insofar as it claims to be rigorously scientific, it is evident that Marxist analysis is able to establish these relations and this subordination firmly only at the level of the material foundations of the social edifice. In respect to what he called "social ideological relations", Lenin ("Who are the friends of the people?") proved to be really very reserved. The major objective which ought, in my opinion, to shape present research in social history is precisely that of showing how conflicting currents that influence the evolution of infrastructures and superstructures are connected, and how these currents interact. The break-up of personal relationships of dependence in the heart of the medieval seigniory seems to follow directly the activity of long-term trends, improvement of agricultural techniques, population growth and the widespread use of money. In this case then, supposing that at that time one had means of analysis similar to those now used, prediction would have been possible insofar as extrapolations go. On the other hand, who could have predicted the sudden appearance, in constructions undertaken at Saint-Denis by Abbot Suger, of an aesthetics of light, the placement of rites of courtly love in counterpoint to a structural evolution of the aristocratic family and to marriage ethics as proposed by the Church, or the fate of the Vaudois heresy and the forms taken on by the Franciscan movement when submitted to papal authority? At the present stage of the sciences of man, it is apparent that the "morphological" prediction of the future of a civilization could not, without being far too bold, take into consideration anything else than the probable course of deep-rooted trends which involve the history of economics, population and techniques and perhaps of scientific knowledge. All this while keeping in mind that the repercussions of a current of opinion, propaganda, or decisions of powers, are, at any moment, liable to alter these trends.

c) Which does not mean that the historian cannot offer the futurologist certain methodological propositions applicable to the observation of value systems. If one admits that the ideological framework, which we have seen to be flexible and which did not shatter suddenly like a chrysalis, is from all evidence affected by the activity of the infrastructures but that it tends to respond by gradual changes of direction, it would seem important to observe in the first place today's hard trends, all of which, at the level of the demographic evolution and the transformation of economic relations, are likely to bring on such adjustments, by disturbing the thought patterns, by stimulating or curbing communication between groups, by favouring transfers, uprootings, exchanges and fusions. To find out, secondly, the points where resistance to tradition seems weaker, to test the rigidity of educational systems, in the heart of the family, of the school, of all institutions dealing with initiation and apprenticeship, to measure their capacity to accept external influences, and to assimilate a certain world view with regard to possible irruptions of elements ejected by foreign cultures. But the event must also be taken into consideration. It is present essentially at the level of politics. One can no doubt take it as a superficial phenomenon, determined largely by the arrangement of deep-seated structures. Yet, to the historian, having already observed how limited was predictability at the level of long-term trends that affect demographic or economic evolution, the event appears to be of an accidental nature, if not its appearance, at least its development proves especially difficult to predict. However, its effects are never negligible when considered on a short-term basis. The event affects institutions in which the transmission of knowledge, beliefs and rites takes place owing to its encouragement of attempts at revolution or reform as well as the transfers of activity it incites. In the end, the historian must insist on the importance of history itself, as an element particularly active among those making up a practical ideology. To a very great extent, the idea a society has of its destiny, the meaning it gives, rightly or wrongly, to its own history, acts as one of the most powerful weapons for conservation or for progress, that is to say as one of the elements, among the most decisive, supporting a determination to preserve or destroy a system of values, as the brake or accelerator of a movement which, depending on the different paces, causes change in mental attitudes and behaviour.

Here, we come back, I believe, to the very heart of the debate which this

conference hopes to engage by inviting the futurologist to place the following question at the very top: What place has history in present-day cultures? What role does history play in these cultures and under what
disguise? What faith is history expected to support? What instructions to
act do the men of our day expect history to justify?

NOTE

1. "In memoria del Manifesto dei communisti" in *Saggi sul materialisme storico*,
Rome, 1964.

RAYMOND ARON

Postface

It is impossible to summarize a dialogue, especially when those taking
part in it belong to different countries and different disciplines. The group
dynamic, to use the language of the psychologists, leads everyone either to
overstate or to play down his views, and thus to betray himself by either
excess or default. It is not easy to resist the temptation to score points at
other people's expense, or even sometimes at the expense of fair argument.
I feel I sometimes got carried away by the heat of the debate and neglected
my duties as chairman. A conference, which can be analyzed sociologically, might also, if it deserved such honour, be chronicled historically.
It develops like a plot, with flurries of activity and lulls, alternations of
passion and indifference. But reports preserve hardly anything of the
emotions, states of mind, clashes and reconciliations of personality which
make the interest and sometimes the charm of such gatherings.

Perhaps I am inspired to write this postface by the rather childish
desire to express what my position as chairman prevented me from saying
at the time. But I hope it will also realize a more serious intention – that of
comparing the problems posed by the organizers of the conference with
those selected by the participants; of bringing out measures of agreement
and underlying disagreement; and of suggesting how future research may
correct some rash assertions and make other arguments more precise.

The primary idea of the conference, as expressed to me by Professor
Bullock, concerned not so much the relationship between history and the
social sciences as the characteristic attitudes of at least part of the younger
generation towards the past and historical knowledge. When I called our
symposium "The Historian Between the Ethnologist and the Futurologist," I was translating a British idea into a Parisian vocabulary.

Ethnology occupies a privileged position at present in the "intellectual field" of the Paris intelligentsia. This is due partly at least to the prestige of Lévi-Strauss and to the fact that structuralism – contrary to the explicit wish of Lévi-Strauss himself – has been transformed into a philosophy or pseudophilosophy. Social anthropology, the British equivalent of ethnology, continues a glorious tradition and perhaps enjoys as much favour there as its counterpart on this side of the Channel, but it does not seem to me to exercise the same fascination, to disturb pure historians in the same way, or to convey a philosophical or epistemological message. As for futurology – speculation on the future, or science of the present – that wins both public and private subsidy more easily than historical research can. This is true from Japan through the United States to France; perhaps even Britain is no exception, though unless I am mistaken Oxford and Cambridge have so far been spared.

The reference to the two extremes – on the one hand that part of the past which falls before the so-called historical period covering the six or seven thousand years of higher civilization, and on the other the short- or medium-term future, inevitably seen in the light of our present situation – tended implicitly to devalue or call in question historical knowledge in the ordinary sense of the term, since, bearing as it does on the "historical period," it is concerned with social phenomena which change or seem to change faster than in archaic societies and more slowly than the G.N.P. and techniques of industrial economies. I had at the back of my mind the thought that, at least at first sight, what are called historical societies differ both from the apparently more stable archaic societies, and from the apparently less stable industrial ones.

But discussion at the conference went neither in the direction suggested by Professor Bullock's question nor in the one I myself had been thinking of; or, at least, the two questions were only dealt with indirectly. But I do not think the speakers were wrong to avoid both the Oxford and the Paris ways of posing the problem. On the contrary I see ample justification for their preference for a more roundabout approach.

Indifference to the past – a phenomenon not at all characteristic of modern civilization, even in its present phase – has two main causes, or, to put it another way, can take two forms: either a different conception of what constitutes a "man of culture," or a preoccupation or even obsession with the present, regarded as something fundamentally new in comparison with all previous human experience. What might we have said about the first of these two forms, in addition to the answer implicit in Mr Trevor-Roper's account? It is an answer which corresponds to certain value judgments and to a certain existential attitude, and both the judgments and the attitude are as incapable of rigourous proof as their opposites. Moreover, historians in the narrow academic sense of the word, while mostly admitting the Eurocentric nature of the historical knowledge dispensed by the universities at the time when historical con-sciousness was developing, and while accepting that Greek and Roman antiquity and the past of the West have no special exemplary value, go on *in fact* according special treatment to those who pass for our ancestors. An alleged indifference to the past is often accompanied by an increased interest in foreign civilizations which have come into their own as a result of the revolt against the West and against colonialism.

Confronted with the despisers of history, historians in the academic sense of the word plead the cause of historical relativism – the multiplicity and equal dignity of different civilizations and even different societies, archaic societies included. But in practice these same historians continue to reflect a hierarchy of value and interest, which may be implicit or un-conscious, and perhaps even legitimate. The other form of rejection of history, which derives from an exclusive concern with the present, formed a continuous background to our discussions, especially when we touched on futurology, which is usually based, implicitly at least, on the postulate that our particular destiny is unique. If futurology nearly always takes its stand on the social sciences and the analysis of the present that is because it declines to foretell the future on the basis of precedent and therefore asserts at once the *Einmaligkeit* and *Einzigarkeit* of our experience.

So we did not discuss either the place which knowledge of the past should occupy in modern education, nor the relative importance, in-trinsic or for us, of archaic and historical societies. In one way or another the discussion always came back to the relations between social science and "history", sometimes seen as knowledge of the past and sometimes as that particular mode of knowledge of the past offered to us by academic historians. Even the debate on futurology only formed a part of this dialogue, though it did lead beyond specialist rivalries to a more radical inquiry into present societies' notions of themselves and their future.

Why did the discussion follow such a course, and was that course in-evitable? All the participants in turn felt themselves called in question, the historians by the ethnologists and sociologists, the ethnologists and sociologists by the historians. Not that the historians constituted a common front: those who claim to be "modernists" and use the quantitative method to reconstruct economic and population patterns are quite ready to throw to the wolves such colleagues as continue to "narrate" the episodes of politics, war and peace, revolutions and the rise and fall of empires.

The direction of the debate was largely determined by the contributions, on the first day, of Ernest Gellner and François Furet, and the choice they made among the many problems raised by the relationship between ethnology and history. The first stressed the opposition between *narrative* and the *structure* which the social sciences attempt to reconstruct; the second emphasized the opposition between *repetitive data*, quantifiable and capable of being expressed in serial form, and *unique events*. These two sets of distinctions, though they often make use of the same words, have each an independent and separate significance.

E. Gellner used different terms to bring out the central theme of his analysis. He mostly employed the term *structure*, but sometimes too referred to the *rules of the game* as distinct from the progress of the game itself. The ethnologist and, I gather from him, the social scientists also, are characterized by the "systematic manner" in which they work out concepts or systems of concepts, giving events intelligibility by inserting them into a "structure" or by demonstrating the way the rules of the game work. As the historians – Mr. Trevor-Roper their bluntest spokesman – replied that they too tried to make events intelligible by bringing out the "context" or background, the discussion came up against an obstacle which was not surmounted: is the conceptualization of ethonologists and sociologists different in kind from that of historians? Do historians make use of the concepts which ethnologists and sociologists make available to them? Should they make more use of them than they do? Probably these are questions which cannot be answered at this level.

Ernest Gellner cited segmentary societies as an example of a concept which makes it possible to understand a structure. There are certain societies which lack a "central authority" or supreme power, and in which the relationship between those who command and those who obey does not function through an individual or a group. To use Gellner's own terms, the systematic elaboration of such a concept makes it possible to compare and explain a large number of cases. Another day it was the concept of "charisma" that was cited – a concept worked out by sociologists but now so much a part of the public domain that ethnologists and historians use it quite naturally without even acknowledging their debt. Mr. Trevor-Roper, fortified by his historical imperialism, said that if need be he would be quite happy to replace "charismatic chief" by "prophet", but his term, though perhaps better, is certainly not the same thing. Both Huey Long and General de Gaulle can be described, in Weber's terminology, as charismatic, but neither of them could be called a prophet.

These two examples of segmentary society and charismatic power suggest by their very difference the need for a twofold distinction – between archaic and modern societies, and between society as a whole and sub-systems. Because of the nature of its raw material and the documentation at its disposal, ethnology rarely tells a story, but nearly always endeavours to make out "structures", whether of rules of kinship, circulation of goods, or relations between temporal and spiritual authority. Of course there is an enormous difference between an ethnologist who describes a particular society after on-the-spot researches and one who, like Lévi-Strauss, constructs a general theory of kinship relations into which all particular cases should fit. But even the most empirical of ethnologists could not embark on his descriptions without making use of concepts. Is it a question of analytic or of historical concepts, to use Talcott Parsons' antithesis? I wonder if in this case the distinction has any meaning. Matrilinear, patrilinear, crossed cousins, parallel cousins – are these analytic or historical concepts? I can see just as good reasons for choosing one alternative as the other. But if, as I think probable, the first is preferred, we must also admit that experience suggests concepts in such a way that analysis and description are almost inseparable.

The situation is quite different with the economic analysis of archaic societies. In this case the analytic concepts – administrative distribution, markets, parallel circuits – have been largely suggested by modern societies, and there is some doubt whether they may legitimately be applied to archaic societies. But in fact the bringing to light, in modern societies, of multiple mechanisms of distribution and redistribution tends to support the trans-historical validity of certain economic concepts. There is nevertheless a contrast between kinship relations and economic relations, between exchange of women and exchange of goods; while it is archaic societies which reveal kinship relations in their most primitive and most instructive form, it is modern societies that make possible the economic conceptualization which will enable us to understand all systems of production and exchange. In the first instance the diversity of history is overcome by getting as far away as possible from the present, while in the second it is dealt with by fixing the attention on the temporary growing-point of the development process.

The fact that the ethnologist naturally aims at "structures", again in Gellner's vague sense of the word, does not mean either that he ignores events or that he achieves a structure true of society as a whole. Archaic societies change, even though they have no contact with "civilized" people, and as far as I can judge no ethnologists would exclude the possibility that structures, such as kinship for example, might in their present form have been affected by such "events" as the extinction of a line, increase of numbers, or struggle between groups. What Lévi-Strauss observes is the tendency of these societies to reconstruct a classifying order despite changes, and to conceive of themselves on the plane of being and not on that of becoming. Thus the distinction between structure and event has no absolute or metaphysical character. Every act performed by an individual, *hic et nunc*, at a point in space and a moment of time, may be called an event, presenting unique traits simply because of its spacio-temporal localization. At the same time, if the act conforms essentially to the particular individual's rôle and to the rules governing the system, it maintains the structure and is not considered an "event." A structure is made up of events repeated according to the "rules of the game." More or less frequent violations, of limited consequence, appear even within the structure. (A *coup d'État* in the United States preventing the presidential election would constitute an "event" in the larger sense, a change of political structure; a military coup in Argentina confirms rather than modifies the structure.)

The relativity of the structure-event antithesis is accentuated further by the fact that both the ethnologist and the sociologist arrive not at *a* structure, but at structures in the plural. Everyone will agree there are connections which are not fortuitous between kinship, political and economic relations and ideological systems. But in fact comparative studies like those of Murdock bring out the irregularity of such correspondences, even within kinship relations – they do not uncover an over-all system in which the different sectors are interdependent or governed by one sector which is predominant. Such studies suggest to me a sort of combinative in which individual items are brought together neither by some irresistible order nor by pure chance. There is an affinity between certain items which is confirmed by the frequency with which the correspondence occurs and of which we can often see the cause. But there are also other, unlikely combinations which are perhaps the result of a history we know nothing about.

Let us turn now from archaic societies to those known as historical and which are at any rate more complex. Each structure now becomes more difficult to grasp in itself, and comes to have more fortuitous links with the others. One has only to think of all the various definitions of the word structure as applied to the economic system or political régime of a modern nation. Take the Germany of the Weimar Republic and Hitler's rise to power, what structural data – economic, social, political, ideological – constituted then the rules of the game which the historian must reconstruct in order to set his account in an intelligible context?

Clearly "events" or series of events will figure among the data – the traumatic shock of defeat, resentment of the Treaty of Versailles, nostalgia for traditional societies, divisions over the legitimacy of the régime created after the collapse of the Empire, and so on. The assertions which historians keep insisting on, namely that the distinction between structure and events is entirely relative, that events leave their traces both in institutions and in men's minds, and that ignorance of events would make it impossible to understand the course of history, are supported particularly strongly by this example. But agreement of this kind reopens the argument instead of settling it. Can the historian do more than describe the "structures" of the Weimar Republic, *i.e.*, recount their rise and fall? Can he explain their inner order or disorder? Can the sociologist help him to grasp their logic, at least in part? Of course the historian must cover both structures and events. But does not their placing depend above all on his skill? This creates the illusion that he is explaining, when he is in fact juxtaposing and aligning. At the very most the illusion is based on the general outlook of an age or a society.

At this point we come up against the problems raised by François Furet, Wolfgang Mommsen, and Peter Wiles, those of *serial history, the crisis in political history*, and *historical explanation*.

Nowadays, at least, the polemic against "narrative history" is not so much a matter of scientific controversy as of rivalry between schools and individuals for prestige and place. The "narrative history" that the "modernists" never tire of condemning is supposed to limit itself to recounting the succession of governments under the French Republics or the succession of wars in international relations. But once this condemnation is registered, what can be said to be new?

Perhaps in the heat of the argument some might maintain there has been nothing new among professional historians but an improvement in the methods which the best of them have employed ever since Gibbon. But on reflection they would probably have admitted what F. Furet calls the "metamorphosis of the landscape" – the increased interest in the condition of the common man, in the survival of ideas and beliefs rooted in the distant past, and the reconstruction of quantitative series on demography, prices and incomes. Agreement could easily be reached, I think, on the two reasons for this widening or especially new orientation of curiosity: a society which aims at being democratic seeks out its ancestors just as aristocracies and revolutionaries did before it; and the study of series, population figures and price levels seems to achieve a higher scientific value. On these two points a few comments occur to me.

From Herodotus to Max Weber, historians and those who have devoted thought to historical knowledge have always noted that research into what has been or happened has always been dictated by a kind of purpose either prior or subsequent to scientific purpose properly speaking. If Herodotus wanted to save from oblivion the noble deeds of the warriors to whom the Greek cities owed salvation and liberty, it may be that the historians of today want to strip the veil of ignorance from the way peasants and artisans have lived and suffered, thought and dreamed, throughout the ages. As F. Furet said, historical knowledge tends to draw near ethnographical knowledge in proportion as it draws away from the noble history of ideas – in fact the history of noble ideas – and concentrates on the peasant mentality or the common intellectual equipment of an age. One might almost say that through a reversal of values or of curiosity the eternal "fellah" whom Spengler with aristocratic contempt excluded from the Pantheon has come to occupy the front of the stage. F. Furet himself recognizes the exaggerations this method might lend itself to: French historians have insufficient knowledge of the aristocracy which, though less numerous than the masses, has nonetheless throughout the ages exercised a major influence on both "structures" and "events".

Democratic ideology is reinforced by the desire to be scientific. The concepts and methods of demography or economic statistics are applied to the past, and historical knowledge becomes the demography or economics of the past. There is no reason why the same technique should not be applied to political history, which would then be presented as political science applied to the past. But do "politics" exist in the same way as "demography" and "economics"? And can political history become scientific in the same way as the study of populations and prices?

Discussion began at this point, launched by W. Mommsen's phrase, the "crisis in political history." On the one hand, while recognizing the work accomplished by the *Annales* school (which throughout the conference was tacitly accepted as the representative of modernism), Alan Bullock was afraid of a possible dwindling of interest in the political sphere as such. On the other hand W. Mommsen said that political history was going through a crisis because its traditional postulates have been either shaken or destroyed: the State no longer appears the chief agent of historical changes; men, with their ideas and intentions, make *a* history but a history quite different from the one they were aiming at. On the one hand stress was put on the predominance of politics even in the régime which claims to be Marxist; on the other, the emphasis was on interaction between various spheres and the influence exercised by social and economic forces on the political sphere despite the latter's partial autonomy.

Now and again the discussion would veer towards the old and by nature interminable quarrel over the role of great men and of accident. And what contemporaries of Stalin of Hitler could deny the effect of such monstrous heroes? At other times the debate came back to the methodological or epistemological question: can political history become "scientific" by borrowing from the social sciences? And inevitably the discussion also turned towards yet another aspect of the *problématique*, that of *historical explanation*.

A historical narrative – the temporal alignment of events – does not constitute a science, either in the rigorous English and American sense of the word or even in the weaker sense of the German *Wissenschaft. Post hoc ergo propter hoc* is an ancient example of a sophism. Narrative alone would become mere chronicle or as Peter Wiles said, "and then, and then, and then..." How then is one to *explain* a consecution which as such is singular and unique *(einzigartig* and *einmalig)?* This question has taken a central place in those studies of analytic philosophy which have been devoted to historical knowledge.

No one doubts, or should doubt, that the Hempel model represents the objective ideal of this scientific explanation of a unique sequence: given a theory, an event is explained insofar as one can, at least retrospectively, deduce it from the theory. Every proposition according to which A is the cause of B on condition that circumstances C, D and E are present makes it possible to explain B if A were present in a context defined by C, D and E.

Are explanations of this type possible in the case of historical knowledge? Obviously. Economic theory in particular usually makes it possible to *explain* conjunctural events (though not always to foretell them because of the varying values of parameters and because of the intervention of man himself). It remains to be seen if this model applies in all cases, and what historians do when it does not, for the lack of a theory or general proposition, or because of the singularity of the event (*e.g.* a decision by one man).

In his contribution Peter Wiles suggests, implicitly at least, a method which though less "scientific" is indispensable and legitimate: the accumulation of facts and the comparison of cases. We have no general theory to teach us the necessary consequences of centralized planning, or the political implications of increasing State intervention in economic life. But we can describe socio-economic organizations in terms over and above a quantified system of variables, we can formulate types and learn what actually happens in given circumstances, without going beyond the stage of empirically observed correlations.

The historian of politics also makes use of this description, reconstruction or analysis of socio-economic or state organization in order to rise above the simple chronicle of "and thens," but political science does not provide him with a theory when it comes to Hitler's decision to attack Russia. Is the Hempel model still valid, then?

Of course the political historian can and must compare; even a chronicle of the fall of the Weimar Republic implies an underlying comparison of Germany with the other Western democracies. Why did the German masses react to crisis and unemployment differently from the masses in England and America? Such comparisons involve at least an implicit conceptualization and a more or less conscious discrimination between the chief variables. But is this conceptual elaboration and attempt at comparison the business of the historian or of the sociologist?

The question itself concerns the ethnography of academic tribes rather than the logic or philosophy of knowledge. In the course of the discussion both Brinton and Parsons were mentioned more than once. The first is a historian, and his book confines itself to historical concepts, while the second is a sociologist, and his two books attempt to apply concepts which are strictly analytic. According to Nisbet, historians – *i.e.*, professors of history – are hostile to attempts like that of Brinton. Alan Bullock told us he once thought of making a comparative study of revolutions but gave it up to write an essentially narrative account of *one* revolution.

I think a sociologist would consider that Brinton's comparative study keeps very close to concrete circumstantial data, scarcely using the concepts and methods of the social sciences and aiming exclusively at one of the objectives, though not the only conceivable one, of a comparative study – *i.e.*, the demonstration of a pattern which seems to be repeated more or less identically in the course of the four revolutions studied. Equally interesting is the bringing out of differences – in causes, social situations, and phases of development. Whether the comparison aims at showing similarity or difference, whether it limits itself to the political sphere or covers the relationships between different spheres, I can see no reason why the historian should not regard it as his business, at least if no theory exists or if it is inaccessible to non-specialists.

This last reservation brings us back to economics. The historian is obliged to take the economic theory from the economists because it has reached such a degree of rigour and complexity that the non-professional cannot think it out for himself. As far as politics and the analysis of régimes is concerned, it may be that intervention by the sociologists is not yet indispensable. Perhaps the historian can construct the concepts he needs for himself, or take them from one or other of the conceptualizations put forward by the sociologists. Parsons' aim was to set out a coherent system of trans-historical analytic concepts which would make it possible to determine the main variations of all the social systems that have ever existed. But as his system has not been accepted, and has not become the common theory and single language of both sociologists and historians, Parsons himself attempted to outline a universal history based on the application of his conceptual system to the various civilizations. But I do not think his outline convinced either the historians or the sociologists.

But beyond this marking out of territories to the various academic tribes there lies, nevertheless, a real question. To what degree may historical knowledge disregard the unity, more or less marked, which constitutes a society or a civilization? How far may the historian ignore the temporal sequence to which the phenomena he is studying belong? The repugnance many historians feel for certain kinds of comparison has its origin in a vague but strong feeling that the revolution brought about by Hitler can only really be understood in the context of the *Zeitgeist*, against the whole sequence of German history. The historian is not restricted to narrative, but should he elude altogether the law of temporal sequence? We shall come back to this question later. For the moment let us return to the event in the strongest sense of the word and to the Hempel model. The event, situated at a moment in time and occurring at a point in space, symbolizes the constraint of spacio-temporal localization which many historians neither resent nor consider it right to escape from.

Let us take as an example Hitler's decision to attack Russia in spring 1941. Do the historians *really* explain it by deducing it from a general proposition? I have no doubt that with a little ingenuity one could reconstruct their practice in terms of a parellel with meteorologists explaining a cloud or economists a crisis. Hitler's character and psychology would take the place of general propositions or theory. Unless one preferred the platitudes of popular psychology, positing Hitler's desire for a European empire and interpreting the destruction of Russia as a necessary consequence of the rule that the sway of empire cannot be shared. Or perhaps a more historical generalization is more attractive: everyone who aspires to dominate a historical field must eliminate his earthly rival, and the same necessity led Napoleon to Moscow and Hitler to Stalingrad. But even if Hitler had attacked in the Mediterranean in 1941 and continued the air raids on England, there would still be a general proposition to meet the case: anyone who wants to rule a continent must eliminate all other maritime power – the final defeat of both Napoleon and Hitler can be deduced from this.

I have two objections against reducing the practice of historians to the Hempel model when they are dealing with *events*. Historians who do not read the analytic philosophers are not conscious of proceeding in this manner. What in fact are they doing? They are trying in the first place to reconstruct the situation in which the decision occurred – but, it should be added immediately *the situation as the agent himself saw it*. Such reconstruction is relatively easy in the case of our own contemporaries, though the British and Americans had great difficulty in understanding the decisions of General de Gaulle because he perceived and articulated the world in a way and according to values, positive and negative, which to them were unintelligible. But it is a long and more difficult task when it comes to agents who saw a different reality from ours and sometimes reasoned differently. The comparison suggested by P. Wiles between the actions of Marius and Caesar brings out the differences between the modes of perception and behaviour of historical agents at two different phases of the Roman Republic. Similarly, in our own day, the attitude of the American Senate towards the military budgets of President Kennedy in 1961 and President Nixon in 1971 reveals and symbolizes a change of mood in the people of the United States or their representatives.

The historians' interpretation of a decision taken by a historical personage consists, characteristically, of this double reconstruction – of the situation and of the agents' perception of the situation. Only secondarily, if at all, do they have recourse to the psychology of the moralists or of everyday life. In the strict sense in which analytic philosophers use the word explanation, this method is not an explanation: it makes the unique decision or sequence intelligible, but it does not make them necessary. But when the matter in question is an act or an accident, it seems to me that an explanation which created the retrospective illusion of necessity would *ipso facto* be a wrong one.

Opponents of the Hempel model point out that historians interpret actions, or at least some actions, in relation to their ends, or sometimes with reference to the motives, interests or passions of the agents. I think they are correct, but they leave out the most important factor: the historian concentrates on certain decisions all the more because *he thinks they might have been different.* Beforehand, *i.e.*, in September 1940, Churchill did not know Hitler was going to attack Russia. Hitler might have deferred the attack, just as the Japanese might have attacked the Soviet Union instead of America and Britain.

What does it mean, "might have"? What is this *possible future* that never happened? It does not imply any metaphysical thesis about determinism or its opposite; it simply signifies that the observer, *post eventum*, goes back in thought to the moment of the decision, analyzes the various decisions the agent had to choose between and between, which very often he hesitated, and comes to the conclusion that the situation did not impose the decision finally taken, or in other words did not make it inevitable. In such cases we include in the situation both the perception of the situation by the agents, and the agents' personalities.

Criticism, as advocated by Clausewitz, represents one particular kind of what I here call *comprehension* of historical decisions. The procedure consists in comparing the decision actually taken with others which would have been possible given the tactical or strategic goal aimed at. Decisions are interpreted in terms of means or military objective *(Ziel)* and political end *(Zweck)*. A *counterfactual history*, one that never happened, contrary to the facts and reconstructed on the basis of another decision which was not taken, makes it possible to criticize the real decision and show whether it was right or wrong, always referring to the moment when it was taken and not using any knowledge which the agent himself did not possess. The relative sameness of the end in the case of military operations facilitates criticism in Clausewitz's sense. But the procedure can also be legitimately applied to historical action, of which military action is just a special case.

Perhaps we have incidentally hit on one of the scarcely conscious contrasts between sociologists and historians. The first are inclined, because of the very questions they put to reality and to themselves, to postulate that the past could not have been other than it was. The second, insofar as they retain the narrative form, try to preserve the dramatic element in human history. Narrative is justified insofar as it retraces a story, insofar as it brings out both the intelligibility and the non-necessity of what happened. What Sartre holds to be the essence of the novel – that the reader should feel that the characters act freely yet at the same time that their acts are never arbitrary or indifferent – is also the final justification of historical narrative. Narrative, at least detailed narrative with individual agents and historic days, would disappear or become a purely literary genre if acts and events were deduced from "structures."

I agree with the historians that they are *not* deduced from them. Thus the difference between the historian stubbornly narrating and the sociologist who despises narration is not only that one uses concepts *ad hoc* and the other systematically, as E. Gellner seems to suggest. Even if he employs the concepts of the social sciences systematically, the historian who narrates what happened in the past still retains a characteristic curiosity in the *course of events* and in *human actions*, which are at one and the same time intelligible and slightly fortuitous. It is not surprising historians feel there is a crisis in history if they think men do not act but are acted upon, puppets manipulated by "underlying forces" which are easily converted into such monstrous entities as Communism, Capitalism or Imperialism. But again, why, if not to disclaim all responsibility in their own destiny, should the contemporaries of Stalin and Hitler have denied the efficacy of human will? Individual wills are like "underlying forces" and mythical entities: by nature they are neither good nor bad. For the last fifty years the charismas of the great simplifiers were chiefly promises of atrocity. But Roosevelt and Churchill were charismatic figures, too, and they also, in the setting of a constitutional régime, are among the leaders who print the seal of their personality on an age. General de Gaulle, too, twice transfigured some of the darkest hours in the history of France, once into an epic of liberation, once into an epic of renewal. A crisis in political history? Yes, if historians take a scientific model unsuitable to their subject. Yes, if they are no longer interested in *res gestae*, in the deeds of men. Yes, if they too want to eliminate the actors and just compare systems, régimes and structures. What more does all this mean but that a certain kind of history tends to disappear when the impulse which directed it and gave it life dies out?

This brings us to two other themes: futurology, and the break between historical ensembles and temporal sequences.

The repugnance many historians feel towards futurology came out in all Mr. Trevor-Roper's contributions to the debate. He used two arguments which were slightly divergent if not actually contradictory. On the one hand no one could have foreseen the triumph of Christianity, the spread of Islam, or the restoration of the Catholic Church in 1571; nor could Marxism or any other historical theory help people to predict the virulence and near-victory of fascism. On the other hand, the poet Heine did predict the German revolution, and the historian Burckhardt foresaw the age of the masses and the great simplifiers through intuition or imagination.

The futurologist, in the person of Daniel Bell, had no difficulty in answering with a distinction which was not put conceptually but which lurked somewhere between *prevision, prediction*, and *prophecy*. Heine's observations about the future German revolution fall somewhere between prediction and prophecy; they announce a future which is too far away to be contained in the present or to call for action to precipitate or prevent its coming about. The abolition of the exploitation of man by man after a socialist revolution belongs to prophecy. To announce in 1970 the population figures for the United States in 1980 or 2000 belongs to prevision. Men have always foreseen the future because all human action as such is directed towards a goal, and presupposes a foreknowledge of the ends produced by the means or of the environment in which the consequences of the decision will take effect. Insofar as it aims at being methodical, futurology or reflexion on the future tries to make its forecasts as rigorous as possible, even if this means a sacrifice in accuracy. Sometimes, by claiming exactitude, *prevision* is transformed into *prediction*, which is bolder and makes a stronger denial of uncertainty.

For easily discovered reasons, modern societies make a greater use than others of prevision. Their management implies a vision looking forward over several years because of the time-lag between the taking of a decision and the full effect of its consequences. A defence system chosen in 1970 will only be operational between 1975 and 1978. Nuclear power stations ordered in 1971 will not provide electricity until 1974 or 1975. Errors inevitably occur when there are unforeseen variations in prices. In 1946 and even as late as 1950 France was afraid of a coal shortage and insisted on having access to the production of the Saar. Ten years later, the government was trying to reduce coal production without causing labour unrest. All managements, whether public or private, whether concerned with economy or defence, look forward to the future. How many years of it, and by what means, depend on sector, circumstance and knowledge.

Previsions are inspired by pragmatic considerations. So are speculations about the future, though they result in multiple *predictions* or *scenarios* intended more for information and less for practice. The demographers' forecasts for the year 2000 are derived at once from facts, extrapolations and hypotheses. What will be the size of the population of working age thirty years from now? Most of them are already living, so if, by way of methodic postulate, we exclude any great catastrophe like war, the forecast figures carry only a narrow margin of uncertainty and inaccuracy, since the relevant birthrates are those for the next ten years, during which it is improbable that there will be a large swing either way. To forecast the proportion of the population of working age that will actually be working involves additional hypotheses about such things as school-leaving age, the percentage of women employed, and so on.

Forecasts about G.N.P. (Gross National Product) are well to the fore in all the books about the year 2000, particularly the best known of them, by Herman Kahn and J. Wiesner. These previsions are rather more risky because they derive for the most part from extrapolations; they are a projection on to the future of tendencies observed during the recent past, corrected by the analysis of growth factors insofar as these and their influence are known and calculated. Population trends over periods of twenty or thirty years sometimes vary in an unexpected manner, as was shown by the rise in the birthrate in Western Europe as a whole after the last war. It may be the same with trends in G.N.P. and economic growth rates. Nevertheless it is probable that in the next twenty or thirty years growth will continue at a rate comparable with that of the last twenty years. But this is a prediction, and it would be better to express the hypothesis as a forecast and say no more than that if present tendencies continue, with variations in terms of known factors taken into account, such and such will be the G.N.P.s of various countries in the year 2000.

The forecasting of technical changes usually makes use of a different method. Although in a sense the science of tomorrow is not foreseeable – if one knew in advance one would know already – experts do make hypotheses as to the date when certain discoveries which the present state of science shows to be possible will actually be made. By questioning enough experts in enough spheres one can arrive at reasonable previsions – I use this term insofar as such forecasts may legitimately be used in planning programmes.

French futurological studies speak of hard tendencies when confronted with trends in population and production – thus stressing their more or less irresistible character, tendencies which human will has to adapt itself to or influence rather than *oppose*. Let us dwell for a moment on the quasi-inevitability of these strong tendencies and the interesting problems raised by Daniel Bell. Is it possible, and if so how, to make forecasts relating to other sectors, such as politics, value systems, life models? And do such sectorial forecasts derive from an analysis of the sector in question or from the supposed relationships between it and another sector (or several sectors, or society as a whole itself)? All futurologists will admit that these questions go to the heart of the matter and they mark the limits of our knowledge.

Futurology begins with a science of the present, of society as it is. It therefore cannot go beyond the present state of the science of society. Insofar as this relates to the over-all whole (a notion ambiguous in itself, for what are the spacial, geographical and temporal limits of this whole?), it must break it down, analyze it and reconstruct it. There is no over-all theory universally accepted by sociologists. D. Bell accepts one analysis, which is that of rational economics, irrational politics, culture-mimesis, or in other words action dictated by the search for efficiency, action dictated by the struggle for power, and action dictated by life- or value-models. Parsons adopts a fourfold analysis, breaking Bell's last term down into two, with values on the one hand and on the other maintenance of the system or regulation of conflicts. All this kind of breaking down is based on analytic concepts, according to Parsons: the over-all whole itself is not broken down, and the interaction of its component sectors is like that of the limbs or organs of a living being. Partly at least, distinction between sectors simply expresses the questions we ask of reality, questions which are neither arbitrary nor imposed from without.

Despite the fact that economic action is defined analytically by the calculation of profit and efficiency, and political action by rivalry and competition for power, these two classic positions do not of course exclude the other fact that economic and political action mutually interact, and that the calculation of profit is affected by the value (or relative importance) of the various consequences of an economic decision. In other words, analytic distinctions involve the reciprocal influence of the terms which are distinguished, and the effect of an economic state on life models or political régime may be a subject of speculation or even of likely propositions but certainly not of proven knowledge.

One discussion at the conference illustrated this uncertainty, which was recognized by all the participants. The family has lost most of its economic functions: the handing down of either property or occupation from one generation to another has become the exception instead of the rule. Does this mean the family will cease to transmit values and cultural continuity? Will it, as Toqueville thought, take on increased importance as a refuge or pocket of emotional relationships in an anonymous universe, or will it give place to other communities? There is no evidence that we know the answer to this question, or even that there is only one answer.

Similarly the indefinite extrapolation of the current tendency towards the breaking of all taboos, particularly sexual ones, is only one hypothesis. Despite the link between secularization, the weakening of traditional religions and the breaking of taboos, the hypothesis of cyclical movements in value systems and life modes does not strike me as absurd. It is impossible to decide exclusively for one or the other hypothesis, *i.e.*, between cycles and a unilinear movement in one direction. Even if one accepts Mr, Daniel Bell's thesis of a limited number of life models, the probable combination between a certain G.N.P. and a certain political régime and life model is beyond us, or gives rise to different hypotheses each equally plausible.

In this respect the limits of prevision result from the limits of our social theory. The political régime of the United States is only partly determined by the current state of the economy: it is influenced much more by the past, the achievement of the founding fathers and the authority deriving from it, by the handing down of respect for democratic legitimacy, and by the law. No society is entirely contemporary. The development of the various sectors is neither mutually independent nor entirely mutually interdependent.

This does not mean that previsions or predictions are useless or to be condemned. It does mean that futurology is as valid as the social science on which it is based, and that it is properly described as the *science of the present* or *hypothesis about the future*. What strikes me most about the literature of futurology is the absence of any surprising, revealing, imaginative vision. Ever since the hippies taught us the precariousness of traditional values and the possibility of the rejection, by smaller or larger groups, of the established order and currently accepted ways of life, there is hardly a book on the year 2000 which does not feature this kind of phenomenon among the probabilities, and describe modern cynics rejecting and fleeing from the rationalized society, or living within it indifferent to money and success, searching for spontaneity, "creativity," or for a meaning to life, and so on.

Once one admits the pragmatic nature of previsions or even predictions (*i.e.*, the opting for one hypothesis or scenario rather than the other), I see no reason why the historian should deny the legitimacy of an activity which derives both from the social sciences and from the nature of modern society itself. Of course, he is right to recall the fact that it is impossible actually to foresee events and their impact on political history; to point out that our imagination is not strong enough either to foretell the international situation or the *Zeitgeist* in 2000 A.D., or even to list the options, problems and compulsions. The historian is right to insist that there are more choices in heaven and earth than are dreamt of in our philosophy.

But the best way to make this reminder is to take part in the debate, not merely to make the statement, which is undeniable and illustrated by countless examples of corrected forecasts, unfulfilled predictions, and prophecies confirmed.

Perhaps the historian's distaste for futurology arises consciously or unconsciously from another source – from the fact that futurology derives from the social sciences, which themselves tend to concentrate on modern societies, to postulate that these are original and unique, and, consciously or unconsciously, to aim at a knowledge of the nature of society comparable to that which the other sciences have obtained over non-organic, and to a lesser degree, organic nature.

Is sociology the science of modern society or of the crisis in modern society? This question represents an old, practically commonplace idea which goes back to the founders at the beginning of the last century. It is an idea which is only partly true, and certainly untrue if sociology is taken to cover all the social sciences. Ethnology obviously studies societies which still exist today and are chronologically contemporary yet not modern. I see two sorts of links between the social sciences and modern society. On the one hand, certain of the methods and techniques used by sociology, social psychology, and even economics (such as field research, interviews, and the quantification of data) are scarcely applicable to other societies. On the other hand, there is an affinity between research into quantitative relations and correlations and the structure of modern societies. Only these made it possible to work out the models and schemas which constitute the scientific theory of economics. Sociology is doubly linked to modern society; as macro-sociology it aims at being a rigorous study of the crisis brought about by the industrial and democratic revolutions out of which sociology itself was born; as micro- or empirical sociology it applies to modern society processes of analysis and explanation inseparable from the scientific spirit which impregnates both subject and object.

Do the modern societies to which certain disciplines owe their development and identity represent a turning-point or break in the history of mankind? Are they fundamentally original and unique? Some insist on their originality, which is difficult to deny; others on permanence and continuity. I do not see how anyone can deny that for the last few centuries and above all for the last few years modern societies have presented hitherto unknown characteristics, in numbers, production capacity, rapid population increase, growth rates, communications, reserves of proven knowledge, and rates of accumulating knowledge. Only the neolithic or agricultural revolution is comparable with the scientific or mechanical revolution as a watershed in the human adventure. But at least up till now neither politics nor beliefs nor ways of living or reacting have become so different that they cannot be compared with the experiences of the past. These two contrasting aspects of our present experience suggest two views of things, one of which is preferred by the sociologists, the other by historians.

For historians of the *Annales* school, population and production trends were characteristic of long periods and slow changes. But in our own day they represent the most mutable and shifting sector of all, just as changing if not more so than the political sector. If an American Senator of 1815 returned to the Capitol he would recognize the place and many of the ways of doing things. But he would have difficulty in recognizing a nation of more than 200 million inhabitants, with an economy whose national product is more than 1,000 milliards of dollars. The relationship is reversed so that sometimes it is politics which seems to preserve the past, while production is the realm of the unexpected, the crucible of the future.

Some fifteen years ago Professor Lazarsfeld said to me, "Read Tocqueville if you want to understand the American system of values" – and his jest had something of truth in it. Have the last fifteen years abolished that truth? I'm not sure. The violent or spectacular breaking of taboos may signify the survival of prohibitions in a new form rather than their abolition. No one can say whether the troubles of the present herald great catastrophes, or the approach of another period of culture, or if they are simply an ironic and ephemeral answer to the economic success of the last twenty-five years, to teach those who have forgotten it, Marxists of East or West, that men do not live by bread alone, or, to put it another way, that the changes and chances of causality remain impenetrable.

These various observations, taken together, lead to a conclusion which will please the historians better than the sociologists: the Promethean ambition of understanding social progress has not yet got beyond the stage of Icarus' dream. The old tag that "men make history but don't know what history they make" has lost none of its sharp truth. It holds its own against both the revolutionaries and the futurologists, who are often inclined to accept certain strong tendencies as inevitabilities. The margin of our freedom depends partly on our own estimate of it, on our own confidence in ourselves. As a matter of method we have to exclude from our forecasts accidents, personal decisions, reversals of values, changes in governing ideas. But if he transformed his method into a rule of action, historical man would fall into the trap of self-fulfilling prophecy. The romantic revolutionary of the younger generation also gives an ironic reply to the wisdom of the futurologists.

Just as it lacks a theory concerning the reciprocal relationship between sectors, so sociology possesses no general theory of change. I even wonder whether such a theory is a legitimate subject for research. Professor Nisbet presented the image of growth or evolution on the one hand, and the image of genetic causality or the narrative of origins on the other hand, as the two which still dominate the thought and practice of sociologists and historians. But his account left his hearers uncertain. Is the representation of a unilinear development *ipso facto* erroneous? Should not the historian retrace the development of a single country, religion or civilization? Or should we remember that the aligning along a single thread of the successive states of a historical entity is not the same thing as an explanation and does not lead to scientific knowledge?

Criticism of "unilinear representation of history" can mean various things, and it is important to distinguish between them. Here are some, though the list does not claim to be complete: 1. Such a representation may conceal what Sir Karl Popper calls "evolutionism," a slanting of the whole history of man in relation to the present, and, more particularly, to the present of European or Western societies. This is an illegitimate slant insofar as it presupposes the exemplary value of a particular society or civilization and assumes implicitly that the values or social organization of Europe or the United States *must*, in both senses of the word, be universally accepted. On the other hand, if one compares the mechanical or scientific with the neolithic revolution, there is no reason to exclude *a priori* the hypothesis that both revolutions mark stages in human development, and that both create compulsions which no group can evade without paying the price. Does the present bear the future within it? Yes and no. To foresee the future it is not enough to know the present because except perhaps in limited spheres we do not possess a theory that enables us to explain in advance, *i.e.*, scientifically foresee, the future which the present will produce. But where will the future come from, if not out of the present? And where shall we get the elements of our forecast, however vague, except from what is and from what is taking shape?

2. This bias on the present may also conceal another subtle form of ethnocentrism or centring on the present, which would make all societies and civilizations find their only meaning and purpose in or in preparation for our own present. The pure evolutionism of Auguste Comte is a prime example of the historicist trap. But it is one which professional historians have never fallen into: they all remember the oft-quoted phrase of Ranke, "Every age is immediate to God." In more prosaic terms, every age is valid as such and relates only to itself. Nowadays, rather than ignore this diversity, we are more likely to go to the opposite extreme. Having abandoned the search for a universally valid criterion, some seem tempted to fall into relativism, forgetting that scientific knowledge progresses and accumulates even if governing ideas and philosophies make up a discontinuous series rather than an ordered, unbroken development.

3. Both the above illusions are found in what might be called the genealogical interpretation. Historical curiosity is inspired by several things: curiosity about *others*, the desire to save *noble deeds* from oblivion by graving them in brass, the search for *ancestors*. It is this which gives rise to the genealogical interpretation, but this interpretation can result in quite different conclusions sometimes. Ancestors incarnate tradition; their prestige gives authority to manners, laws and men. But they can also be seen as precursors, deserving children to be patronized by their elders. Epistemologically, criticism of genetic causality can be reduced to the classic argument that succession does not constitute cause, though conversely cause usually does imply succession. Philosophically, the same centring on the present is to be found in the interpretation of any society, age or sector, any artistic form or doctrine, as a necessary stage on the way to the present.

But the genealogical interpretation can occur in various forms. Hegel's account of the history of philosophy leads up to his own present and to the whole of his own system. But in a sense it does respect the originality and truth of each of the previous systems.

4. Above all the double rejection of growth and genealogy applies to historical reality regarded as a real over-all whole. But at the same time it raises a paradox: historians and even certain sociologists themselves accuse empirical sociology of isolating certain sectors from the social

whole, and thereby of missing the most important thing, both in space and time. Can the educational system be considered independently of the political and economic régime? Can the political régime of the Fifth Republic be considered independently of France's many experiments since 1789? In other words, sociology, the science of the present, tries to neglect neither the over-all structure of society, nor the constant survival of the past in the present. Historical knowledge must accept the task of changing directions as required and of breaking down both societies and processes of development in accordance with the questions it wants to ask.

Despite the resulting paradox, it seems to me that two tendencies emerge. Knowledge which aspires to be scientific is no longer content with narrating the development of an entity which is a nation, or a nation's economy, or even a group of nations; it is conscious of the distinction between *narration* and *explanation*, and of the illusion of explanation created by temporal alignment. Nor are historians unaware that contemporary realities do not as such constitute a totality; they know they cannot necessarily be explained in terms of each other or by one single or ultimate cause. So they ask questions of the past, as scientifically as possible, so as to *explain* with as much rigour as they can any event, great or small, whose uniqueness is revealed by comparison with other events. Why National Socialism? Why anti-Semitism? Why did Britain escape revolution in the nineteenth century?

Thus historical knowledge, in those sectors where a theory has been developed, becomes a theory of the past. Where theory does not or does not yet exist, even then historical knowledge tends towards the "scientific" by abandoning juxtaposition in space and succession in time, and by dividing up and questioning instead. I neither deny nor reject these tendencies. But one day there will be another Marc Bloch who, as Bloch did for feudal society, will reconstruct an ordered and significant whole which will *be* a reconstruction and not an explanation, despite all the analytic philosophers in the world. Must we say historical knowledge does not *explain* and is therefore not a science? Or should we say with Trevor-Roper, on the contrary or simultaneously, that it retains its supremacy, queen not of the sciences but of the humanities?

Mr. Trevor-Roper's words were received with a respectful silence which neither approved not contradicted them. Only Professor Nisbet replied on a marginal point: he doubted whether historians were influenced by the social sciences until the last thirty years, except in France, where Durkheim and his school had an effect on neighbouring disciplines. Professor Trevor-Roper riposted vehemently, perhaps to a certain extent unjustly. For although some historians, some of them among the most famous, have perhaps borrowed from ethnology or economics, on the whole the tribe of historians, in the United States and even in France (despite Durkheim) and Britain (despite Trevor-Roper) have gone on with business as usual. But we may now leave this argument of historians about history.

What, though, does the word history mean? What sense do we give to it, or ought we to give to it? In the course of the discussion we often used the word to mean the sort of knowledge possessed and the sort of writings produced by people at universities who are called historians. But we still need to distinguish two categories in this kind of literature: books of synthesis or instruction which do not break with the practice of narration, however much simplified it may be in terms of the field covered, and books of research, dealing with some neglected aspect or unknown facts. Only those in the second category belong to science in the making, and their results are more or less rapidly incorporated into those of the first category.

If, instead of holding to the formula that history is what is produced by historians, we look for a logical or epistemological definition, we have to make a choice. On a primary level we may say the word history designates not a science but a subject or a method. In general it deals with the past, the past of human societies – but why should this past be the business of a single discipline? Every human science deals with the past, distant or recent, of human societies. So the subject, the past of human societies, is not enough to specify a discipline. What is called historical method – the use of documents and monuments, of the traces left by the dead on stone, brass, parchment or paper, to reconstruct the deeds of our predecessors – remains the indispensable instrument of knowledge. But is the combination of human past and historical method enough to define the essence and draw the frontiers of what historians call history? What history was Trevor-Roper thinking of when he accorded it regal supremacy?

He laid stress on the *empirical* nature of history. The word *empirique* in French does not convey exactly the same thing. The French distinguish between *empirique* and *expérimental*, the word *expérience* in French meaning both "experience" and "experiment." History cannot perform experiments comparable to those of physics or chemistry, but certain procedures of the social sciences present an equivalent, and sometimes make it possible to determine and demonstrate correlations or causal relations. In this respect history is inferior to disciplines which deal with that recent past which is called the present.

If we use the word empirical in the same sense as the French *empirique* the mystery deepens further. No strictly empirical knowledge rises to the dignity of science, in the English sense if not that of the German *Wissenschaft*. The more history tries to be empirical in this sense the less it claims or has a right to claim to be scientific. So it can only aspire to the throne if its superiority consists in its modesty.

What did Professor Trevor-Roper have in mind when he proclaimed the imperialism of history? As history clearly does not elaborate a theory or a system based on hypothesis and deduction, or even a system of concepts subject to experimental control, as it therefore neither can nor wishes to rival the sciences properly speaking, its superiority must reside elsewhere; it must be that in abandoning the claim to be scientific it gets nearer to reality and attains another kind of knowledge. So the question arises again: what knowledge? I can see two possible answers: narrative on the one hand, and on the other hand men, men of flesh and blood, as they live, as they are conscious of living.

What is the value – *i.e.*, interest or validity – of narrative as such? Professor Nisbet answered that historians have gone on recounting the French Revolution in the same way as novelists tell "stories". But while novelists' stories are not true, those of the historians claim to be. A tale has the same intermingling of necessity and accident, it creates the same sense of over-all determinism and liberty in detail, of momentary choice and irreversibility after the choice had been made, as are created by the art of the historian. Is this art of reconstructing the plot of a true story the historian's art par excellence, or only one of his minor characteristics? Even if Professor Trevor-Roper thought the first, could he call it a *royal* art and put it above scientific knowledge?

Let us turn to the other path for a moment. The historian tells us not of social agents, roles or laws, but of the people we meet in the street or at the office, men who act, dream, suffer, quarrel and make up, hate or love, live and die, try to find a meaning in their life and in their death. I can imagine an argument in favour of this knowledge, treating of men of the past just like those we see every day. In the last analysis all sciences have as their objects constructions or abstractions. Knowledge of life as it has been lived would at least have the virtue of not being scientific. There is no doubt that historians make use of this argument, more or less implicitly, even unconsciously, when they justify their activity to themselves.

But it is a defence not easily established. Most of our contemporaries, even of those we meet in the street or at the office, we know only through the intermediary of abstractions. We know them as social agents, and whenever they cannot be reduced to their role we resort to the psychology of the moralists or even of the analysts, to account for their deviation, anger or passivity. Moreover, anyone who has not actually lived in political circles is not really familiar with the professional language and way of thinking and acting in the Palais Bourbon or the Capitol. But even experts in politics do not know all this? Agreed – but neither do historians. They all need to reconstruct the universe of the American Senators, French deputies and Russian *apparatchiki*, just as they try to reconstruct that of the citizens of Athens in the 5th century B.C. It is true the political experts often mistake their own schemes and correlations for reality and may more frequently be in error than observers who lack prejudice as well as method. That may be. No specialist can do without intelligence, and in the absence of theory or abstract science a historian of Bolshevism and Russia may do better than a political expert without experience of Russia or of Marxism-Leninism. But this is neither a proof nor an example of the superiority of the historian over the political commentator. Supposing the first aims rather at general propositions and interests himself in the system, while the other concentrates on the oddities of the Soviet régime or the development of Marxism-Leninism since 1903 or earlier; it is only two different aspects of the same curiosity, and each kind of research involves the other. It is hard to see why one should be singled out for supremacy.

Do we find a more satisfactory answer if we combine the two ideas of narrative and knowledge of real men? Apparently not. It is true that the narrating of men's experience, the reconstruction of their consciousness of it, and the juxtaposition of that with our own consciousness of it, seems to have been the supreme ambition of the traditional historian, though it does not accord with the scientific aspirations of today. But this narrative, this reconstruction, this juxtaposition, calls for all the resources of the social sciences, including those resources which are desirable but not available. How can one narrate the development of a single sector or a complete entity (*e.g.* a country or empire) without a schema or theory for that sector or entity? In order to surpass the economist or the sociologist, the historian must be able to argue with them on equal terms.

I even wonder whether the historian, in order to justify his claim to the throne, should not abandon the empirical vocation usually ascribed to him and flirt instead with philosophy. Whether he is narrating an episode or an evolution covering several centuries, the historian chooses, reconstructs, seeks out the essential, in relation either to the men of the past or to ourselves. Whether he compares all societies regardless of time, or aligns them in temporal sequence, he is trying to preserve the experiences of mankind, to compare them and grasp their significance. A great historian rarely has an explicit philosophy of history. But Nietzsche was right when he said that the value of the history depended on the personality of the historian. To understand in depth the experiences of mankind one must be capable of living them. Anyone who does not look for a meaning in existence will find none in the varieties of society and belief. In this sense the historian is like the philosopher: both ponder on the destiny and destination of man.

Participants

Aron, Raymond	*Academy of Moral and Political Sciences; Professor at the Collège de France*
Bell, Daniel	*Professor of Sociology, Harvard University; Chairman, Commission for the Year 2000, American Academy of Arts and Sciences; Co-Editor* The Public Interest
Besançon, Alain	*Professor at the Ecole Pratique des Hautes Etudes, Paris*
Besson, Waldemar	*Professor of Political Science, University of Konstanz* (died in June 1971)
Bracher, Karl Dietrich	*Professor of Political and Contemporary History, University of Bonn*
Bullock, Alan	*Master of St. Catherine's College, Oxford University; Chairman, Board of Directors, IACF*
Duby, Georges	*Professor, Collège de France*
Furet, François	*Director of the Center of Historical Research of the 6th Section of the Ecole Pratique des Hautes Etudes, Maison des Sciences de l'Homme, Paris*
Gellner, Ernest	*Professor, London Schools of Economics*
Graubard, Stephen	*Editor,* Daedalus, *Journal of the American Academy of Arts and Sciences, Harvard University, Cambridge, Massachusetts*
Le Goff, Jacques	*Director of Studies, 6th Section of the Ecole Pratique des Hautes Etudes, Paris*
Momigliano, Arnaldo	*Professor of Ancient History, University College, London, and Scuola Normale Superiore, Pisa*
Mommsen, Wolfgang J.	*Professor of Modern History, University of Düsseldorf*
Nadel, George	*Editor,* History and Theory, *London*
Nisbet, Robert	*Professor of Sociology, Unitversity of California, Riverside*

Papaioannou, Kostas	*Athens*
Peckham, Morse	*Distinguished Professor of English and Comparative Literature, University of South Carolina*
Rossi, Pietro	*Professor of History of Philosophy, Università degli Studi, Turin*
Tenenti, Alberto	*Director of Studies, 6th Section, Ecole Pratique des Hautes Etudes, Paris*
Trevor-Roper, Hugh	*Regius Professor of Modern History, University of Oxford*
Wiles, Peter	*Professor of Russian Social and Economic Studies, University of London*
Yamamoto, Tatsuro	*Professor of Asian History, University of Tokyo; Member of the Japanese Academy*